Unemployment

ALSO BY JEREMY SEABROOK

The Unprivileged
City Close-Up
The Everlasting Feast
Loneliness
A Lasting Relationship
What Went Wrong?
Mother and Son
The Way We Are, Age Concern

Unemployment

Jeremy Seabrook

Quartet Books
London Melbourne New York

First published by Quartet Books Limited 1982
A member of the Namara Group
27 Goodge Street, London W1P 1FD

British Library Cataloguing in Publication data

Seabrook, Jeremy
Unemployment.
1. Unemployed—Great Britain
I. Title
306'.3 HD5767

ISBN 0-7043-2325-7

Typeset by MC Typeset, Rochester, Kent
Printed in Great Britain
by Mackays of Chatham Ltd

Contents

Acknowledgements

I wish to express my thanks to the following:
Canon Ken Stock, St Columba's, Southwick, Sunderland; the people at the Southwick Neighbourhood Action Project, especially Angela Cadaxa, Ian Smith; everybody at the Lane Neighbourhood Centre, Birmingham; Betty Birch and family in Bolton; Sue and Neil Turner in Wigan; Sheila Ramsdale in Wigan; Keith Home in Newcastle; Barry in Selly Oak; Ken and Jean in Coventry; Professor Bernard Crick for his kind comments and suggestions; Paul Barker, *New Society*, for his interest and encouragement over many years.

Some of 'From the Thirties to the Eighties' appeared in the *Political Quarterly*, vol. 52, No. 1 and in *New Society*; and part of 'The Survival of Poverty' in the *Guardian*; and I gratefully acknowledge their permission to reproduce them here.

'The basic aim of modern industrialism is not to make work satisfying, but to raise productivity; its proudest achievement is labour saving, whereby labour is stamped with the mark of undesirability. But what is undesirable cannot confer dignity; so the working life of a labourer is a life without dignity. The result, not surprisingly, is a spirit of sullen irresponsibility which refuses to be mollified by higher wage awards but is often only stimulated by them.'

(E.F. Schumacher, *Good Work*.)

Foreword

Many people wonder how it can happen that unemployment has reached figures comparable with those of the 1930s, in spite of the apparent social and economic transformation that seems to have occurred since then, in spite of the alleged power of the trade unions, in spite of all the assurances that there would never be a return to the demoralizing conditions of the years between the wars. All those things which, it was serenely assumed, had been banished for ever, are being discovered all over again, and in what seems to be a quite different context. More than this, it has all become acceptable again, just as it was then in those shadowed, bitter years. Of course there is no lack of justification for what has happened. We are told that the recurrence of so many ugly features that disfigured society in the thirties has a more exalted purpose today: it is the price we pay for the process of modernization, becoming competitive in the world again; if we pass through this painful time, we shall emerge into a future of leisure and ease. This is the official explanation, the explanation of the rich and the powerful. When they talk of the price we pay, they do not mean themselves, but the poor and the unemployed.

But the question remains. How are the dramatic changes that took place in the common experience of living through recent decades compatible with what is happening now? Why are more and more people being thrust back into poverty – not the destitution of the Public Assistance Committees and the Means Test of course: poverty has been modernized like everything else. Many older people say they thought they had fought for a better world; only they find with time that it looks more and more like the old, worse one. And yet the altered circumstances are obvious: the city centre slums have been largely demolished, most people do not want for shelter, food and warmth. How can the old pain, the same feelings of worthlessness and despair still be there? Or is it perhaps a different kind of pain, another despair? Is the suffering of those who lose their livelihood, and with it often a sense of purpose, a different kind of suffering now?

Making sense of people's sense of profound change within a static system is one of the main themes of this book. The recurrence of that despair in the eighties which afflicted the inter-war years cannot really be understood unless we examine the changing context in which unemployment occurs now. It is easy and tempting to document similarities between the contemporary experience and that of the thirties. Adrian Sinfield in *What Unemployment Means*,[1] says 'Unemployment strikes most harshly and frequently, those who are among the poorest and least powerful in the labour force and in society as a whole', and this echoes what Cook and Stevenson say in their book *The Slump*.[2] Similarly, Orwell in Wigan in 1936[3] has a sharp contemporary resonance when he says

> When I first saw unemployed men at close quarters, the thing that horrified and amazed me was to find that many of them were *ashamed* of being unemployed . . . At the time nobody cared to admit that unemployment was inevitable, because this meant admitting that it would probably continue. The middle classes were still talking about 'lazy idle loafers on the dole', and saying that 'These men could all find work if they wanted to', and naturally these opinions percolated to the working class themselves.

Even J. B. Priestley's comment in his *English Journey* in 1934[4] has an added poignancy in its lasting relevance: 'I think I caught a glimpse then of what may seem to future historians one of the most dreadful ironies of this time of ours, when there were never more men doing nothing and there was never before so much to be done.'

It all seems to make the eighties of a piece with the thirties; but that takes no account of what has happened to and within the working class in the intervening period; and it is there that the reasons are to be found for the new acceptability of what was thought unacceptable, the inevitability of what seemed to be avoidable, the tolerance of acute suffering and sense of loss in the old industrial areas. Since the last war, the changes in working-class life have been such that many working-class leaders were tempted to see in them a secular victory of labour over capital. Because the Labour movement has increasingly concerned itself with what capitalism has shown it can and will give – money – it has neglected the struggle against the deeper subordination of working people to its values. The concessions to the working class coincided with a reduction in the oppressive and debilitating burden of work imposed upon people at an earlier stage of capitalist evolution, and this made it appear as if a new and benign symbiosis had been reached.

Yet during that period in which the Labour movement seemed to relax its vigilance over the wider issues, an epic change occurred within the working class, a transformation that appeared beneficent because it took place within an atmosphere of ostentatious rewards and concessions, but which, now it is so far advanced, looks more ambiguous. In other words, even during the greatest period of affluence and apparent working-class power, so many forfeits and penalties were being imposed on people that the result begins to appear as net loss and not gain, as damage and not progression, as distraint and not bounty. It may well be that the much-commented changes turn out to be simply another wound inflicted on the working class, and this time a very deep one, a wound against work itself. Has there been a blow against the very thing which, it was always assumed, would never be superseded – the work function of the working class – and hence, against the source of its power against capitalism? If the labour exacted by capitalism has for the most part been harsh and ill-rewarded, why should we now believe that what it now promises – or threatens to impose in the same arbitrary way that it imposed work and hardship – will be any more fulfilling or rewarding? E. F. Schumacher, in *Good Work*,[5] says 'Until quite recently, I heard it said everywhere that the real task of education was not education for work, but education for leisure. Maybe this extraordinary idea has now been abandoned. Fancy telling young and eager souls "Now what I really want you to envisage is how to kill time when you have nothing useful to do."'

In recent years I can recall many conversations with elderly Labour councillors and trade union leaders, who sat serenely behind their heavy office desks and said, 'Yes, well we've achieved most of what we set out to do. It's only a question of tinkering now, the nuts and bolts.' Their eyes are fixed firmly on their past, and they evoke, movingly, the orange-box furniture, the Means Test, the memory of the people they loved prematurely old with work and worry. The elimination of those things became their life's work. They do not see that nothing stands still, and that the damage inflicted by capitalism on the working class, the toll it takes can also move; and that the price paid by working people for the 'successes' of capitalism has been in terms of the breakdown of the old neighbourhoods, the destruction of human associations, the loss of solidarity, indifference between people, violence, loneliness, mental illness, alcoholism, drug-dependency, a sense of loss of function and purpose. And here we are at the beginning of the eighties, and it is capital, with its harsh triumphalism that is in the ascendant, while the Labour movement is in a state of turbulence and disunity.

What the decay of work and the changed function of the working class means for people is the subject of this book; not in a visionary futuristic way, but as it has already happened to people in the places where they have lived and worked.

What I have tried to do is absorb the feeling of people in those districts badly affected by unemployment, to attempt to reach emotions and reactions not always accessible to social science, and therefore I have relied on an older tradition of reporting and interpreting. I have allowed people to speak for themselves as far as possible. I was deeply touched by the kindness and hospitality of so many people I met, and this book is, if nothing else, a testimony to the warmth and resilience of people, temporarily discarded by a society that does them the injury of not knowing where its real resources lie.

1
From the Thirties to the Eighties I: Contrasts

The most common response to the surge in unemployment in the late seventies and early eighties is that, however disagreeable it may be, it is less humiliating than it was in the thirties, because of the protection afforded by the state against destitution. This feeling is so widespread that even with 3 million people out of work, it isn't difficult to find those who insist that it is all caused by the lure of easy dole money which undermines the will to work. A typical reaction is 'There's work for those who want it. If I lost my job this week, I'd be working by next Monday' (Electrician, thirty-four, Bolton). And W. W. Daniel[6] has observed that the number of long-term unemployed is relatively small to the total number: most people's experience of unemployment is of lengthening gaps between work, rather than continuous spells of being without work; although naturally, as the figure rises, more and more people will have been unemployed for longer periods. (In autumn 1981, out of 3,000,000, the number without work for more than a year was 600,000.) It is important to remember that people do go in and out of jobs in a casual way, which may shock many of those who are accustomed to think of their own work as a career, with long-term goals beyond the immediate wage-packet.

A second, widespread reaction is that we are living through a return to the thirties; that we have learnt nothing from those unhappy years. And the suggestion of the thirties, despite the sad memories it arouses, does at the same time offer some reassurance. However unpleasant, it is at least familiar. We have seen it all before.

Both these reactions are, in their way, deeply comforting. To the Right, they demonstrate the resilience of the social fabric. To the Left, they offer the hope that hardship will re-kindle some of the old fire and passion in the working class. Many people on the Left find it hard to conceal a certain satisfaction. They feel they are being vindicated. What they've been saying all these years – that capitalism hasn't changed – is now being proved true. In their tone, you can sometimes detect a hint of *schadenfreude* against the working class for having resisted their warnings all through the easy years.

But it isn't the same. It isn't a return to the thirties that the purposes of capitalism require now, even though the echoes are there, sometimes startlingly so across the years.

In an old-fashioned parlour in a house in Sunderland, an elderly man reaches down a painted biscuit tin in which he keeps, not family photographs, but pictures of the people in Sunderland taken during the depression of the thirties. 'I take these pictures out sometimes to remind other people. I don't need reminding myself. There's not a day goes by but what I feel the bitterness and shame at what this country did to millions of its working people.' The photographs, faded and cracked with age, fan out across the threadbare chenille tablecloth. He indicates a young woman with braided hair and a graceful plinth of neck. 'She came from a TB family. You knew who the TB families were, you knew not to marry into them if you wanted your children to survive. She died when she was nineteen.' There is a picture of a misty street, with a cluster of old men on the corner, hands in pockets, bodies arched against the cold. A man looks unsmilingly into the camera, flat cap, muffler parted to reveal collarless shirt. 'He was a miner. After the General Strike, he never found work again. He cut his throat one afternoon in July 1931. I can remember it like yesterday. I came home from school and found him. He'd written a message on the looking-glass with a cake of soap, saying he was sorry. He was my father.'

A council flat in the same town, October 1980. A young man with a beard, a few threads of silver in his dark hair, tries to pacify his nine-month-old son, while his wife, nineteen and pregnant with their third child, pushes her three-year-old out of the door onto the landing, and tells her not to come back until she is ready to say she's sorry. The child starts to scream, and the mother buries her face in her hands. The room is piled with washing, clothes, towels, nappies, and a few scraps of children's toys. The double-bed and cot leave room for nothing but a sideboard, with a television standing on it. There is an electric kettle, a teapot, a pint of sterilized milk, a sugar bag, a sliced loaf and a tub of margarine. The young couple live with the girl's parents in their two-bedroom flat. The electricity has been cut off in their own house, the arrears of rent having reached over a hundred pounds. The husband went to London to find work, but was offered only low-paid catering jobs, and could find nowhere for his family to live. He came back, even more heavily in debt, and with an even more overwhelming feeling of failure.

'My wife has known nothing but debt and poverty ever since we've been married,' he said. 'I know I ought to feel glad, being able to spend so much time with my kids while they're young. But what can I give them? I just feel empty. I'm ashamed I can't provide them with everything they need. What kind of a father is that? We have no life together, even though we're never apart. I've even stopped looking for work. Some days, I feel like topping myself, I'm not kidding. If there's no hope for me, what chance will they have? Life won't be worth living. I feel like topping myself and taking them with me.'

But the similarities distract from the vast changes that have taken place within the working class since the thirties. One way of describing them would be to say that working people have moved from a position of being for the most part excluded from the benefits of capitalist production to a state of captive dependency on them, with all the implications that has for the sensibility of the working class, for what Raymond Williams in the *Long Revolution*[7] calls 'the structure of feeling'. Alternatively, in the words of an old lady from Sheffield, 'Working-class people used to be proud of how much they could do with very little money; now people feel ashamed of how little they can do without a lot of it.' This change has coincided with a weakening (or at least a profound alteration) in the function of large sections of the class, kneaded as always into whatever new configuration circumstances demand. It is very important here to distinguish between the welcome sense of release of those who have been the victims of back-breaking toil, and the destruction of a sense of purpose and meaning, an undermining of the feeling that working people have an indispensable contribution to make. We should not for a moment lose sight of the relentless and destructive influence of work on the lives of generations of working people. E. P. Thompson in *The Making of the English Working Class*,[8] says

> It is neither poverty nor disease, but work itself which casts the blackest shadow over the years of the Industrial Revolution . . . New skills were arising, old satisfactions persisted, but over all we feel the general pressure of long hours of unsatisfying labour under severe discipline for alien purposes . . . After all other impressions fade, this one remains; together with the loss of any felt cohesion in the community, save that which working people, in antagonism to their labour and to their masters, built for themselves.

But equally, it was out of that resistance to those wrongs that an alternative to the degrading, brutalizing values of capitalism was to be forged. If the old crippling restraints on working people strengthened the capacity to conceive, in those bitter circumstances, the idea of a different, more human kind of life, what can we expect of the changed impositions – the decayed function and the disabling licence which have come with the evolving needs of capitalism? What will be the effect of these on the hope of an alternative way of life?

The epic of work, with its demands for the last ounce of human energy and more, is giving way through time to something else. As the labour of extensive sections of the working class becomes more detached from products and services that are directly identifiable with perceived human need (as opposed to those that can make money), its whole context is transformed. The idea of *redundancy* has a resonance now that goes far beyond the lay-off of workpeople in a given industry; and this being so, the contemporary experience of unemployment cannot be separated from the circumstances and values of those who are still in work. A former shipyard worker in Sunderland, a man in his seventies, said, 'I pity those who haven't got work now. When we were on the dole, people were generally more sympathetic than they are now. When we marched, there was always a few who stood on the pavement calling us Commies and Reds, but on the whole people's good will was with you. Nobody ever called us scroungers. I'd never heard the word layabout. But now, they make the poor sods feel it's their own fault. And what really appals me now is that they don't have hope, and we did. We felt, not only that work would pick up again in the yards and the pits, but that time was on our side. We saw a future possibility for socialism. We knew the Labour Party hadn't reached the full height of its development, in spite of the fiasco after the General Strike and 1931. There hadn't been the disillusion over Soviet Communism. We were still waiting. But not now. The young have no such hope now. Their only hopes are centred on individual salvation – the dream of the pools, the big win, the stroke of good fortune. We hoped for the whole of the working class, not just for ourselves.'

Many of those who recall the twenties and thirties insist that much work was relentless and harsh, without satisfaction for individuals, often an affront to their intelligence and abilities. But there were two great consolations: the sense of the indispensability of their labour in occupations that were plainly essential, however poorly rewarded, and the sense of a shared predicament. It was this collective dignity and stoicism which constituted what we may call, with bitter irony, the moral capital of the Labour movement, on which dwindling resource it has been living ever since. Unemployment in that atmosphere had its particular pain – absence of work in places that were built for no other purpose; whereas unemployment in a context of a function already eroded is more like an aggravation of processes already pervasive and widespread, especially as it affects the young. Of course the transition from one context to another has not been abrupt. It is a continuous process. J. B. Priestley[9] in Stockton on Tees in 1934 already foreshadowed much of what is familiar today:

> Stockton has shipyards that have been closed for years, so that the grass is growing in them, and it is very unlikely that they will ever be opened again. It has big marine engineering shops that are now empty shells of brick, though the engines they sent out are still driving good little tramp steamers through every sea in the world. And it has a large number of citizens, excellent skilled workmen, who have been unemployed not merely this year and last year but for seven and eight years, who might as well be crossbow-men or armourers, it seems, for all the demand there is for their services.

And equally, the heroism of the old working class is not extinguished by any means, even though so many of the industries in which they worked are in decline. Many of those who work in coal and steel, construction and fishing, although only a fraction of the work-force, can still call on the epic associations of their past. This is especially true of the miners who, with their heroic past and elemental work, are the subject of a whole working-class folklore and literature. Zola expresses this at the end of *Germinal*:[10] as Etienne walks away over the fields quickening with springtime growth which covers the coalmine, he hears the sound of thousands of his comrades tapping out their warning under the earth: 'Men were growing there like seeds in the dark, a black and vengeful army, germinating slowly in the ground, preparing themselves for the harvest of future centuries when their final flowering would burst forth and open up the whole earth.'

But increasingly the essential work of production can be carried out more effectively with the decreasing participation of the British working class, whether this production is transferred to workers in other parts of the world, or whether through technological innovation. Many of those who are relieved of their traditional labour, both here and elsewhere in the West, are redeployed. But they do not, for the most part, move to work that has the same obvious relationship to human purposes; for instance those who move from agricultural production to food-processing factories; and this is reflected in the economy of many working-class towns. In Northampton, where I grew up, the change has been from the making of boots and shoes to the credit industry and the manufacture of cosmetics. If the pressure of relentless work prevented millions of people from developing their real powers and abilities, the changed and easier conditions, instead of releasing them, demand less and less of working people, and just as effectively inhibit and lock up their strengths and possibilities as poverty ever did.

This tendency is currently hidden by a rhetoric that promises a future of leisure and freedom from work – a kind of mass aristocratic society. This vision is offered by capitalism to the descendants of those it abused and injured in the past – an ex-gratia bounty to make up for the breaking of bodies and destruction of the spirit of so many people now dead. This vision, however, belongs securely to the future. It is to be aspired to, earned, achieved only on certain conditions, the principal one being that the working class should acquiesce in their own erosion, if not extinction. They must lend themselves to a painless and terminal effort to make themselves even more expendable and powerless than they have been in the past. The words that cloak these processes are familiar to us all: modernization, rationalization, streamlining, renewal, regeneration – all words that sound dynamic and thrusting, but which smuggle in ideas deeply damaging to their victims. (This is not a recent phenomenon either, although it has accelerated in the last few years. J. B. Priestley wrote in the 1930s:[11] 'A rationalization of industry that suddenly leaves a whole mass of men sinking into the bog of permanent unemployment cannot be very rational.') These processes all imply the growing expendability of people; and this has been dramatically highlighted by the present increase in unemployment. In the past, it has often been difficult to decide which is worse: the capitalist imposition of work, or the arbitrary removal of it at times of recession and slump. The experience of both should perhaps make us wary of any promises about a future of leisure; it may well be that unemployment in the eighties turns out to be an anticipation of that future, and most of those who have been subjected to it do not, on the whole, recommend it.

But it is only now that we can begin to see in a longer perspective the meaning of some of those changes that have occurred in working-class life in recent decades. We should perhaps look again at all that has been conceded to working people. Concealed until now by constant insistence on material improvements – the least that capitalism had to offer – the extent of the continuing expropriation and dispossession of the working class is only just becoming visible.

In response to the seductive clamour of the market-place and a promise of plenty, much of the resistance of working people to the destructive power of an earlier stage of capitalism has been unwittingly surrendered. The old defences have broken down, and the modest gains only serve to shroud much greater forfeits.

The pain of unemployment in the eighties does not come only from the ruin of the old industries formerly associated with essential work. It is aggravated by the loss of the human response to the cruelty of the conditions which those industries imposed upon people. Even the least sentimental writers about the working class have dwelt on the positive values of the old neighbourhoods, however poor. Robert Roberts,[12] in *The Classic Slum*, certainly no romantic, writing of the early years of this century in Salford, says:

> People, en masse, it is true, had little education, but the discern-

ing of the time saw abundant evidence of intelligence, shrewdness, restraint and maturity . . . Very many families, even in our 'low' district, remained awesomely respectable over a lifetime. Despite poverty and appalling surroundings, parents brought up their children to be decent, kindly and honourable.

Their sense of a shared predicament was so intense that at times it became more than a reaction to harsh economic conditions. At its best, it reached a metaphysical level; it became a metaphor for the heights men can reach in their response to suffering, as they contemplated the brevity of their life and its sure extinction in pain and struggle. It is this feeling that runs through Hoggart's *Uses of Literacy*,[13] and the poignancy of that book lies in that it was written in the 1950s, at the time when the working class was losing much of what Hoggart describes. That process of loss has intensified since then, but it has not been recognized for what it was. Dismissed or devalued by academics as romanticism or nostalgia, it has been sentimentalized by politicians and the media for their own purposes.

As the importance of work has been eroded, so has much that went with it. The working class has been gutted of much of its substance, and dependency on commodities has been substituted for it, what Illich[14] calls 'an addiction to paralysing affluence'. Those who seemed to own nothing have nevertheless had priceless things stolen from them: wisdom won through effort and struggle, the knowledge of how to respond adequately to their own and others' suffering. These are things of such worth and beauty that it is impossible to believe that they have been yielded without a fight. And yet such is the case; what has happened has scarcely been acknowledged, let alone resisted.

In their calm certainty that nothing has changed, and that they know their enemy, even large parts of the Labour movement have been enlisted in a crusade on behalf of those processes which are necessary to the evolution of capitalism. I mean, in particular, the turning over of so many areas of human experience – those things in which the old working class was proud and self-sufficient – to the market-place. This mysterious alchemy transforms everything. Intangible things, moral, human and spiritual qualities are changed into commodities that can be bought and sold. If working people have been complaining about the loss of community, the destruction of traditional relationships and associations, this is what has happened to them. 'Expectations grow while hopeful trust in one's own competence and the concern for others rapidly decline' as Illich puts it.[15]

Nothing illustrates more clearly the sense of being trapped, functionless and without purpose than the lives of the working-class young. They have been nurtured in a closed world of material things brought to perfection, goods that cry their competitive desirability at them from the moment they are born. Their only business, it seems, is to yearn and strive for possession of them. The increase in violence, disturbance and destructiveness among the young, which puzzles so many people, seems to me to have more to do with the obliterated function of which they are the inheritors than with an insufficiency of money to buy all the things that are supposed to constitute the 'full' life. Their part in the production of all the wonders that have been spread before them is pitifully reduced. It is not for them to wonder where they came from, how they were made, nor what effort and pain went into their making, what suffering may be contained in the most trifling ornament or plaything. Nothing is demanded of the young but their continued passivity and quiescence. Nothing is asked of them. They seem to have no place in the world, except as obedient and abject competitors for all that is tantalizingly held out to them. And the real choice is obscured from them – the possibility of another context in which this would not be so. In this way the primary determinant in their lives has been, not work, not doing or contributing or creating anything, but the lopsided insistence on buying, getting and having. In other words, a most important aspect of the lives of the young – their social development – becomes a function of market relationships, a by-product of selling things. In its way this is as cruel and disabling as the old poverty was. And if people are treated like this, their energies denied, their will to create suppressed, we should not wonder if their reactions are disturbed and violent.

Anyone who spends time in the emptied towns and wrecked communities where the old industries are in retreat and a sense of aimlessness pervades everything must be appalled by the feeling of shock that hangs over them. In these places, where people gave everything and received nothing in reward for their labour ('My mother and father and his brother gave 150 years between them to one firm; and none of them had so much as a 'thank-you' on the day they retired,' said one old man in Sheffield), a mirror-image of that relationship tries to hide the violence that has been done to them. In most towns and cities the only sign of dynamism has been in the construction of new shopping malls and plazas: these now offer everything, and people have nothing of themselves left to give. Skills, strengths, powers and possibilities lie choked and unused within.

In the changed circumstances of recession, the clamour and excitement of the expanding consumer economy which grew throughout the fifties and sixties, have different, harsher echoes. Those caressing voices – which urged people to get more and to do less; to spend their human substance as easily and unreflectingly as they spent their money; to set aside skill and forget struggle and effort – now seem to have been, not only a delusion, but also a terrible trap. Those who resisted the blandishments of that capitalist plenty, its promises and seductions, were right to be wary. The transaction that has taken place between the working class and capitalism has been, as always, profoundly unequal.

The golden age of the consumer society may come to be seen simply as an interval. The working class was persuaded that capitalism had changed radically. Poverty and poor rewards for work seemed about to disappear for ever. But in fact it was a time for only paltry concessions, under cover of which a great deal more could be spirited away by stealth.

Writing of an earlier period, E.P. Thompson[16] says:

> If we can now see more clearly many of the elements which made up the working-class communities of the early nineteenth century, a definitive answer to the 'standard-of-living' controversy must still evade us. For beneath the word 'standard' we must always find judgements of value as well as questions of fact . . . Any evaluation of the quality of life must entail an assessment of the total life-experience, the manifold satisfactions or deprivations, cultural as well as material, of the people concerned. From such a standpoint, the older 'cataclysmic' view of the Industrial Revolution must still be accepted. During the years between 1780 and 1840 the people of Britain suffered an experience of immiseration, even if it is possible to show a small statistical improvement in material conditions.

Observations of such critical sensitivity should not be confined only to an assessment of the past: our contemporary experience is in even more urgent need of them. The fact that material conditions have conspicuously improved in recent years is not in dispute; but this should not inhibit us from trying to judge the effect of the accompanying loss of intangibles – relationships, satisfactions, values – the human things, to which everything else is, after all, only a means.

We can see now that the subordination of the working class to the needs of capitalism for the sake of necessary work has been evolving into the subordination of the working class for the sake of nothing but its continuing subordination. One kind of meanness and indignity has been replaced by another. And because of its impaired work contribution, the working class has less strength and power to oppose the process. This means that much of the work achieved by the Labour movement has to be done all over again, and from a far more difficult starting-point. We have believed that capitalism, which visited on so many working people pain and degradation, was capable, even willing, to bring those same people plenty and comfort. The effects of our compliance in this belief are beginning to be discernible, not only in the values in which so many of the working-class young have been nurtured, but in the feeling of impotence of millions of people in the face of what it had been calmly asserted was the unacceptability of 3,000,000 people without work.

The future of Western society begins to look less like the age of leisure for the working class, as it is sometimes represented, than a time of drugged somnolence, an even greater subjection than has been known before. It suggests a world in which the working class, having had its potential for the creation of alternative values taken from it, can only answer back with 'mindless' violence, rioting, perhaps racial conflict – anger detached from conscious political objectives. In so far as the riots in the summer of 1981 were a reaction to a sense of despair, the images they produced of looting and destruction do not suggest a resistance to capitalist values, much less an expression of the desire for an alternative. Such reactions are a measure of the growing political impotence of the working class, and suggest evidence of its greatest forfeit of all – confidence in its ability to fashion a more just and humane society in opposition to the continuing indignities which capitalism reserves for it.

The similarities between the experience of unemployment in the 1930s and the 1980s are not hard to find. There is the recurring sense of hopelessness, the same general acceptance, a repeat of the individual's feeling of a lack of worth, the same waste of human abilities. The same images are evoked – the scrap-heap, people rotting away, the laying waste of human lives just as the old industrial areas have been devastated. One of the things I set out to discuss with working people in preparing this book was whether the most significant difference between the thirties and the eighties was not what appears at first sight to be yet another similarity: a sense of defeat. This was a powerful theme of the 1930s in the aftermath of the General Strike, in spite of the efforts of the NUWM, and the sporadic disturbances of protesters against the Means Test and at the reorganization of the administration of unemployment relief in 1935. One of the questions this book asks is whether the defeat of the working class in the eighties isn't even more radical and enduring than it was then because of the assault on its very purpose and function. It is a complex issue, and one which easily lends itself to exaggeration and hyperbole. But it is possible to look for tendencies and patterns in the overwhelming confusion of reaction to daily events. There is some contradiction in the evidence of the effect on people being without work. A great deal depends on the temperament and internal resources of individuals, and I have met a fair sprinkling for whom unemployment has meant personal liberation in quite unexpected ways. These should not be discounted. But they are a minority. For most people, everything confirms Harrison's view that 'Prolonged unemployment is for most people a profoundly corrosive experience, undermining personality and atrophying work capacities' (quoted Sinfield 1981).[17]

2
Family on the Dole

What unemployment feels like has been presented to us extensively in the last few years in the form of media portraits, newspaper reports and political speeches. Most people are familiar with the television interview; the young man sitting on the leatherette sofa with the foam rubber exposed through the cracks in the seat, and the wife sitting on the edge of her chair, hands clasped in her lap, shoulders rounded in despair. The furniture is decrepit, and everything in the flat seems to be falling apart after only a year or two without money for replenishment and renewal. There are the pieces of ornament already tarnished and dingy, the stains on the carpet, the biro marks on the wall where the five-year-old scribbled while mother was trying to get the baby to sleep. The children, half-shy, half-fascinated by the tv camera, suck lollipops, bought no doubt out of the petty cash allocated to the film-makers to keep the kids quiet during the interview, and the baby lies in its second-hand cot with just the basic necessities allowed by Social Security. The man rolls thin cigarettes from the shreds of tobacco in a battered tin; his fingers tremble as he talks about the boredom of being at home and the dispiriting walks all round town to find work. The camera lingers on the tattoo on the back of his hands or the bitten fingernails. His wife manages a weak smile when she says he gets on her nerves being around the house all the time; and then she becomes serious and the tears stand in her eyes when she says how guilty she feels that she can't give her children the things other kids have. She has to dress in second-hand things – she can't remember the last time she had a new dress. They say how they are ashamed to go out because some of their neighbours who are working think the husband hasn't tried hard enough to get a job. He no longer even goes to the pub to enjoy a pint as he used to, but stays at home all day watching television, even the women's and children's programmes. They look at each other and admit to the interviewer that they have had more frequent arguments in recent months. In fact, their marriage has come close to breakdown. If it hadn't been for her Mum and the occasional pound or two and the little treats for the children from her, they don't know what they would have done.

These images are powerful; but they are soon gone. They give no sense of the elasticity of time, all those empty hours in the middle of the day, the temptation to sleep more and more as an escape. The fact that employment imposes a time structure on the waking day is the first of the most important 'latent functions of work', as identified by Marie Jahoda (as opposed to its manifest functions, pay and conditions).[18] That this is so is an impression I was able to deepen by a few days spent with a young couple in a Midland town at the beginning of 1981.

Mike and Jean live in a three-bedroom house on an early post-war council estate about two miles from the town centre. The houses are half red-brick, half grey concrete slabs. The estate is bleak and dingy, but not badly run down. Each house has a spindly metal porch supporting a concrete slab, and the patches of green are muddy with the winter rain. Mike's last official job finished almost a year earlier: he had worked as a warehouseman in a factory that had closed, making about 300 people redundant, almost a third of them from the estate where Mike and Jean live. At that time the unemployment rate was already 12 per cent in the town. Mike then worked briefly and unofficially with a friend who had opened a second-hand spare-parts yard; but they quarrelled because the money he had been promised wasn't paid.

Mike and Jean have two children, Neil, six, and Natalie, four. They have been married seven years. They say they still love each other, but communication between them has become limited and functional. When they eat, the whole family turns towards the television – an old black-and-white set balanced on top of an even older tv set which hasn't worked for years. 'You feel you have nothing to say to each other. What have I done in a day that interests her?'

I've never had a stronger feeling of the actual effect of television on people's lives than I had with Mike and Jean. It is not only the jingles of the adverts, the impossible holidays in the Caribbean, the invitations to get an American Express card, the urgent necessity of acquiring a hover-mower – the hollowness of that speaks for itself. Rather, it is the intensity of life that takes place on the screen, against the emptiness of what seems to happen in that threadbare living-room with its old moquette three-piece, the buff-coloured fireplace with the bag of coal in the hearth, and the battered, tarnished saucepan with its mince stew that Jean serves directly over large chunks of bread on each plate (carrots, onions, some Bisto with half a pound of mincemeat makes a meal for four). On the screen there is a sustained intensity of emotions, but expansive, passionate emotions, lust and greed, love and violence; not the irritation and tetchiness of a domestic interior. The television seemed to disturb their lives by this insistence on stormy and powerful relationships, more often than not allied to great wealth. The week I was there an American four-part serial seemed to shriek at Mike and Jean their own inadequacy. I had the impression that they felt their life was diminished, their relationship denied. Their own experience is nowhere validated publicly; and even the attempt to escape from it only gives another twist to the screw. The children, too, seemed hallucinated. Neil was so engrossed that he spilt his dinner or knocked over his cup of tea; and then Jean lost her temper and shouted at him; and it didn't sound at all like the shouting that had been coming from the television a few minutes earlier.

Mike and Jean are fighting demoralization all the time. They try to impose some structure on their lives. Tuesday, for instance, is child allowance day, and Jean always dresses up a bit to go to the post office because it makes an outing. She often runs into one or two women she knows, and they stop to have a chat. It was a cold drizzly morning when I went with her, and there was a small cluster of mostly young women with small children, standing in the cold, stamping their feet, exchanging a wry joke or two – a sad sketch of a social life. They never go to each other's houses. Jean said, 'I don't want people coming in here, seeing how shabby it is.' Mike told her not to be so stupid; 'they've got no more than we have.' 'Yes they have. Carol's Dave is working, they've got a nice house, she's always wearing something new.' 'People don't come to see what you've got, they come to see you.' 'I don't care. I don't want them here.' This makes Mike angry because he can feel her hostility towards him, and he feels keenly his own failure to fulfil what remains to him of the male role – which basically means providing money; and he sulks and recklessly put too much coal on the fire. She says, 'It's not that cold, don't waste it.' Then – because I am there – the quarrel stops and they say: 'This is how it is all the time. The only things you've got to say to each other are things that hurt. You can't do anything for each other except lose your temper.'

Jean walks to town twice a week. The fare is thirty-six pence each way on the bus. She pushes Natalie in her chair, but when Neil is not at school he stays with his father because four miles is a long way for a six-year-old. Jean goes to three supermarkets because she knows where the cheapest items are to be found. She buys the supermarket brand of whatever is available – Co-op washing-up liquid and toothpaste, for example, even though the quality is not so good. Her weekend shopping, heaped on the counter at the checkout, looked sad and not very appetizing. The only meat was some frozen New Zealand lamb chops which looked like a block of wood painted crimson. There was processed cheese, a 5lb bag of potatoes, some carrots and parsnips, two sliced loaves, 12 eggs, a box of cup cakes, cornflakes, half a pound of butter, a quarter of tea, 2lb of sugar, and a tin of sardines for Saturday dinner. The only luxuries, as she called them, were a packet of streaky bacon for tea on Saturday and some chocolate Penguins for the children.

On Thursday Mike goes to sign on. There is a line of about fifty people stretching out of the reinforced glass doors of the plain rectangular building. A few children, one or two with dogs, wait outside. The people in the queue do not speak to each other. Movement is slow; a slightly anxious shuffling, as each individual signs at the counter, and then goes on to the desk, which is a sort of glass cage partitioned off from the main counter. The rubberized buff and pale-blue floor tiles are covered with crushed cigarette ends and the imprint of muddy boots. You can tell which people in the queue have been out of work the longest: some wear clothes that were in fashion a few years ago – bell-bottomed trousers, particoloured imitation-suede jackets, cork-heeled shoes.

Mike says, 'You always get nervous when you go to sign on. There's always the worry that your giro might not be there. You watch them fingering the bundle of giros behind each letter of the alphabet, and you think "What will I do if mine isn't there?" Only once it wasn't. It was terrible. They swore I'd come to the wrong place. You panic, you don't know what you're doing, you can see the wife and kids without any grub. I had to go to Social Security. It was all sorted out, but it scared me.'

Inside the office there are a couple of blue plastic chairs, chained together. There is a notice board with a large poster of the Samaritans, inviting those close to despair to phone them. Mike sees me reading the notice and laughs. 'The reason why most poor buggers'd want to phone them would be because they don't have the five pence for the bloody phone call.' His laugh has a bitter edge in that silent shuffling crowd.

The post office is about a hundred yards away; and most of those go at once to cash their cheques. A few women are waiting outside. Mike says 'Hello' to one of them, a pale-faced thin woman of perhaps thirty-five, hair once dyed blonde, but darkening again at the roots, wearing an old blazer, torn jeans and plastic sandals. 'Her old man can't be trusted with a week's money in his fist. If she's not standing there when he gets paid, she'll not see a penny of it. They've got three kids.' Some of the childen who were waiting outside the Department of Employment office run past, into the tobacconist's, and come out a minute or two later with ice lollies and packets of sweets. 'That's their week's money gone,' says Mike.

On Friday, Jean is going to a jumble sale at the church. The church is a red-brick building, dim with the soot of vanished industry. The church hall adjoins it, and there is a piece of garden in front with laurel bushes and a holly tree. On a piece of cardboard fixed to the gatepost is written 'Jumble Sale, Friday at 6.0'. Jean gets there by quarter past five, and she is by no means among the first. One woman says she has been waiting since three o'clock. She is very knowledgeable about the jumble sales in the area, knowing which ones have good quality stuff and which ones aren't worth waiting for. St Luke's has a good reputation. One women tells how she once found a five pound note in a jacket she bought for her husband. 'I took it back.' 'Barmy bugger.' 'No, the Vicar said he knew the woman who gave it, and she put the money in it on purpose. He gave her another fiver for being honest.' 'Get away.' At six o'clock the door opens, people pay their five pence, and rush to the clothing stalls, seizing garments which look good.

'You don't go with anything special in mind' says Jean, 'you just have to make sure you don't get a lot of stuff you don't need. But if I see anything decent for myself or Mike, I'll take it.' There is a hectic quarter of an hour, by which time, most of the things worth having will have been taken. Nearly all the customers are women; the husbands of many of them are out of work. Jean indicates two who are single parents, one deserted, one unmarried. 'At least we're together', she reflects, 'though sometimes I wonder how much longer if things go on the way they are.' She has a pair of children's jeans for Neil, a bit too long, but they'll turn up, and a dress for Natalie, and a pair of shoes that Natalie will grow into. She has spent 95 pence.

On Friday evening, Mike goes out for a drink to the WMC – a rather gaunt and cheerless room, with snooker, darts, and a space invader machine, which the same group of boys monopolizes for almost two hours. It is a wet night, and coats and umbrellas drip onto the rubber tiles. Most of the men are middle-aged or elderly. Mike comes here in preference to the pub, because the older men are more sympathetic. There is a group of younger men out of work who come in only on Fridays and Saturdays. The talk is all of the Yorkshire Ripper, who has appeared in court that week; how many times the police had already interviewed him, how the joker who made the Geordie tape had contributed to the deaths of the last five women. 'He was a fucking animal' says one of the older men, 'and he should be put down like a fucking mad dog. Hanging's too good for him. I don't know about bring back the rope, what he wants is something slow and fucking lingering.' 'Try my missis' says one of the others, and everybody laughs. Mike says 'Don't take Harry too seriously, he just don't want anybody to know what a kind heart he's got.' Harry denies it. 'Fucking stone mate,' he says, patting his chest. Later, Mike tells me that Harry and his wife lost their only child when she was seven; that his wife has been in hospital, prematurely senile for ten years, and that Harry goes to see her three times a week. Harry has the role of offering a defining edge to the others. Later he says he thinks Mrs Thatcher is the best thing that's happened to this country for years. 'She put you out of a job.' 'The world don't owe me a fucking living. I don't need her to teach me that, like some of you silly fuckers. Eating seed-corn, that's what we've been doing for years. Eating seed-corn.' The conversation comes back to the ripper and sex. Harry says 'Sex on the brain, that's the trouble. We never had all this sort of thing years ago. We had better things to think of.' 'Better than sex?' 'It's all got out of hand.' 'Not out of mine it hasn't.' He makes a wanking movement. Everybody laughs. 'They'll have a fucking minister for sex next.' There is a sense of release that is quite out of proportion to the modest jokes – it is a way of dealing with all the pent-up frustrations, not only the enforced monogamy of having no money to be anything else, but the long days at home in the week, sleeping in the armchair in the afternoon, inventing things to do in the house that don't cost money, the lack of social contact, which most unemployed people mention as the thing they miss most about work after the money. Mike drinks three pints, and he is visibly more relaxed when he gets home.

On Friday evening Jean takes Neil and Natalie to see her mother. Alice is fifty-eight, and works full time in a baker's and confectioner's near the centre of the town that specializes in lunch-time take-away sandwiches. She has been there since her husband died, eighteen years ago, and she always provides good things for tea on Friday; and two or three times a week takes the odd cakes and left-over sandwiches down to Jean. She is generous to the children, and most of their Christmas presents and birthday toys are provided by her. Nan has a colour tv, which is still a novelty for the children. Jean goes down to see her in mid-afternoon, after she has collected Neil from school. The journey is about a mile. On Friday, Mike gets his own tea. Jean is close to her mother, and often has a moan and a weep – a very similar kind of release to that of Mike's. Today, Alice looks at Jean and wonders if she's all right. Jean has been to the doctor's, and takes out a cylinder of Valium, 2 mg, one to be taken three times a day.

She started taking the sleeping tablets because she found herself lying awake all night wondering how she'd get through the next day without her proper sleep. She says that she is bored a lot of the time, and sometimes she and Mike go for two or three weeks at a time without sex. Jean says she can't bring herself to initiate it.

'Even after all these years. I feel now he's at home all the while, I don't know him as well as I used to. I see more of him, but it's like it's too much effort. You can feel time slipping past, and you know you ought to do something about it, only you don't know what. Sometimes I panic, I think "This is it, I'm on the downward slope, I'm going to get old, and the kids'll grow up, and then by that time there'll be nothing between me and him, only a lot of years together." Do you know what I mean?' Jean worries because the relationships of so many other people on the estate are all breaking up. 'Half the marriages are on the rocks, they go their separate ways. Not that there's much chance of that, we're forced to be together like bloody convicts.'

Alice doesn't try to deny her daughter's feelings. She knows that what she is expressing are her fears – not her real relationship with Mike. She always leaves her mother's before nine o'clock, partly because she feels afraid walking through the streets after dark, and partly because she knows that Mike will be home soon after ten; and she stops at the chip shop on the way for another of their little luxuries. She buys some peas and roe and chips, and puts them in the oven to keep warm; and he brings her a bottle of light ale, and they have supper when the children are in bed.

Saturday morning isn't a happy time for the family. Perhaps it is the start of the weekend, the time of leisure only reinforces Mike's sense of inactivity. Jean tries to get him to dig the garden, which is neglected and untidy. 'At least we could grow a few things, some vegetables or something. But he won't.' Mike says if he did dig the garden, he would grow flowers anyway; he doesn't see why he should have to grow his own food. 'My Mum said they all did it in the War.' 'We're not in a war.' 'That's what you think.' 'What do you mean by that?' Half-exasperated, half-affectionate, she thumps him; he seizes her by the wrists and she falls onto the sofa, laughing and crying at the same time.

Jean says that their life has become very tense: it's touch and go whether they have an argument or whether she sits down and has a cry for no apparent reason. Mike takes the spade out of the porch, and turns over a few spadefuls of earth in the garden; but the grass has grown so high, and the ground is so stony that he gives it up, and comes in a few minutes later saying it's hopeless. He doesn't have the will to do it. He knows he should; but the rewards seem remote and thin. He sits in the armchair by the fire; and Neil comes to sit on his lap; he buries his face in the child's hair. He says 'What is my kid going to think of me? You feel so useless. You're a failure.' Natalie climbs up onto the other side of the chair, and pushes Neil slightly to make room for herself on her father's lap.

Jean gets ready to go shopping. When she has gone, he goes round to the local shops and goes into the betting shop to put 'a few bob' on a horse. He won't tell Jean unless he wins.

Saturday afternoon is spent watching sport on the television.

Mike's sister sometimes comes in at tea-time: her children, Kerry and Donna, are the same age as Neil and Natalie. Jean and Mike don't have friends. They know a lot of people in the neighbourhood 'to speak to', but they don't visit. Jean says that when people first move, they're in and out of each other's houses for the first few weeks, then they fall out, and then your life is all over the estate. Mike's sister and her husband are the only people of their own age they see regularly, and they go out with them at Bank holidays and occasionally weekends; but Roy is working, and since Mike hasn't worked, there has been an awkwardness between them. Roy is generous, but Mike won't accept the outings in the car without paying for some petrol, and it embarrasses him to have Roy buy ice-creams for his children. 'It messes up your relations with everybody,' Mike says. 'You have to budget for the last penny, and you know if you go over that any week, something's got to be sacrificed.' They don't have a newspaper except on Sundays; Jean's mother keeps the *Mirror* for them, but it's nearly always two or three days old by the time they get it.

On Saturday evening, Mike and Jean play cards when the children have gone to bed. They have a bottle of beer each; and Mike is always rolling cigarettes so thin that they disappear in two or three puffs. The television plays in the background all the time. Somewhere on the estate a party is in progress and the thump of the music throbs through the house, making Jean irritable. She gives up the card game, and goes to the window. She says she can't remember the last party she went to. Mike tries to be cheerful. He says, 'Well we'll have our own.' 'What on, fresh air and tap-water?'

On Sunday morning an absolute silence lies over the estate until 11 o'clock. A few children on their way to get sweets or a Sunday paper; one or two people perhaps going to church. Mike and Jean don't get up until 11.30. She makes tea; and Neil and Natalie creep into bed with them. Mike reads the paper. Natalie goes downstairs, and Neil is sent with her to make sure she doesn't come to harm. She gets out a plastic tricycle, a flimsy white moulded thing, and pedals down the garden path. Jean is just getting up, when suddenly Natalie is heard screaming. She runs into the garden: the trike has struck a stone in the path and overturned and Natalie has cut her forehead on the clothes'-line post, which is set in a concrete base. Jean picks her up, but the child continues to scream. Mike runs down, half-dressed. He pours some disinfectant into a basin and dilutes it with water to wash the cut. They have no antiseptic apart from the pine disinfectant they use to clean the lavatory. The thick brown liquid dilutes to a whitish colour in water. There is no bandage in the house; but Jean keeps an old torn sheet for the purpose, and cuts a strip from it. There is a wad of cotton wool in the bathroom. The wound is not deep, but it is bleeding a lot, and Natalie is frightened and continues to scream. As soon as the disinfectant is applied, she screams even louder. Jean tries to comfort her while she is cleaning the cut. It doesn't stop bleeding. Mike says 'Do you think she ought to have a stitch in it?' Jean is more worried that Natalie has never had a tetanus injection. Mike goes to the neighbour to see if he will run them down to the hospital in his car. He isn't at home. Mike comes back. 'I think we should get her to the hospital.' He suggests a minicab; but the telephone has been vandalized. The bus runs only once an hour; it would be 40 minutes before there's another. 'I don't think it's too bad,' says Jean. 'We've cleaned it. There.' She winds the piece of frayed sheet around the child's head. Natalie is still crying, but the screaming has stopped. 'I think she'll be all right.' 'Are we going to take her to hospital?' 'She'll be all right.' 'Are you sure?' 'I think so.' The wound wasn't as bad as it seemed at first; but if they had had the means, no doubt they would have taken her to hospital. Later, Natalie begins to enjoy the attention, and everybody says she's been in the wars, she is a proper little wounded soldier. Mike takes her down to the shop, carrying her on his shoulders, and buys her some Smarties; and some for Neil so he doesn't feel left out.

Sunday dinner consists of the lamb chops, and Jean makes some sauce with the mint that is just beginning to grow in profusion at the bottom of the garden. There are potatoes and carrots, and an Instant Whip for afters, with ice-cream as an extra. When he has finished, Mike goes and eats two slices of bread and jam because he is still hungry. Sunday afternoon is a quiet time after the emotional upset of the morning. Later on, Alice is coming for tea.

When she arrives, the children jump up and run to her; she carries an old leather bag; there is bound to be something good in it. She has half a dozen custard tarts, two Florentines. She has brought the last two days' *Daily Mirror*. She makes a great fuss of Natalie, and gives her ten pence. Jean frowns; she doesn't like her mother to give them money. Natalie wants to go to the shop to spend it, but Mike says no. She starts to cry. 'Nana'll go with you in a few minutes my love.' Alice looks at the bandage around the little girl's head. 'Is that the best you could do?' she asks. 'I can't afford anything else Mum.' Jean's voice is strained. Alice looks at Mike. 'I know what you're thinking,' he says to her. 'I never said a word.' 'No, you don't need to.' 'Well, is there anything in the offing?' 'No there isn't. Do you think I'd be bloody sitting here every day if I had any choice?' 'I only asked.' 'You're always only asking. How do you think I spend my sodding time? Do you think I'm on some sort of holiday? Do you think I want my kid to wear a bit of sheet round her because we can't buy bandage?'

One of Mike's complaints about Alice is that she doesn't realize how impossible it is to get work at the moment. She's always just heard of somebody who's got a job; Mike thinks she is criticizing him for being feckless. To make matters worse, she tells an anecdote of a pensioner who's just got a part-time job doing somebody's garden; and Jean says Mike can't even do his own. Mike gets up and storms out. Jean is alarmed now; and she turns on her mother, saying 'Now look what you've done.'

Mike stays out for several hours. In fact, he has been to his sister's; and by the time he comes back Alice has gone. There is a tense silence between him and his wife. She says she is sorry; but for an hour or more, Mike is unrelenting. Later, he yields and says that he knows that Alice is good to the kids, but that doesn't give her the right to disapprove, and behave as though she doubted his efforts to get a job. Jean is soothing and they are reconciled, curling up in the same chair together.

On Monday morning, Mike is up and out of the house by half-past eight. He says he won't come back until he's got a job.

Spending time with people out of work, you can see how love is stretched and the relationships wear thin. Mike and Jean are more resilient than many others I met. People turn on those who love them best because there is nobody else you can take the pain and humiliation to. Jean and Mike say they know a lot of people who've left each other, because in a way it is easier to run away from responsibilities than to stick with them. My memory of time with them is of a house that was shabby, never quite warm enough. The food they eat is not very tasty and never quite sufficient. Many basic household items that most people take for granted are simply not there; everything runs down and cannot be replaced.

Adrian Sinfield[19] says, 'Observing the pressures and strains that poverty and prolonged unemployment place on many families, my own research has made me much more conscious of the many ways the double impact wears them down and turns them in on themselves. The silent endurance of deprivation and rejection does not make headlines, and is astonishingly often dismissed as apathy or lack of will.'

Certainly, poverty is the greatest nightmare of those who fall out of work; perhaps we should wonder how this should be so in the richest societies the world has ever known.

3
The Survival of Poverty

Many people wonder why our poverty, the poverty of the rich world, remains so ugly and hard to bear, when it should be easier than the poverty of our own past and far easier than the destitution of much of the Third World. Perhaps the word 'poverty' covers too wide a range of ideas. After all, the experience of poverty in a monastery bears little relation to what it means to be poor on a rundown council estate in the North of England. What is important is the context of poverty; and its function in the society gives it its particular feeling. If the poverty of nineteenth-century Britain was largely an unhappy product of powerless and inadequately compensated labour, if the poverty of certain religious groups is a discipline in the service of higher truths, what shall we say of our poverty now, in the rich societies of the West? Why have the vast material improvements over recent decades done so little to relieve the shame and humiliation of being poor?

One of the most obvious achievements of Western society since the Second World War has been its ability to eliminate poverty; and its failure to do so. The survival of poverty has been a project second in importance only to the conservation of wealth by the rich. The wonder is, in the midst of the abundance we have seen, not that the misery of being poor has been mitigated, but that the poor should still manage to be present at all. And since it is difficult to believe in the attachment of the poor to their condition, their permanence must have other causes.

It is not so much that the poor are indispensable as a foil to the rich that is remarkable; that is an old story. The fact that the poor should be still with us, and the manner of their survival, demonstrate the wonderful flexibility, the Protean nature of the capitalist processes. The persistence of poverty in spite of the capacity for enormous material advances shows that the poor are there for reasons which have nothing to do with scarcity of resources (in any way that scarcity could be interpreted by common sense) but everything to do with ideology.

The very idea of sufficiency is one which capitalism cannot acknowledge. The possibility that a society could produce enough to ensure the well-being and comfort of all its people is a terrible blasphemy against the deep purposes of capitalism. The drive for more, for accumulation, for increase, the generation of wealth, imply dearth, want and loss elsewhere; and the unchanging symbiosis of rich and poor only reflects this simple equation. In this way, concern for the poor is always tempered by the secure knowledge that we are never going to be seriously upset by their sudden disappearance. It is in this context that the suppression of the glaring fact that poverty is no longer 'necessary' has been the overriding aim of those who have led us through the last three or four decades. Their momentous and ignoble achievement has easily overshadowed that other possibility – the dream of an end to the ancient scourge of poverty – even though that too was a project well within our reach. The senseless dynamic of the *status quo* has reaffirmed itself in the face of common sense (human needs are only as elastic as an economic or social order requires them to be), in the face of morality (by our insistence on the rights of the rich to strive beyond satiation, we ensure that those parts of the world in absolute poverty become even poorer), and indeed in the face of feasibility (even with the prospect of ruinous effects on the resources of the earth, the only real 'hope' held out to the West lies in a resumption of growth, however cancerous that growth may prove to be). In other words, ideology is triumphant; and the affairs of continents continue to be conducted on the assumption that the only way for the world's poor to become a little less poor is for the rich to become very much richer.

In Britain we had all the conditions for the easy abolition of poverty, given the frugality, the modest needs of the old working class, the traditionally deprived, the previously poor, and given also the possibilities for post-war plenty. But here we are thirty years later, and poverty is as securely installed as if it had never for an instant been threatened. The spectre at the feast is an essential, if not honoured, guest. And in order to avoid admitting that we have failed to eliminate poverty when it was well within our power to do so, some elaborate justifications have been necessary. All the complex and ingenious academic and sociological constructs which seek to account for the persistence of poverty are mere decoration which shrouds the damaging absurdity at the heart of the way we live; and we continue to look to economists and social scientists for answers to moral problems. Of course they cannot solve the conundrum, but they offer some impressive theories.

For instance, we are told that deprivation is relative; and by that simple assertion the idea of sufficiency is abolished. Poverty and wealth become symbolic and are 'liberated' from any relationship to human need. Set free in this way from subordination to human purposes, the capitalist process achieves a kind of inviolability, and its power to assert its cold tyranny over us is legitimized, ensuring that the poor will indeed be with us for ever. In the same way, politicians can call Britain a 'poor' country and not be contradicted, in defiance of the evidence of our daily experience. We are told that we suffer as a country because we have failed to modernize, we haven't kept up with the necessary application of technological progress etc. What this really means is that the mythology which we apply internally has been also projected outwards until it embraces the whole world, so that we are doubly trapped in its absurd unrelenting mechanism. In other words, we are securely imprisoned in ideology.

And we accept it with a kind of fatalism which isn't normally associated with the West. If ever we need an example of the tenacity of belief in the face of reality, we should turn, not to the triumph of Islam over self-interest in Iran, nor even to the ugly contortions of Soviet communism. The subordination of millions of people in our own society to our belief is actually a form of human sacrifice. It is our tribute of living flesh to ideology. It is, of course, an aspect of the very thing which we claim to abhor in the Soviet Union, with its stifling of individuals for the sake of inflexible beliefs. And even if we were to concede the analogy, we would no doubt say that we conduct these things with much greater subtlety in the West; even though there is nothing subtle about the cruel consequences of the ideology for all those people who continue to live out their lives in a state of wretched hopelessness in the richest societies the world has ever seen.

For in order to accommodate this lie – that poverty is irremediable – people have had to change. In order that poverty might survive human beings have had to adapt; and considerable violence has been done to them in the process. Humanity has had to be relentlessly, ruthlessly 'modernized'; and poverty has endured.

The poverty of the old working class, however harsh, did develop in people a certain response – a human resourcefulness, frugality, self-sufficiency, and the ability to share. Clearly these values militated against those that accompanied the advent of the consumer society. And so they had to be broken, in order to open up markets – the almost virgin territory of the traditionally deprived and under-rewarded. A whole culture, based on extreme scarcity of material resources, which nevertheless still managed to furnish some dignity and pride to people denied access to many basic necessities, had to be swept away. It was in effect the same kind of colonization which capitalism imposed on other cultures all over the world. People of course accepted it readily enough: they knew nothing then of the hidden costs, the measureless price they would pay and go on paying. They didn't know that out of the destruction of the positive and defensive response to the old poverty, a new experience of poverty would be forged.

In a one-storey terraced cottage in Sunderland, an old man sits among the plain furniture and modest ornaments acquired over a lifetime. He says 'Poverty has changed'. He speaks, not in the tone of so many old people who lament everything that is past, even the poverty, but with great feeling. He says that instead of curing one sort of poverty, we've exchanged it for another. If he says it's worse now, this is because there is even less need for people to be poor now than there was when he was young; and because the poor of this generation have lost the consolations that he and his wife had, despite a lifetime of hardship.

On the same estate, Grace Daly, a widow in her late sixties, describes her life as a girl. It is the kind of testimony to be heard every day in working-class areas, part of the common discourse of the last quarter century, but which has found no answering echo in political debate.

'We slept five to a bed, top to toe. There were thirteen of us living in two rooms. There was a kitchen table with a white wood top; my Mam scrubbed it snow-white, and she covered it with newspaper to keep it clean. We never had cups. My father used to take these empty tins of condensed milk, smooth all round the jagged edges, and then he soldered metal handles onto them, fettled cups for us. We never thought there was owt to be ashamed of; only how clever he was to think of it. He worked in the shipyard, but he never got a decent wage for it all his life. But don't get it wrong; the work he did wasn't degrading or worthless. And the way we lived, the way we looked after one another, we kept our dignity. My mother learned to make and mend, she could create a meal out of next to nothing. We learned to be frugal.

'I can remember the street on an afternoon; all the women'd be standing round the doors, talking to each other. One would say "Ah've got nowt for tea, what have you got?" The next one would say "Ah've nowt either, I don't know what Ah'm going to do." Then one of them would say "Why don't we make up a parcel and take it down the pawnshop?" One would say "Ah've got a pair of pillowcases"; another would have a pair of sheets, another some curtains. So they'd make up a parcel and take it to the pawnshop, and whatever they got, they'd share it out between them, get something for tea . . . The hardships of life didn't bother us like they bother people now. We learned to do things. When I was eight, one day my mother was called away sudden, just as she was getting all the week's baking ready; her sister had took bad, and she had to go to her. She stood me on a cracket and said "Get on and bake that bread." I'd seen her do it so many times, I knew by instinct what to do . . . Many a time I've seen my mother take the skirt off her back on a Sunday night to make a pair of trousers so the boys had something to go to school in on Monday. Whatever was wrong with life – and there was plenty – it wasn't the people, and the care they showed each other.

'Out of the week's money, rent always came first, then a good warm fire, then food; they were your priorities. We had nowt, but we shared it.' As she talks of her time, I am reminded of Orwell's evocation of the working-class interior in *The Road to Wigan Pier*:[20]

> In a working-class home . . . you breathe a warm, decent, deeply human atmosphere which it is not easy to find elsewhere . . . especially on winter evenings after tea, when a fire glows in the open range and dances mirrored in the steel fender, when

Father, in shirtsleeves, sits in the rocking-chair at one side of the fire reading the racing finals, and Mother sits on the other with her sewing, and the children are happy with a pennorth of humbugs, and the dog lolls roasting himself on the rag mat – it is a good place to be.

Grace Daly's neighbour, a man in his late seventies, says 'Oh, we suffered all right. As a lad, I was up at six o'clock on Saturday mornings to go and stand in the queue for two pennorth of stale cakes for the weekend. I've seen my father weep at the wages he had to offer my mother . . . And Mam, she had a baby a year; and she seemed to lose a child a year as well. But you had too much to do to be unhappy; and you had a whole street full of friends.'

The same place, Sunderland, January 1981. The male unemployment rate is twenty-eight per cent (reaching forty-five per cent in parts of the area), and one in four of the houses has had the gas cut off, according to a report by the Southwick Neighbourhood Action Project.[21] This advice and community centre – a former shop – acts as mediator between the poor and those agencies designed to serve them, but whose workings have become too frightening and labyrinthine for the poor themselves (the public utilities, DHSS, housing department, even Social Services).

On a late January afternoon, a low sun gilds the front of the houses, and their windows burn for a moment; but as soon as the sun goes, all colour is drained away. The brick dulls to the shade of dried blood, the green is sparse and faded. The privet hedges spike out in all directions, a broken fence collapses in a fan of creosote planks into a front garden. The neglected grass rustles in the biting wind that comes off the North Sea; an Alsatian dog turns on his chain on a patch of worn earth; a child plays with the rubbish spilt from an overturned dustbin. One house, blackened by fire, had been boarded up, but the plywood at the windows is torn away: inside, the litter suggests kids' glue-sniffing parties, and there are empty bottles of Newcastle Brown and cheap wine. The roads glitter with splinters of broken glass. Many windows are smashed; rough pieces of cardboard cover the cobweb of shattered glass; newspaper to keep out the draughts flutters in the rusting metal window-frames.

It is the context that gives poverty its definition. To see a child doing his homework by the light of a street-lamp on a freezing

December evening because the electricity in his home has been cut off; to hear the half-sad, half-proud voice of a mother saying of a handicapped three-year-old child 'He's just had his first clothing grant', as though it were a rite of passage from infancy to childhood; to listen to the woman whose husband has been out of work for five years, and who allows herself one pot of tea that has to last all day – all this would not be shocking if you felt it served some other purpose than the humiliation of those who suffer it. But it doesn't. As one poorly paid railway worker said 'Poverty has become a crime.'

In these towns, with their ruined industries, exhausted collieries and depleted shipyards, there is a sense of broken purpose, a draining away of meaning. What has been lost is that which sustained an older generation of the poor: their function and its importance. The poverty of living memory is allied to people's indispensable labour. An old miner said 'Even at the worst of the depression, you knew you were waiting for trade to pick up. You never lost that feeling that you belonged to the working class. Those who had work helped the poor and the unemployed. Nobody in the community called the unemployed scroungers. Even those who were a bit feckless, they were helped just the same as canny folk, those who could cope. They were still your neighbours.'

It seems that the purpose of the poor now is more nakedly ideological: their purpose is to be poor. Not to produce, but simply to serve as a contrast, a defining edge for wealth and success, and a warning and example to the rest.

It was the experience of work and an inadequate reward for it that produced such a profound collective resistance to the idea that poverty was the fault of those who were poor. Everybody had daily evidence that this was not so. But as the work function, and the sense of a shared predicament that went with it, have been eroded, so has resistance to the idea that the individual is not responsible for his plight. In this sad place, collective hope is being extinguished. In its place, the only hope most people are aware of is individual escape – the big pools win, a good night at bingo, something on the horses. This has had the effect of immeasurable impoverishment on communities whose only strength lay in the hope of sticking together and in shared action: something imposed upon them by their work and living conditions, but the forfeit of which leaves a sense of vast shock and emptiness.

As the traditional associations that grew up around the workplace and the streets have been discarded, people are set increasingly against one another. The pain of this process is keen in Sunderland, where memories of the pooling of resources – not only money – to fight destitution are still fresh. You can feel the sense of injury in everything people say. The old grieve, while the young become hardened against the sufferings of others. In the clubs and pubs, much of the talk is about who shopped someone to Social Security for doing a little job on the side; who grassed to the police about a break-in; who wrote an anonymous letter to a neighbour about what her husband was doing, working overtime 'with a woman in the next block'; who told the court when a husband disappeared to avoid paying maintenance; who neglects his kids and yet can walk out of Social Security with £300 special needs' payment in his hand.

One man, just out of prison, said 'My missis left me while I was inside. She divorced me and got custody of the bairns just to get her hands on the stuff in the flat. Then she sold it all up, dumped the kids on me Mam and pissed off with her new bloke.' A woman, a widow of twenty-nine with five children under the age of ten, a loving and conscientious mother, had been visited by a social worker in response to an anonymous letter that said she was going out every night and leaving her children with no one to look over them. 'When the social worker saw how I kept them and looked after the home, she said she was sorry and that I deserved a medal. The neighbours said they would all speak for me. But that's not the point. People know how to hurt you by hitting at you where your pride is, where it'll do the most harm.'

There is a competitive vigilance about who is getting more benefits than he should, who has given up work for easy dole money and a bit of undeclared on the side. The poor law lives on in people's attitudes towards each other; and the law of less eligibility has found a new impetus in these once solid working-class areas: 'Why should they get everything when they're not working, and I can't get any of the things I need.' The stories people are telling each other are about violence and assault, break-ins and vandalism, the fear of going out after dark, the nightmare of being alone, abandoned, unable to cope; all metaphors of loss and the stripping away of something vital.

The young, many of them out of school and out of work for two or three years, take refuge from the cold in the coffee-bar.

'I've took cars and driven them away loads of times. I don't care about getting put away, don't make any difference. I take things, not out of poverty, but because I'm bored. Take a car, it's the only thing that gets me high. Something to do.' His hair is shaved, and his face looks bony and hard. He wears an ear-stud, and a tattoo over his left eyebrow says 'Skins'. But his eyes don't change their expression all the time he is talking; nothing touches the sadness there. He is the oldest of seven children; his father died nine years ago, when he was nine years old. He goes home as little as possible. 'Sometimes I go and nick groceries from the supermarket and tell my Mam I bought them and she gives me the money. But I have to be hard up to do that.'

A boy of sixteen, still at school, with long hair that covers his forehead and eyes, says 'My Mam died last July. She died of a stroke I think it was. I was away at camp, and when I got back they told me. I don't go to school much. I've been eight days this term. They don't listen to you. I kicked somebody, and this teacher took all the kids and said to them they could all kick me if they wanted to.'

'My Dad's on disability benefit. But I've got older brothers behind me so I'm all right. If anybody picks on me, I can get my brothers to go and crack 'em. We were at this disco, and this kid said I insulted his girl. So him and his mates waited outside for us when we come out. He threw my mate through these doors, all the glass broke, and his mates were waiting in this car, and they chased us up this alley under the club. They gave my mate a yoking, they smashed his face in, broke his nose. The only way we got out – we started smashing their car with bricks, that was the only way to get them off us; we had to smash our way out.'

'My mate won ten pints at the club last night in a competition. So I got pissed. I stayed in bed till two o'clock today. My mate's about thirty. He's married. He don't sleep with his wife, she comes into the bathroom and sees him wanking himself . . . He's always making a grab for your bollocks. You can have a laugh with him.'

'Life is boring. There's nowt to get up for in the morning.'

'Anadin, crushed up with tobacco. That makes a good smoke. You don't know what you're doing.'

'You never do know what you're doing, you cunt.'

'I know a lad, you can get these pills, 50p each, crushed up in a pint.'

'Up Town End Farm, they sniff glue. They're losing what bit of brains they've got. You see them, like the walking fucking dead. I wouldn't do that.'

'There was a lad I knew, he was sniffing petrol or something, and then he was drinking and they took him home flat out, and laid him on his back, and he choked in his sick in the night. His old woman got up in the morning and found him dead.'

None of them has worked. 'My Dad's been out of work for two years now. He used to work on the buses. Then the Pyrex factory till it closed. So he can't say owt to me.'

'I'd like to settle down and buy a house.'

'I was courting this girl for five month. She got too serious. One night I was up her, and she suddenly starts crying. I thought fucking hell, this is supposed to be fun, what does she want to start howling for? She said she loved me. I don't want that yet. Not me. I didn't like to upset her, but I told her it wasn't on . . . She went and married my mate, they've got a kid.'

'I only want a job with a decent wage.'

'You ask Bri how to win a lot of money. He's got a mate in a betting shop, and he stops the time machine sometimes, finds out what's won, then tells Bri and he goes and puts a lot of money on and phones in. He won £350.'

A tall thin lad with dark hair who hasn't said much so far, tells of his ideal night out. He goes fishing at night. 'You go at six o'clock with a few of your mates, and you stay there all night, get home at seven in the morning. You can catch flatties and codlings, take them home to eat the next day. Oh it's beautiful. You light a fire, and you keep the fire in all night, and you sit there just listening to the wind, and watching the water. You take a flask of something hot to keep you warm. Come home at seven in the morning, then you can stay in bed till two in the afternoon. The other day I came home and I was that tired I laid down on the floor and fell asleep. My Dad gets up to go to work, he gives me a kick and says "Get up and get yourself a fucking job." I said to him "Fuck off will you." I wouldn't go too far with him though.'

'I've never worked,' says an eighteen-year-old, 'not for money.'

'Yes, you have, you cunt.'

'I haven't.'

'It's always been for money – nicking, mugging, breaking and entering.'

He thumps him affectionately in the chest.

'It's kill or be killed round here. This estate, it's getting like Belfast.'

They don't mean it all literally. What they are really saying is that they wish something would happen to take them away from the stifling boredom and lethargy, from the diminished sense of purpose which they have inherited. They long to be rescued from their own fantasies of escape: 'staying in bed till two in the afternoon, dreaming of being laid by Raquel Welch'.

They speak in metaphors, images, feelings, because they cannot see the society that has denied them any sense of purpose, and hence any opportunity for self-definition. They inhabit the fantasy of functionlessness, and are at the mercy of values and definitions shaped by the market-place – a peculiar and uniquely contemporary form of captivity, which those who control it like to describe as freedom.

If the formless longings of the young represent a new kind of impoverishment of the working-class spirit, so does the present form of poverty that has been preserved in spite of the great wealth of the West.

Mrs Travis lives with her second husband and five children on the estate. Her husband has not worked for two years. She tries to keep the living-room of their house warm and comfortable, and she succeeds: it is a place apart from the desolation all around. The gas-fire burns as high as she dares set it, the chairs are drawn close to its warmth. On the wall is a little plaque that says 'The only thing ever worth putting on a horse was Lady Godiva'. Mrs Travis is a small, rather nervous woman in her thirties. 'I hate this place. I've been here seven years. The kids round here won't leave the windows alone, the gardens either. It's not the big kids now, God knows what they're up to; it's the little 'uns, they just stand and swear at you.

'My first husband was in and out of prison all the time. Just after Wayne was born, I had the gas cut off. My husband re-connected it when he came out, but he did it illegally, and I took the blame. I got two years' probation. I'm still paying the debts he left. I went to Social Security several times and said "Please let me have the money for me and the bairns separate from his"; but they wouldn't. I had to go and ask my Mam for money before I could get the bairns something to eat. The only time I was happy was when he was inside. When he came out, I'd get pregnant again, then after a month or two, back he went. I was going to kill myself. I got so scared I'd really do it, I had to go and tell my Mam . . . If it wasn't for her, the bairns would've starved.

'I told the bairns their father was in hospital, but the kids at school told them where he was. It upset them; in the end I had to admit to them he was in prison. If you're on your own, the fifteen- and sixteen-year-olds think they can do as they like; they wreck your garden, torment the dog, throw bricks through the window. They knew they could get away with it because I'd no man.

'I lived with him five years before I married him. My Mam said "Don't". But I thought "He'll change once we're married, when we've got somewhere of our own to live." Then I thought "He'll change when we have a baby." He'd been married and divorced before. You think you can change them.

'I rely on the bairns getting free dinners. I spend £20 of the £62 we get a week on food. I get a sack of potatoes, that lasts two weeks. I get cabbage, carrots – vegetables are reasonable in the winter. On Sunday we have Yorkshire pudding, potatoes and carrots. We never have meat. Last time we had meat was last Christmas. I can't remember when I had new clothes. I go to jumble sales all the time. When my husband was in prison, I went to Social Security when the baby was due. They gave me £10 to get everything you need for a baby; and that was only a loan, they took it all back afterwards. I went to them for nappies. When the visitor came, he said "Well, where's the nappies you had for the last baby?" It makes you mad; you have to wash nappies in bleach, and that wears them out because you can't afford to buy decent quality ones on the money they allow you . . . The bairns have got trikes upstairs, but I daren't let them out in the street with them. If the kids see anybody with something they've not got, they get jealous, and they'll steal it or smash it up.

'To get this house I had to get pregnant. We were living with my Mam, just a box room. When I fell pregnant, I thought "Oh, good, we'll get a house now." But one bairn wasn't enough to get a house, so I fell again. I got the offer of this place a week before the baby was born. It was in a terrible mess, it was disgusting. The family that lived here belonged to that lad who'd murdered two little girls; he sexually assaulted them and killed them. There was a big hunt for him; the papers were full of it at the time. His family lived here. It killed his mother. The neighbours set fire to the house, they threw bricks through the windows. There was no door on the scullery; the back had all been burned down and tinned up; there was all bottles and bricks that had been thrown in. People don't want to come and live here. The Squares. This is where you see people at rock bottom, plonkies and criminals, everything.

'I'm lucky now, even if there is no work for my husband. He thinks more of the bairns than their own father does. I've no kids by him yet. I got pregnant, but the baby was not in the womb, it was in the tube. It burst, and I had to be rushed to hospital, have an emergency operation. I nearly died. They told me I would die if I tried again. Only it's bad like, for him, not to have any of his own.'

If we listen carefully to the testimony of the poor, we can begin to see some answer to the riddle of why poverty remains so cruel in spite of the wealth in our society. It isn't so much about low growth rates or relative deprivation; it's all about what yesterday's poor have lost – even those worn, exploited, dispossessed people who seemed to have nothing, have nevertheless had things taken away from them; intangible things, but of great worth and beauty, moral, human, spiritual qualities: the capacity for caring, the wisdom won through pain and struggle in adversity, the stoicism and pride. The bitterness and regret that lie beneath our contemporary experience of poverty come from the fact that instead of building on these qualities, they have been undermined. They were dangerous because they suggested the possibility of a more thoughtful and more sober achievement, a more measured society than that permitted by the unbridled dynamic of market relationships.

And so our poverty is all about forfeits, the forfeits of the lately poor, the giving-up of the human consolations of that poverty. Many of the strengths which people developed to resist its cruelties have been yielded up in exchange for a promise of plenty; but the material concessions that have been granted cannot possibly live up to that promise, nor can they be compared with what they have replaced. It has all been a vast swindle. In a way it makes sense: after all, if the consolations of the past had remained, allied to improved material circumstances, poverty would have ceased to be the distressing and degrading experience it still is; and that would be unthinkable because that would impair the mechanism whereby individuals strive for self-enrichment, which is supposed to give this society its meaning and purpose. In fact, it would no longer be poverty at all. It might even bear some resemblance to the vision of those brave people who struggled for a better world. It would have come closer to socialism than anything we have actually been permitted to experience. It is ironic that many people who have felt uncomfortable with the extravagances of Western society have struggled to live in a way that does not damage or use up more than a minimum of resources. In their search for a life that limits that damage, they have had to start from scratch; even though a starting-point from which such a life could be constructed already existed in the recent past. The frugalities and modest demands of traditional working-class life, expanded only to mitigate the effects of poverty and not to satisfy the exigencies of the market-place, would have presented just such an example. All that would have been necessary was some improvement, of which it could have been said that it was *enough*; but because it is the greatest blasphemy to the market-place and its compulsions that possibility was quickly suppressed. Instead of building on what we had, we delivered ourselves to the ceaseless striving for more, and we behave as though sufficiency were our greatest enemy instead of our best hope. We have cultivated a dependency which exhausts and impoverishes, and which we no longer even dare to think of breaking.

But it will have to be broken sooner or later, and not only to recuperate the sense of injured humanity. That rejected possibility will have to be rediscovered. It is no longer a question of whether it poses a threat to wealth and privilege; it is a question of survival. The dynamic of endless growth – elusive enough – cannot continue without violence to the poorest parts of the earth, with all the risks that implies in a world of spreading nuclear arms. The poor of the world are unlikely to accept for ever that the only way for them to become a little less poor is for the rich to become richer. But what needs to be affirmed is that the end of growth need not be a disaster; it does not have to be a step into darkness and immiseration. Quite the contrary. It need not be a diminishing, but a liberating experience. We have a living model, not of that alternative itself – it was crushed too soon for that – but at least of the values out of which it might have been forged. It is an irony that the vision of the old poor – the hope of sufficiency – finds its echo now, still awaits realization. In this way the experience of the old working class, far from being lost – a subject fit only for labour history – is informed now with a new significance; not of course through the circumstances as they affected a dispossessed industrial proletariat, but in some of the human reactions to those conditions, reactions that remain valid and inspiring through time, and which will make rich our future sufficiency, just as they offer us now the only hope in the wretched market-induced poverty that afflicts us all.

It is not that the old poverty has survived the age of plenty; it is that a new modernized version of poverty has accompanied it. And people have been changed to accommodate the new poverty.* But this violence is intangible, and it lies beneath the notice of most commentators, outside the scope of the investigations of sociologists, beyond the models of economists and below the threshold of politics. It does its work on the spirit and the feelings; it hurts us in the heart and wounds our deepest human sympathies.

To say that working-class people have lost, or rather, have been deprived of many (mostly intangible) things in recent years, is to invite derision. How can it be said of the poorest, of those who traditionally have possessed nothing, that anything has been taken from them? Surely all the material advances have been pure gain. Anyway, where are they, these things that have been given up? How can they be detected, how evaluated? Can you really expect people to respond to such fanciful ideas when their day-to-day lives are taken up with the effort to survive, to pay the heating bills, keep up the payments on the cooker, afford new winter shoes for the children?

And yet, in all working-class communities, so many of them ravaged now by the extinction of their original industrial function, people have been talking ever since I can remember about their sense of loss. Nobody disputes the obvious material changes. But what is important is the conditions on which those changes have been granted, the price that has been paid for them, the penalties that have been exacted for all that has been 'given'. These argu-

*'Modernized poverty appears when the intensity of market dependence reaches a certain threshold. Subjectively, it is the experience of frustrating affluence that occurs in persons mutilated by their reliance on the riches of industrial productivity. It deprives those affected by it of their freedom and power to act autonomously, to live creatively; it confines them to survival through being plugged into market relations. And precisely because this new impotence is so deeply experienced, it is with difficulty expressed' (I. Illich, *The Right to Useful Employment*).[22]

ments are so familiar that we have become deaf to them, and it is tempting not to take them seriously. Why can you no longer leave your doors open day and night? Why can you not go out after dark in the street where you have spent your whole life for fear of being attacked? Why are people not as they were? Why has our solidarity been undermined? Why is the sense of shared existence no longer there? Why does it seem that everybody is out for himself? Why is there a cruel discontinuity between the generations? Why do our deepest relationships seems to be less stable and enduring? Although these questions have been asked repeatedly, there has been no satisfactory answer.

What seems to have happened is that these intensely political questions have been isolated from the area designated 'political'. The pain implicit in them has to be accepted as the necessary price to be paid for what the Labour movement has 'won'; and therefore they may not be acknowledged as issues at all. These things, which are part of the common discourse in all working-class communities, are not admitted into political debate. Apathy is not always the state of sullen indifference it is made out to be: it is a direct response to that other silence, the official silence on so many issues of daily concern, to the narrow and selective range of political argument. What we need to do, above all, is to reclaim those forbidden areas and restore them to where they properly belong – at the centre of the discussion about the way we live and why we live as we do.

It is not difficult to see why these issues have been placed out of bounds. They represent the obverse of those concessions made to working people that the Labour movement is pleased to take credit for as its finest achievements. There has been a collusive silence between capital on the one hand and the representatives of the working class on the other, on the price that has been paid. It is true that these costs have been borne in ways that nobody foresaw; they are in part a result of earlier, heroic struggles already won. But because capitalism seemed prepared to yield what it had traditionally withheld, the Labour movement believed it had succeeded in radically modifying the system. The old mistrust was relaxed, the vigilance not maintained. The damage that has been done is precisely in that solidarity and that resistance which working people developed in response to the harshness and cruelty of an earlier phase of the capitalist process. Although politicians and trade union leaders talk constantly about the gains they have wrested from a reluctant system, and capitalism continues to insist on its further promises and possibilities, no one mentions that other side of the balance, the forfeits and exactions, the tribute that has been paid – in another coin, it is true, but by the same people. The reason for all the shrillness of selling, the clamour of the advertising industry, the lopsided stress on getting and amassing things, is not primarily to persuade people to buy what they don't need (although that doubtless occurs too), but to submerge in the noisy, showy confusion of the marketing of everything that other side of the equation – the assault on working-class dignity, the plunder of working people's traditions and values that have occurred under cover of the ostentatious concessions which have been no sacrifice to capital at all. Above all, they conceal the crucial connection between gain and loss; they shield from scrutiny the continuing process whereby working people are cheated and impoverished. This concealment has skewed political 'debate' into narrow and constricting channels. The only groups which touch that pain (because they are, in part, a product of it) are those on the extreme Right; and that is why their ugly message has a resonance in working-class communities that the Left has lost.

Because the draining away of much of the strength of the working class has taken place under a huckster's cry of gifts, rewards, offers and prizes, it is harder to perceive than that other, older poverty. Its very intangibility makes it difficult to reduce to words. But it is no less real; it is a feeling, gnawing, corrosive, inescapable. It is not by chance that everything in Western culture is so readily turned into the visible, the palpable, image and commodity, what Guy Debord[23] describes as the 'society of the spectacle'. Everything that exists becomes pictures, objects that can be seen and handled, and which give an impression of multifarious richness and diversity. This is perhaps a metaphor for the way in which all the plundered attributes of working-class collectivism have been transformed. The anguish, the pain and loneliness which have been inflicted in exchange for all those positive intangibles are, like them, not acknowledged; and they remain buried beneath the torrent of visual stimuli, the manufactured excitement of the buying and selling.

The denial, the sustained disregard of this pain, gives rise to what seem to be apathy and disaffection in many working-class people. With what sense should we perceive those impalpable losses – the confidence in the knowledge of how to assuage each other's suffering, the proud and unrelenting defence against the ravages of the old poverty, the generosity in spite of inadequate material resources? Perhaps only those who have lived through these appalling distraints can give voice to them. As E. P. Thompson observes, again in another context,[24] 'We forget how long abuses can continue "unknown" until they are articulated; how people can look at misery and not notice it, until misery itself rebels.' Such is the triumph of capitalism that even when that misery does rebel – in the violence and riots of the young – its deep causes can still go unrecognized.

We are seriously mistaken if we assume that apathy has to do with ignorance or a state of numb insentience. The emotional withdrawal of people from the Labour Party has come about because Labour has presided as serenely over these losses as the Conservatives. It is significant that so many Labour activists are those people, often of working-class origin, who are now members of the professional middle class: this movement itself is part of the continuing pillage and expropriation of the working class. It is the guilt and the helplessness of that involuntary betrayal that make so many of us defer to the idea of hope and renewal through the working class – the class to whose erosion and loss we have unwittingly contributed.

It is in these circumstances that the arguments within the Labour Party have occurred. What is being debated there is seen as an enclosed and meaningless struggle by many millions of those in whose name the fight is waged. People find it hard to see the link between their lives and the conflict between Left and Right in the party: the defection occurred too long ago, capitalism has moved on too far for the immediate connection to be obvious; while the Labour movement seems sclerotic, fixed, no longer capable of illuminating for working people the shadow that capitalism still casts on their lives. The capitalist processes have marched on, while working-class institutions are static and have failed to keep pace. Capitalism's promise of plenty has evoked no imaginative response from the Left except the faltering claim that it could do better. The Left can no longer connect the sense of pain in the working class with its own visions. People ask, what difference will all that make to us? Sceptical and wondering, they feel the arguments are esoteric, detached from their preoccupations – the great losses in neighbourhood, kindred and workplace, the plunder out of which this new intractable experience of poverty has been created.

Because the Left thinks everything has been revealed and it knows what has to be done, it has lost the sensitivity to listen, and it misses the note of pain, the unacknowledged ache, the unassuaged loss.

There is something intensely moving, and at the same time tragic, in the revival of the Left and its rhetoric. Beneath the resounding phrases lie, ossified, the aspirations of a nineteenth-century proletariat, those who slaved in their millions in the traditional industries, and out of whose collective response to almost identical living conditions the trade unions and the Labour Party grew organically. They were an expression of the way people lived, projected into an idealized future, and they sustained people with the hope of something accessible and intelligible because they were guided by values that were an embodiment of living, daily experience. And it is the eclipse of that way of living and its informing defence against the ravages of capitalism that gives the attempts at revivalism their tragic dimension. The imposition of the programmes of the Left on what we have become would be a cruel infliction: the old structures of work have so far decayed, and the consequences for the working class have created a quite different kind of human being from anything resembling that old proletarian type in whose cause the old struggles were engaged. To people whose role as the hands of capitalism (i.e. labour) is at least equalled by their role as mouths and stomachs (i.e. markets) the rhetoric of the Left sounds hopelessly one-sided and inadequate. If there is a tragic quality in the Left, it is because they are the ones who have striven to keep faith, not those who have broken it.

But the things that belong to politics must be restored to their proper place. The issues are rich, vital and complex, and those who live them every day of their life are well aware of them; only puzzled and hurt that they find no echo in public debate. Raymond Williams in *The Long Revolution*, puts it:[25]

> It has been the gravest error of socialism, in revolt against class societies, to limit itself, so often, to the terms of its opponents: to propose a political and economic order rather than a human order. It is of course necessary to see the facts of power and property as obstacles to this order, but the alternative society that is proposed must be in wider terms, if it is to generate the full energies for its creation.

It is only when people hear the mean and disfigured definition of politics that reaches them that they turn away, because it rejects so many elements of our common experience. It is as though the working class had been quarantined from the living issues, isolated from certain forbidden areas – precisely from any discussion of those things that would open up, call into question the continuing dynamic of the capitalist process, and the damage it still inflicts in pursuit of its cold unchanging purpose.

4

From the Thirties to the Eighties 2: The Feeling of Unemployment

When you compare the experience of unemployment in the 1930s with that of today, it is the similarities that strike you first, the survival of responses through time. Even in the thirties, it was widely reported that apathy, fatalism and passivity were characteristic of the majority of the unemployed. The absence of widespread political unrest – as compared with the unemployment associated with depressions before the First World War – was attributed to the existence of relief measures and their success in protecting people against destitution and despair. Furthermore, many of the poorly paid and irregularly employed were felt to be better off on the dole than they had been previously.

However, when we compare remembered experience of the thirties with the direct testimony of today, it is the differences which are emphasized despite the persistence of feelings of shame, humiliation and futility.

Mrs Lily Jarrett is seventy-five. She lives in a Lancashire town badly hit by the depression; and during the thirties she, her parents and her husband were all out of work for long periods. But as she evokes her life at that time, it is its remoteness from the contemporary experience that is most striking. The young unemployed on the estate where she lives do not see any continuity between her experience and theirs. They find what she says archaic and crude, of no interest, and certainly of no use to them when she talks of the efforts she and her family made to survive. She is puzzled and hurt by this: she would have expected them to listen because she feels that she has something to offer them.

Mrs Jarrett has no children, but she has nephews and nieces; and none of them sees any relevance in what she has lived through for their own lives. The problem is that the feelings and the reactions remain the same; only the circumstances are different. The same responses occur, yet through vastly altered contexts, and perhaps we look only at the context, not at the feelings which would bind us more closely across the years to those who have lived through the identical sense of rejection and shame.

But it is wrong to compare the stories of poverty in the thirties with the stories of poverty now: it leads only to misunderstanding and impatience. 'They don't know what poverty is,' say the old; 'What's all that got to do with us?' ask the young. The old say 'They're lucky, they can sit at home and watch television, they don't have to worry about where the next meal is coming from.' 'We're bored, we don't know what to do with ourselves,' is the apparently graceless response. The spread of affluence has had the effect of turning more and more areas of human and social intercourse to the market-place; so that by the time the grandchildren of those who were poor in the thirties come to maturity, they find their lives more seriously diminished without money, even though for most of them the basic necessities of food, clothing and shelter are not in question. It is a different kind of impoverishment from that of the thirties: then, great resourcefulness had to be deployed in providing even those basic requirements; and there was no question but that everything else – all the things which the young cannot conceive of without money (mutual support, occupation, amusement and entertainment, the comfort extended to each other through pain and loss) – had to come from their own human resource and capacities. The young believe that money can make good all deficiencies; the old never believed that, even though they were crushed by severe poverty. And the young are damaged by their losses, just as the old were damaged by material insufficiency; the only link between the generations is the continuing subordination of their lives in the unrelenting mechanisms of a system in which everything appears to change and yet somehow remains the same.

Mrs Jarrett lives in an old person's bungalow on a council estate in Bolton. She lives in greater comfort now than she has ever known. But she is alone. On the morning before I first visited her, she had received a poison pen letter. In neat, pot-hook handwriting, it said 'How many men do you need? You've got them at the Labour Club, at the Pensioners' Lunch Club, why can't you leave them alone. Why can't you be satisfied with what you have, and not lower yourself. You should know better at your age.' It was signed 'From a Well-wisher'. Mrs Jarrett sat and cried all day. 'Why would anybody do that to me? I don't do any harm to anybody. Just because I like to go out and have a drink sometimes. Why should I sit here on my own and just fade away? I've nobody in the world.'

She talks about the twenties and thirties, a lifetime with the poor of industrial Lancashire – not the poorest: the fact that she was the only surviving child of her mother's eight worked to her advantage in that respect. She mixes the laughter with the inextricable sadness of life in that curious blend which was so much part of the old working-class tradition. The women of her generation still keep vestiges of that power and strength, and the intense theatricality of their performance as they discussed their own and other people's lives, the laughter that ends in a sigh, and the sudden change of mood to a reflective melancholy.

'In the twenties, every man had a pigeon run in the backyard; and when they weren't working, they used to lay bets on these pigeons, you'd see them all looking up at the sky, waiting for their bird to come in. Well, I had an uncle, and he used to bet on the horses, and he was always winning, and nobody knew why. In those days, it was all done on the quiet, you'd have a bookie, and he'd take bets right up to the last minute, even after the races had started. Well, this lad were always winning and the bookie couldn't understand why; it was the first time he'd ever been so much out of pocket. Well, what he was doing, his mate always went down to the town centre with this pigeon, and as soon as the news came through of which horse had won the race, he put the name on a bit of paper, tied it to the pigeon's leg, and then, whoosh, it flew straight home. So my uncle would know what had won the race, and he'd send his kiddie round to put sixpence on this horse that had already won. He was getting the winner every time, and nobody knew how. They found out some road in the end. I expect somebody got jealous and gave the game away. (Compare a modern version of this story, p. 34.)

'Oh you had to try and outwit them, the Means Test, the PAC. You had to be sharp though. You'd tell them that your son or daughter had left home, and you'd send them to sleep with a neighbour on a night. But the beggars'd stand there all night if necessary, to make sure nobody was sleeping there who shouldn't be. There was one woman we knew, she swore to the Means Test her son was dead; and of course they didn't believe her, and she said "I'll take you up to see his bloody grave if you like"; and the lad was under the stairs listening all the while.

'People tried to make an odd copper any road they could. They were so poor, everything you could imagine would get sold, bits of wood, filthy old rags, bits of glass bottles. Even now, when I see the kids smashing glass on the road, I think to myself "Oh don't do that, that'll fetch a copper or two", the habit goes so deep in you.

'I was sixteen and a half when I first went on the dole. You had to go to dole school to get your shilling a day. Dole school, one week you went mornings, the next afternoons. They used to teach you things there – dancing, dressmaking, how to make things, domestic work. Well, in them days you were born to work; it was how many pair of hands was there in the family. I had a sewing-machine when I was nine – that was my ninth birthday present, and I was too small to reach the treadle. But I can remember being at the dole school and unpicking all these old-fashioned bodices and making new things out of them, underskirts, jumpers.

'A lot of people left Bolton, looking for work. The dole used to flit people if they found a job. A lot of girls went in service. They trained them up in a big house here in Bolton, then they went away . . . They wanted to send me, I said I wasn't going. I had my Dad to look after at that time. My Dad never worked after the strike in 1926. He was only in his forties. He went picking coal in the strike, and standing about in the cold, never having enough to eat, he got rheumatic fever. He did try to go back after the strike finished, but he couldn't lift a thing. That was it, that was his working days over.

'I don't remember getting bored like they do now. We were always on the look-out for something to do to earn a penny. In the summer we used to go to the park. Then I had a friend who had six children. I'd go and help her, and she'd give me a meal, and I'd take the babies up the park for a couple of hours. Most of the men used to go poaching. If they got enough, they'd go and sell the rabbits round the houses. They'd go over to Garstang, take the nets with them. If they got caught, they went to gaol. There was nothing unusual in that.

'But people were good-natured. If anybody was ill, they all went in to make sure they didn't want for anything; they'd take it in turns to take in some gruel. There was no thieving; of course there was nowt to take, but even if there had been, nobody would take it. People were all friendly with one another. One girl near where we lived, she bought some chips for her dinner one day, and she'd just been paid, slipped her wage-packet in the paper the chips was wrapped in. Well, she and her sisters ate these chips out of the paper, and her mother threw the paper on the fire. She said "Oh Mam, my wages was in there, a pound note." Well it was a tragedy, that. She was the only one in the family earning. Well, the whole street had a collection for her . . . Would they do that now? . . . Aah. I've even seen children lick the grease off paper that chips have been wrapped in.

'I was married on the dole. Love on the dole, that was us. My husband was very poor. He came to me as he was, with no second shirt, no change of clothing, nothing. He was a nice lad. I'd known him around the town, like you do, for years. Then, it was after his father died, he had a new suit on because his father was dead. And I said to my pal "Eh, don't he look nice in his new suit?" It got back to him; and that was how I got together with him. I was twenty-nine then. He was out of work for five years. Then it was munitions that got him back to work. I'd just got a-gate working nights in a cotton mill, and then he had to go in the army. After the war, he went working in the pits, but he had a dropped stomach and had to come out. Then he worked in a quarry, then a brick croft; and then he went into an iron foundry, and that just about finished him. When I think about him, bless him, I don't know which was worse, having no work at all, or watch his health go down doing the jobs he hated.

'Oh, people was brow-beaten. I had a rough life, because my father left home when I was two. He just walked out one day. There was no work, it got too much for him. Then eight years later, he walked back in. I was ten by that time. I used to go picking coal; there were these women who used to empty the waggons, truckers-off they called them, and you used to go and help them fill these bags of coal, and for every three you did you got one. My father was a miner, but he was out of work after the War, the First War. My mother had to go out to work on the brow, emptying coal. She went as a pit-brow woman because she couldn't stand the mill. I remember we lived in a little house, single house – one up one down – and there was no sink in the kitchen. There was just a tap with a bowl on a chair underneath it. When my mother came in from the pit-brow, she was filthy with coal dust. She used to fill this big black iron bath. She always had a poor life; she told me as a girl, she'd had to take 2*d* for her schooling every day. One day she spent it instead of going to school, and didn't she get beaten by her father! Her father had come out of Staffordshire to Lancashire to work in a forge. My father's father came from the same place, Hanley, but he came to Lancashire as a miner. Before that he'd been a page-boy, and his wife was a cook in service. That was in the eighteen-sixties. They were only seventeen when my father was born. My Dad was once thrashed for stealing an apple out of the orchard of the place where he worked. There was a great orchard, apples falling from the trees, but nobody was allowed to touch them.

'My father remembered the good times in the country that his parents used to talk about; you could get a big paper full of cheese for 2*d* . . . That was why, when he left us, he walked back to Staffordshire. What was he looking for there? I know he never found it. He went on the tramp, and finished up in the work-houses. He lost a finger breaking stones. He was following something he'd got in his head, I don't know. And all the time he was away, she never got a halfpenny. When she went to the Public Assistance, all they said was "Find your husband".

'When he'd gone, she tried to look after us. She had a toffee shop one time over. I was about four. It wasn't a proper shop, just a front room. I can remember going in the shop window to pinch the toffees. Afterwards, she tried to support us with making clothes, but she always used the best materials, and made a loss. It was the same with the toffee shop. She lost that because she took ill, and had to go to the hospital. My auntie came to look after it, but she pawned everything. So when my mother came out of hospital, that was when she had to go working at the pit-brow. She stayed there till she collapsed and couldn't work any more. In the house where we lived it was damp and cold; it made my mother ill. After that we went to live in the parlour of a house of some relations of my Dad. I was the only child of my parents that survived; and I was born after they'd been married seven years.

'When my father came back, I was only ten. I had to go on holiday to me Auntie's, so that me Mam and Dad could get used to each other again. They just took up where they left off. My Dad was all right. He was a drunkard; he liked his ale. But going on the tramp like that, it broke him. But he could drink. One day, that was before he left home, I can remember him hitting my mother, and I was sitting on a little stool by the fire; and I got hold of my clog and I hit him over the head with it. My mother started yelling "Oh my child, he'll kill my child", but little as I was, I was off down the road. Oh, but he could drink. I remember, he'd be sat in his chair of a night, upright Windsor chair, and my mother would wind the clothes'-line round him, so he shouldn't fall on the floor. And many a morning we've got up and found the floor all flooded where he'd weed, tied in this chair.

'My mother was a good woman. All her sisters were Sunday School teachers at the parish church. She once bought a family Bible for £2, shilling a week. It was felt you ought to have one in the house. My Dad used to go and pawn this Bible; but he always carried it under his jacket because he was a bit ashamed of pawning the Good Book . . . She always called him "that man". I can see him now, all the men watching for their pigeons. There was a bit of a brow where we lived, and there they'd be looking up at the sky; and then they'd fight over which bird got home first.

'I had nearly three years working before I went on the dole. I left school on the Wednesday when I was thirteen, and I started work on the Friday, spinning. I started at 19*s* 10*d* a week, with £1 once a month. That was good wages in 1919, just after the War. But they were the best years, they were soon gone. Our wages went down and down; they kept knocking a shilling off and a shilling off till they went down to 11*s*. But they worked you for it. There was no time to go to the toilet; you were spinning, doffing, the toilets were too far away for you to spare the time . . . And all the girls sat on the floor in their break-time, you had to step over them to get past; there was nowhere for them to sit. I worked in bare feet; we all did then. The hours were 7.45 till 12.00, then 12.30 till 5.30. I lost that job and went to a bone works, where they made sausage skins. Oh but the smell was awful, nobody'd talk to you. Then I got took on again in another mill. They talk about getting more on the dole than you do working, well when our wages kept on dropping, there was one time when I would have got 15*s* on the dole and 12*s* working. When I started, I was a ring-spinner. When the bobbins were full, it was your job to put new ones on. We used to sing while we worked. We sang parodies to the tune of popular songs. This one is the tune of "In the Shade of the old Apple Tree":

In the shade of old Eckersley's mill
The doffers are doffing there still.
The clothes that they wear, the style of their hair
Are enough to make anyone ill.

We sang together, all these rows and rows of women; it helped you through the day

At the frame where I used to doff my share
The bottom of me tin rolled away.
The scoppie-winder said she'd break me blooming head
If I didn't doff my share off right away.

When you were in work it was all right. If you got with a lad, you'd be bragging on a Friday, I'm going to the pictures tonight; a quarter of a pound of chocolates for fourpence, 4*d* each at the Pavilion.

'My mother was very strict. I had to do what she said. When she said no, she meant it. Even when I was eighteen, she stopped me going to second house at the pictures . . . I was nineteen when she died. And even though she never dressed up fancy, never went out anywhere, she always kept a good table. She made all her own bread, pickles, jam. We'd go out and pick the blackberries for it. She was a good housekeeper. Only once the bum-bailiffs came while she was in hospital. That was a disgrace. I remember they always used to be waiting for my Uncle Jim on his way home from the pit. It wasn't fair; they worked them all hours for a pittance, and then, when they were coming home, there'd be these bailiffs waiting to claim him for the debts they'd built up. And they weren't debts to get luxuries – it was the necessities of life. But poverty, I'll tell you what, people learned to do things for themselves. My mother always cut my hair, soled our shoes, painted and decorated. We did our own rugs, made jumpers, all this embroidery.' (The covers at the back of the chairs and sofa are all worked with garlands of daisies and leaves in many colours of silk cotton.) 'I'm not clever, but I can do plenty. We made rugs out of old coats, because when I was young the floors had no coverings. They did get lino, and you thought that was luxury. Carpets were unheard of. People today are always wanting more. When you know that tomorrow's going to bring the same as today and that's beggar-all, you don't yearn for what you know you can't have. I made all my own bedding, all my own blankets. I never took charity. Only one Christmas when my father took bad, I gave up my job to look after him. I couldn't get relief because I'd given up my job voluntary. The woman next door said "Go to the Minister and tell him. You might get a well-wisher parcel." I got a charity voucher for £2, and a pint of milk a day over Christmas. I looked after my Dad when mother died.

'There was a woman near us who lent money. I don't know where she got it from. The women would go and ask her: "Can you lend me £3?" And she would let them have £2 10*s*, so she'd taken her interest out of it in advance, and they had to sign for £3. I only borrowed once. The house where we were living, it used to flood, and once when it had all been washed out, I bought some lino for 7*s*. I went to borrow 10*s* from her, and I got 7*s* 6*d*. Oh, they were that poor. A woman might get up a saloon, you know, a charrer for kids to go into the country on an outing. And on the morning, there was a queue all round the houses, grown-ups as well. Nobody ever went anywhere, but we made do with nowt. We might stop off at a pub after one of these outings, a bottle of stout, somebody'd play the piano, and if nobody could, we'd all dance to one note being bashed out. If they went to the sea, they saved up their own food for a year, took our own tins. You used to write your name on the eggs, so as the landlady shouldn't try and palm you off with some that wasn't fresh; oh yes, write your name in indelible ink.

'Of course, I grew up knowing nothing about sex. At one time, we had a couple living in our house, and the woman was having a baby. Well, the doctor came and said we could all go to bed because she'd last till the morning. Her sister had come up to stay while she was confined. She had a baby of her own, and they all went up to bed. And I'm lying there half asleep, I was about sixteen; and I was in the next room to them. Some time in the night I heard somebody ask what the time was, and her husband answered "Three". I thought "Oh bloody hell, there's three of them. Then I heard this sister's baby say "Mama". I said to my Mam, "Hark, it's talking." I didn't know children couldn't talk when they were newborn. I must have been sixteen or seventeen. Next morning, I went in to her and I said "Where's the other two, are they dead?" She said "What other two?" I said I heard Jack say there was three.

'I was nineteen, and I still didn't know how babies came. You used to hear snatches from girls in the mill, girls you knew around like. But you never put it all together, you half didn't believe it. I was nineteen when my mother died; and I don't know if it was the shock or what, but my courses stopped for three months. And I used to sweat real heavy; it all came under my arms, and the girls in the mill assumed I was having a baby. I didn't know anything about it. My periods stopped because I was upset, that was all. But these girls, they all said to me "Come on, tell the truth, you've been with a lad, haven't you? You only need to go with a boy once to get pregnant." I thought "Oh ee, I did go out with that boy to the pictures, and he twisted me wrist. It must be that that makes you pregnant." I was that ignorant. I said "Yes"; and they took me to the doctor, everybody at the mill thought I was pregnant. I nearly lost my job over it. I really thought I was pregnant. When they said that to me I thought "Ee, well I must be." Having no brothers, you see, and my father being very strict – I never once in me life put me stockings on in front of him; and I'd never seen any part of a man, like. My mother had kept me innocent. I knew you had courses, but I didn't know how that had anything to do with sex. I went out with one or two boys. One of them one day did ask me, he said "Have you ever had any connections?" and he showed me this French letter. I didn't know what it was, I ran a mile. I was frightened. He said to me "I'll let you have your own road, but you'll paddle your own canoe if owt happens. . ." I ran away, not knowing anything, it makes you more scared. I think I killed my own nature. My mother used to say she would tell me, as though there was some big secret, but I was always so little. She used to say "Oh I'll tell you one day"; and then she died, so she never did. I thought people just got married and they had babies. I never really wondered how.'

Mrs Jarrett feels sad when she tells this story; the tale of her attributed pregnancy and her own ignorance are unthinkable now. She says without bitterness 'Ee, it was cruel.' She says that now things have changed beyond recognition; and it is these stark changes that conceal the things that remain the same. When we look at the damage social pressures inflict, we should look always at the point where the damage occurs now, not at the point at which it occurred in the past. People look at the kind of poverty and ignorance of those times and are, properly, appalled. But because we compare like with like – the ignorance of a nineteen-year-old about her own body, the indignities of the pit-brow women – everything appears to us immeasurably better. But ignorance, like poverty, has managed to survive the material improvements and the educational advances. It's just that they have shown themselves in other areas of experience: certain aspects of that old poverty and ignorance – certain human responses to them – which were taken for granted then have been suppressed. A different kind of poverty has been substituted, a different sort of ignorance. And when we take account of those, it is not so easy to see where our gains lie.

Gavin Lawrence is eighteen. He lives not far from Mrs Jarrett. His father left home when Gavin was seven, and his mother has brought up her family on Social Security. His sister, Janet, is twenty, and she works in a supermarket in the town centre. Gavin has not worked for nine months. He did a youth opportunities course for six months in a local factory; after that worked in a warehouse, an amusement arcade, and then a timber depository. He was sacked from the warehouse for bad timekeeping; he left the amusement arcade because he was having to work twelve or fourteen hours a day for £40 a week and the timberyard because the work was too hard. He was going to join the army, but a friend of his was bullied and came out after six weeks, and his experience put Gavin off.

Gavin's mother, Rose, is only forty, but she looks older; she is fat and her legs are swollen, and the veins stick out. She has trouble with her nerves, and seems to have entered middle-age prematurely. Most of her companions are older women, and she spends a lot of time in their houses, talking about ailments and tablets, drinking cups of tea with the gas-oven flaring for warmth. She has a great capacity for doing nothing; and this irritates Gavin. He hates to stay in the house, and almost never sits in the living-room with his mother. He sleeps late, goes downstairs only to eat or watch television. The lives of the three people in the house seem to glide past each other. Rose says she worries about Gavin, but she is also afraid of him. Janet is very concerned about her appearance, and ashamed of the untidiness and disorder of the home. Exasperated, she comes home sometimes and cleans it thoroughly; but if she complains to her mother, Rose says 'I'm not well love.' 'You never have been,' is Janet's reply. Rose has never really recovered from the demoralization of her husband walking out. It still burns there, and is the only thing that brings her to a slow smouldering life.

'He thought he was onto something good, but she plays Hamlet with him. His life is not his own. She's got him on a bloody piece of string. Four kids they've got, and he has to look after them; she works in some sort of club all hours. It were the worst day's work he ever done. When she were pregnant with her third, he told my sister he'd come back tomorrow. He knows he done wrong. He told me he was working overtime; I knew, he stunk of her when he come home, a woman knows. I said to him "If you're working overtime, where's the money? It's the sort of overtime you have to pay out for i'n't it?"'

She says the only thing she misses him for is as a father for Gavin. 'He needs a man. I can't tell him what to do. He'll not take any notice of me. I've told him the minute he goes out that front door he's on his own. If he brings any trouble back to this house, I don't want to know. I've done what I can. He's eighteen now, he should be bringing something in.' Janet says 'He can't help it. There is no work.' 'He's had jobs, and he's bloody chucked 'em in because he's a bighead, like his old man. He's not going to do this, he'll not put up with that.'

Janet has just got engaged, and she is saving up for her wedding next year. She earns about £65 a week and she gives her mother £15. She often gives Gavin a few pounds. 'He never asks for it,' she says. She is obviously fond of him; and Gavin says he can talk to her. He feels uncomfortable with his mother; you can see him physically squirming when she talks to him; he bites his nails, his foot works away, his whole body turns away from her. When Rose says she worries about him, you can tell that she really cares, but cannot cope. She is almost playing a role – worried mother – but she isn't really convincing. She hates housework and cooking, and meals tend to be improvised. Janet says she can't remember when they all sat down and had a meal together. Janet cooks a Sunday dinner, but the rest of the week, they help themselves at irregular times. Gavin has just become a skinhead. His mother disparages him all the time; partly it is a way of trying to evoke some sort of emotional response, but it only irritates him more. 'First time I seem him I thought it was Yul Brynner. Frightened me to death. He had a lovely head of hair.' 'You said it was too long.' 'Yes and now it's too bloody short. I don't know what they think it does for them. Baldy.'

Gavin spends most of his time at home in his bedroom. He has forbidden his mother to go in there; if he finds she's touched anything, he says he will smash the living-room up. He doesn't make the bed; and the sheets are dirty, the bed-clothes an irregular heap of faded and threadbare blankets. On the walls are some faded pictures of footballers and pop stars: Kevin Keegan, Gary Glitter,

Barry Sheene. On top of the wardrobe are some toys he had as a child – a deep orange teddy-bear, a grubby panda, and he has drawers full of Dinky toys, tanks, and pieces of plastic from games he didn't want to throw away. On the wall there is a dartboard, and he spends hours lying on his bed, throwing the plastic darts at the yellow and black segments of the board. He is very skilled, and says he may join a darts team. The room is a strange mixture of childhood and adulthood – some horror and war comics, and some old annuals, which he still likes to look at when he feels in certain moods. It is as though his childhood was quickly smothered in the race towards becoming adult, and this has already disappointed him. He has brown eyes, and with the short hair his face looks bony and hungry. For him becoming a skinhead involves a reaching out for self-respect. Rather than drifting, he says he wants to take hold of his own life and make something of it. 'Nobody's going to help you, you've got to make it on your own. It's what you can do, you and your mates.' On the floor are some Hollywood Love-Books, which are hard porn, and under the bed is a towel, dried hard with semen, that he uses for masturbation. He shows me one picture in particular: Two women, one licking the other's vagina, while a man is posed, penis erect, about to enter her from behind. Gavin says 'I only use them when I haven't got a girl-friend.' At the moment, there is nobody. The last one wanted to get married, but they had no money, and nowhere to live. 'I wouldn't bring her here, not in this shithole. Anyway it's the last thing I want. I don't want to tie myself down when I've not had a chance to do anything yet.' He talks about sex as something you have to 'get'. He says he has never been in love. He doesn't know whether it exists; he sees Janet and her bloke – he is an electrician – and he says, 'Well there must be something in it.' Janet looked after him a lot when he was a kid; instead of going off and playing with her friends she always took him with her. When he talks about his sister, he is much softer: the face relaxes, he smiles more fully, his head looks less knobby and bony. He says that he spends most mornings in bed, sleeps till about midday; then when his mother has gone out, he goes down, makes tea, and has some toast and marmalade, reads the *Sun*, looks at television if there's anything worth seeing. He goes out in the middle of the afternoon. He knows where he will find his mates – in a pub if it's not too late, or hanging about the shopping centre. They go to a café, share a cup of tea, play the space invader machines, sit around, talk about what they would do if they had a lot of money. If it's raining, they sometimes go to the house of one of them whose parents are both working. There are three mates in particular, who have all had their hair cut short. They have started going to a gymnasium two or three times a week. One afternoon we talked of nuclear war; and they said they meant to survive it. They have formed a group called the Brotherhood, and they plan to build a hide-out in the country and stock it with food. Somehow, a cult of physical fitness, the fantasies of survival seem to be a response to the de-energized life they actually lead; it is a gesture rather than a concrete plan, as if they are aware of the futility of the way they live, the absence of reward in small-time thieving, getting drunk, occasional fights, visits to the disco, intermittent and always inadequate sex; and yet they don't quite manage to put it into practice.

One afternoon, they came round to Gavin's house while his mother was visiting her sister who was in hospital. They arrived with some cans of lager, and Gavin took a packet of his mother's cigarettes which she had hidden in an empty Nescafé jar. What soon established itself was a sense of inertia and relaxation; they talked about the lad Michelle is going out with; when Gavin told her he didn't want to get married, he nevertheless felt insulted when she went and found somebody else – 'a cunt like that.' He feels it somehow adversely affects his honour to have been succeeded by somebody so unworthy. They believe that you should progress if you're going seriously with anybody; and they need to beat up Michelle's new lad just to show him that there is no order of precedence in her leaving Gavin and going to him. They discuss it without rancour, simply as a practical problem. Should they lie in wait for him when he comes out of the pub on Friday night, or catch him when he finishes work on Saturday when he goes from the shop where he works to the piece of waste ground where the buses stop? They don't actually make any plan, but they talk of scraps they've been in, escapes they've had from the Bill, the times they've been pissed and the things they've done when they were out of their heads. They talk about women they've had, and the name of Cindy recurs, who apparently can't stop herself doing it with anybody; but they agree that's no achievement unless you're desperate: half of the fun is getting girls who make out they don't know what they've got between their legs.

They have all been 'getting sex' since they were thirteen or fourteen. 'Oh you think it's going to be something really big; and you get all scared the first time you do it. But then it's nothing. I mean, you have to do it, because once you start you can't do without it. You spend a lot of time thinking about it. You can't get enough ever, can you? Nobody can.' The only way you could get enough sex would be to have enough money to pay for as much as you wanted; and this leads to one of their most familiar conversations of all – what they would do if they had unlimited money.

'I'd go to Canada and build a big house and have a big wall built round it, and electric fences; then I could keep away from all the stupid people in the world. I wouldn't have anybody near me unless they were people I wanted. Then I could tell everybody I didn't like to piss off . . . And I'd have a recording studio in it, and I'd have all the crumpet I wanted queuing up. I'd never have to take any shit from anybody ever again. I'd hire a hit man to get rid of anybody who'd ever insulted me or made me look small.' 'I'd go on the fucking space shuttle. I'd put all the money I had into exploring space, until I found a new planet.' 'I fucking wouldn't; I'd explore the world first. I'd spend five years just travelling, picking up women on the way. I'd buy a fucking Jensen, and I'd drive it till it clapped out, then I'd just step out of it into a new one.' 'I'd just have people round me who'd do everything I told them.'

Although what they say is only fantasy, and it remains securely detached from the obvious limitations of their life on the dole, it is nevertheless hard to avoid the feeling that the market relationships – which after all are supposed to be simply a reflection of people's demands and the response to them with the goods and services they can buy – have invaded them and shaped them in a way that has nothing to do with the quite neutral role attributed to them by their most enthusiastic defenders. It is as though the market-place has actually formed their conception of the world and their place in it in a way that violates their youthful vulnerability. They are good-natured and likeable; but their knowledge is all about manufactured articles – cars, music centres, cameras, videos, things that can be bought, and they know the price of them too. It is like an ugly implant in their lives.

I've never had a stronger sense of the unfreedoms of the young; and it isn't difficult to see where they join Lily Jarrett and the spoiling of her youth for the sake, not of some voluntary sacrifice, not of some ideal, but for the maintenance of the social and economic order. The knowledge that these boys have of sex is bought; and it has been at the expense of real relationships and feeling. Their addictive dependency on goods and services has been created at the expense of the knowledge of what human beings can do for themselves, what they can create out of their own substance; their fantasies of power have grown at the cost of their own real abilities. Looking at them, in that shabby untidy living-room, as the cigarette smoke grew thicker and the beer cans mounted on the table, it was impossible not to wonder about the effect of the conditions of their lives upon them; and to think of that other, old struggle against malnutrition, rickets and TB: to see them abusing their bodies – talking about getting high, discussing glues and solvents and pills and the effects they have, the reliance on junk food, the search for sensation – a caricature of the possibilities of human inner exploration. It seems that everything about them expresses contempt for what has been done for them in the sense of the achievements of standards of health, education, the possibilities for self-development. It is as though some deep atavism tells them they are not worthy of it – everything that was won with such pain and sacrifice on their behalf – and it is their object to diminish it, to throw it all away. All the cruel things visited on the working class by the circumstances of the Industrial Revolution which called them into existence don't disappear within a few years, or even within a century. They bit so deeply that they lie there in memory, a corrosive poison waiting to reclaim them; ghosts, graveyard recollections of poverty, oppression and stunted humanity rise up as these young people talk about their lives, saying that they're rubbish, worthless, useless, unwanted. Who listens to us, why should we bother, what's the point? And when they express their feelings towards other people, these are marked with selfishness and indifference because they can only echo all the familiar cruelties of which their forbears were victims. The working-class young have all the bitterness of the adult ill treated in infancy, and so haunted by the privations he suffered then that he cannot see his life in any other terms.

And yet they are vibrant with energy and vigour that have no outlet; and it all seeps away during the course of the afternoon. Pete is sick, Gavin falls asleep. In the spillage of energies, you can actually see the processes that deny them self-expression – the obscuring of the self they have to express, lives defined only by what is on offer through the capitalist market-place. It is an ugly and defeated way to treat the young; an appalling betrayal of their 'innocence', an innocence that is the mirror-image of Mrs Jarrett's. It is hard not to wonder about the kind of world for which these children have been formed and what is to become of them.

Both what they say and what Mrs Jarrett says need to be interpreted. Much of what working-class people say is through metaphor and image: they feel the pain of what is done to them, but don't always find it easy to express directly. Behind the memories of Mrs Jarrett and the incoherencies of Gavin and his friends there is the same pain. Even when people speak for themselves, the context in which they do so often falsifies the sense of what they mean. Mrs Jarrett's is the kind of testimony that Labour historians delight in, those twentieth-century equivalents of the great folklorists of the nineteenth century, retrieving memories before they vanish, but missing the violence which the 'improvements' in her life have done to her. And what the young say – listened to, documented, recorded by the media, sociologists, psychologists – isn't heard as an expression of the violence that has been done to them, the unfreedom of their violated and diminished youth.

5
The Inner City: Balsall Heath

Birmingham. Balsall Heath is an enclave of nineteenth-century Birmingham: terrace houses with bay windows and beading between the upper and lower storeys; some of them built in courts, with short gardens in front and a footpath dividing the gardens from each other. The small shops are now predominantly Indian, heaps of saffron-coloured balls and ochre lozenges in pyramids in the windows. Second-hand shops sell ancient black and white tv sets for £20, some of them switched on in the window, images faint and greenish in the bright sunshine. There are old clothes on racks, a lurex dress, baggy pinstripe suits, gas-cookers, old electric fires. Indian and Pakistani films in video are on offer in a shop protected by metal grilles in a building named Percy Villas. Some of the streets are dilapidated: the bays tinned up, the acanthus-shaped chimney pots leaning, the primeval furl of papery ferns thrusting through the slates of a ruined out-house. Some of the houses have been renovated: functional letterboxes, concrete forecourts, and uniformly painted doors, while in others the overgrown evergreens of the old villa luxuriate, the stonework crumbles, the interiors decay with sagging ceilings and an efflorescence of mildew on the walls, the paint in kitchens flakes to show the red bricks beneath, taps drip into discoloured fireclay sinks, back-yards that have never seen sunlight are overgrown with bright green moss.

If you walk out of Balsall Heath onto the Moseley Road, it is like a frontier. You walk under a railway bridge, past the ornate green urinals and the rust-coloured dampness that stains the walls beneath the metal bridge, and suddenly the whole aspect is changed. Ahead, the blocks of flats, symmetrical towers on their grassy ramparts, office buildings gleaming like marble and regular as tombstones fill the space that you look down on between Moseley Road and the city centre. There is a symbolic change here that is more than spatial: look back at the sooty salmon brick of Balsall Heath and the contrast is dramatic. The relationship between the old part of the city and the new is made explicit. Here are made visible the penalties of the ghetto. At the same time, all those distant gleaming blocks are not quite what they appear to be. When you get close to them, the concrete base is covered with ugly graffiti, the lifts stink, there is litter and debris everywhere. Perhaps there are also penalties in moving out of the old decaying area, in passing through the spectacular transition. It may be that for all the scruffiness, with its chipped mouldings and cracked stained glass, the mauve-painted woodwork of the multi-occupied mid-nineteenth-century villa, the steep gables shedding their slates, the tiled hallways with their mail accumulating for tenants who have moved on – perhaps this place still holds vestiges of a way of living that for all its poverty was more human than that which most of those who used to live here now enjoy. Those bland and efficient towers are also, in their way, places of defeat. They proclaim that people have acquiesced in what has been done to them. One kind of struggle has ceased, and they have accepted their place on the fourteenth floor with its view over the city. In Sparkhill, Balsall Heath, people haven't submitted to, or been overtaken by that change, even though the pressure, severe pressure, is on them to adapt. These older streets have become places of deterrent, with their lore of violence and poverty, impelling individuals to make even greater efforts than they have already made to move out. Everything here combines to make life intolerable; and the most important influence is the migrations outwards that have already occurred. The property is now falling into even greater disrepair, there is no work, people don't feel safe, nothing seems permanent. The social forces that create the ghetto seem so remote, the feeling of impotence of the individual is so complete that there is no one to whom you can express the pain and anger of being trapped here but to those you care about most – neighbours and former workmates, husbands and wives, parents and children. In this way, people move apart instead of supporting each other, violence increases especially against the weakest – children, women, migrants; the forces of disintegration grow stronger.

Yet, in spite of that, in these streets, the ghosts of another sort of life still cling; the old networks, faint reminders of the supports of neighbourhood and kinship live on, in the closeness of the families of immigrants, in the way of life of the old who cannot respond to the demands of the changed circumstances of their lives, in the persistence of patterns in the poor, patterns that have faded or been overlaid for many of those who have moved on. The sharing of insufficient material things, the protection of one another against outside threats, the sheltering of shame and loss, solidarity and endurance. But these are precisely the values that are most scorned now. The things that gave the poor dignity two generations ago are now the scarecrows brandished at working-class people to drive them to accept the new form of poverty. It seems almost unbelievable as a social project, this change: the transformation of mutual support and comfort, the delicate tissue of love and duty binding people together into the stigma of a despised way of living. Out of the old working class, it is the values of the minority which have become the norm – the improvident, the self-seeking; while the generosity and the sharing have been eclipsed. What helped people to share pain and hardship – the only consolation human beings have or are ever likely to have – has to be given up; and it is around this change that the wound in working-class sensibility has been inflicted, both for those who have adapted and for those who feel the pressure but cannot adapt, the unreformed, the slow to learn, the old. It is a deep and bitter experience. Nothing can express too strongly the sense of injury that has been done to people. Hoggart,[26] in *The Uses of Literacy*, acknowledges but understates the feeling: 'It seems to me that the changes . . . are, so far, tending to cause the working class to lose, culturally, much that has been valuable and to gain less than their new situation should have allowed.' It seems now that through the experience of the working class, we came close to recognizing what could form the basis for a good way of living together: the frugal habits, modest wants and mutual concern joined to the capacity for plenty now within our reach; but a restrained and equitable plenty that would not have overthrown all those hard-learned lessons and that difficult wisdom. That opportunity has been thrown away because it threatened the richest and most powerful in their riches and power, not by expropriating them, but simply by rendering obsolete the absurd ideological apparatus by which they are maintained.

And the price that is being paid for that defection is still being paid; and it is being paid by the poorest, by those who have least to give.

Ladypool Road. A girl, eighteen, lives in one room with her two children, two years and six months respectively. At the window there is a single faded curtain with a blue floral pattern; but because of the damp, the wire on which it hangs is rusty and has stained the top of the material so that the curtain cannot be pulled and has to be draped diagonally, resting behind the case of an old radio that doesn't work. In a pot on the window-sill there are some plastic flowers, faded lilac with a thick coat of dust. The room is damp and faces north. It looks out onto roof-tops and the blank wall of a disused factory; and the electric light, a single bulb without a shade, burns for most of the year even in daylight. Above the wainscot, painted dark yellow, but chipped and stained now, there are patches of bluish mould, and a kind of black pollen that stains the fingers if you touch it. The wallpaper, a faded yellow Regency stripe, has come away in strips, and has been held back in place with sellotape, but even this has lost its adhesive power, so that the strips have fallen again like the petals of a dying tulip into the room. The ceiling has been covered with polystyrene tiles, but the surface is so uneven that many have fallen down, and the ceiling sags, with great patches of damp. In heavy rain the water drips onto the floor, which has rotted the cheap red lino into a greyish pulp. There is one bed, a black metal frame and a foam mattress. Here Pauline sleeps with Michelle, the two-year-old. The blankets are old and dingy, and there is a strong smell of urine. It was warm the first time I saw Pauline's room; the sash window was broken, so it was propped open at the bottom with an old shoe. The baby sleeps in a cot improvised by Pauline herself out of a box with Palmolive stamped all over it, and decorated on the outside with silver paper. The baby is called Dion.

'I wanted to call him Angel,' says Pauline, 'because I felt he was going to be special.' The child wears a discoloured babygrow. The milk in his bottle has seeped through the damaged teat, and made a puddle in the piece of gabardine material covering the foam rubber. The two-year-old wears a blue dress with tiny puff sleeves; her hair is tangled and her face sticky with sweets she is finishing from a cylinder of Smarties.

Pauline is unmarried; she lived with the children's father intermittently, until he went to prison for a series of violent robberies. 'My Mam hated him. He was good to the kids, even though he used to hit me sometimes. He never set a finger on them, well Dion wasn't born when he was put away, but he knew if he'd touched them that would have been the finish. He wants me to wait for him. My Mam says why should I, he should have married me. My Mam says she'll take the kids. I don't want to part with them, but I expect I will in the end. She's got a house. I don't mind my Mam, but I hated my Dad. I ran away with Gerry when I was fifteen, and they were going to get him for USI, and I said if they did I would have killed myself. And I would. They knew I meant it. My Dad used to be showing himself all the while to me and my sister, right since we were little. He used to come into our room and make out he was going to the lavatory but got mixed up because he was asleep; and we used to be frit of him. Then other times he used to get strict about sex and that. Right from when we were about ten or eleven he used to question us about who we'd been with and what we'd been doing, and he used to give us a good hiding if we went out with boys . . .

'My Mam and Dad are divorced now. She never believed us when we told her what he did. But then he got pinched for exposing himself to some little girls on the estate, and she divorced him. I don't want to leave my babies, but the only thing is, if I keep them, what sort of a life are they going to have? What can I give them? I mean, I couldn't look after them properly . . . Living here, I get depressed. I'm on nerve tablets. I go out some nights. Mrs Khan keeps an eye on them. She's all right. But I've got no life have I? I'm only eighteen. Some days I feel like an old woman. Then nobody wants you when you've got kids. I go out for a drink some nights, I can get a bloke . . . I'm not waiting for Gerry. I get these letters from him; they're all full of what he'll do for me, says he worships the ground I tread on, that he dreams of me every night, and we'll start up a new life when he comes out – 1985. I mean, I'm flesh and blood. He says he'll kill me if I have any other men. What does he think I am? He said he used to do what he done for my sake, but we didn't see much of it, did we? I mean, I wouldn't be here now.'

Three weeks later Pauline was preparing to leave. She was going to Manchester, was going to get herself a job, find a rich man who would keep her. Her mother had been to visit her and threatened to go to the welfare if she didn't get herself somewhere better to live.

'I'm going to leave them with my Mam. I'll save up some money, get a place where we can all be together again. The only trouble is, I can't live on my own. I can't live without a man, my Mam don't understand. Just because she's got rid of hers, she thinks everybody else should be the same. No man wants to know you if they find out you've got two kids. A good time, that's all they want, not responsibilities. I mean, I know a fair few men, when I go out I look good; that's one thing I always do, you've got to keep your self-respect; and if I go to a party or if I go out for a drink, I can look very smart, I know what suits me. But the minute you start to tell them about kids, this look comes into their eyes, I've seen it, time and again. I mean, I don't want any more, but you can't just send kids back once they're here.'

She picks up Dion from the cot, and holds him close to her. Her eyes fill with tears. 'I don't want to leave him, I wouldn't part with him, not for anything, but I've got to live and find somebody who wants me for myself. Maybe then it'll be easier. If somebody loves you, really loves you for yourself, then they won't mind if they find out later . . . But it's when you first start, the first thing that happens if you've got kids, it's like a switch going off, they don't want to know. I could get a job. I mean, a lot of girls I know are prostitutes. There's nothing wrong with it. Only even that isn't easy now; there's too many think it's easy money and it isn't. I'd rather have somebody who'd look after me and love me, and then we could have the children and it'd be all right.'

These streets shelter a population of lonely and damaged people; it is a mercy in one way that there is the haven of this hiding place, but in another it means that their suffering doesn't disturb the majority because it remains invisible. August, from Latvia, whose English is barely intelligible even after thirty-five years in this country, lives in one room. The only thing he has ever done in England is work; and even that finished in 1978. To do the kind of labouring work he has always done, it has never been necessary to learn English. He shrugs his shoulders and says 'Not speak; speak with these'; and he raises his hands, scarred and scaly with deeply bitten nails. He smiles, and his teeth look as if they have been filed to sharp points, wolf-like. Since he finished work, even the limited social contacts he had have ceased, apart from paying his rent and visiting the shops. On Ladypool Road there is a butcher's shop where he can buy pigs' tails; they are sold cheaply because no one else will eat them. 'English people not eat them, too fat, too much fat. But cook them, vegetable, some onion, it is good . . . Last week I buy some beef, 40 pence, I buy two pound, I eat it for a week, but it smell bad. I say "August, you got to eat it because you bought it." I cook it up with vegetable. It stink worse, everybody in the house say "What you got up there, dead body?"'

Even so, there are those who eat even worse than August. A man of about forty, a woman some ten years younger, were eating out of dustbins behind the Commodore Cinema, and gnawing at detritus from a nearby Indian restaurant. The man was wearing a tattered, greasy suit, the woman was dishevelled and dirty, without stockings, wearing odd shoes, and a man's gabardine raincoat. She was opening up the plastic sacks, thrusting her arm inside and retrieving a half-eaten bone, some handfuls of saffron-coloured rice still with its sprinkling of peas. It's no use saying that there is no need for people to live like that: for some – those who have no address from which to claim Social Security, those on the run, those too far corroded by alcohol, those who despair – there isn't a choice. I saw the same couple later the same day. The woman was begging; and a surprising number of people in the poor street stopped and gave them a few pence. Later, they went to one of the condemned houses, looking round to made sure they were not observed by anyone likely to disturb them, and then pressed back the corrugated tin from the door. They stepped inside, and then closed the metal behind them; pulling the metal over the door so it appeared not to have been disturbed.

There are many Irish people in Balsall Heath. I met one man, in his forties, gaunt and ill-nourished, living in a lodging house. His benefit had been reduced without warning to £19; and £10 of that he was paying for the room with its minimum of comfort – a mattress on the floor, a chair with the plastic torn and disgorging yellowish foam rubber, a few pieces of matting, and a bare electric bulb on a long flex draped over a chair, a few greasy magazines with pictures of women with violet-coloured flesh and white boas. A gas-ring, choked with overflowed saucepans, burnt with a high orange flame. On the ring was a saucepan of tomato soup, and near to it a mug stained inside. For the occupant, even casual work has dried up. He left his wife in Liverpool because he was out of work. 'She picked up with a feller that had a job, he had a trade, he was an electrician, and he could buy her what she wanted. I've had a lot of bad luck, I've not had work, only labouring, and as you get older you can't do it; I had a bad chest, I went down with pneumonia and had to go to hospital. I thought coming down here, I'd get work, and she'd come back to me. But it's gone from bad to worse. I was fooling myself. She'll never come back to me now.'

Mr McFarlane came from Jamaica in 1956 to live in Birmingham. His story is that of thousands of others. From a rural part of Jamaica, where his family had a piece of ground insufficient for the seven of them, he came to England in search of a better life. But what happens to many immigrants in the search is precisely paralleled by what has happened to millions of working-class people. All the strengths they developed to deal with that older poverty – the poverty of hunger and hardship – have all been set aside in response to a promise of improvement, a hope of an easier life. When Mr McFarlane talks of the sharing and the contriving in Surrey County, and the inadequacy of the money from the cash crops to pay for all the other things they needed, he talks of a different kind of poverty from the poverty of dependency in which he now lives with his family. Of course they depended then on selling their bananas, sugar and fruit; but at least they still worked their piece of land, and there lingered an idea that they could always return to subsistence farming, even though it was no longer seriously practicable. But there is something about waiting for a giro through the post, standing in line in the Social Security offices, which is experienced as a loss of power over their lives. They are faced now with a granite imperturbability against which no amount of ingenuity or resourcefulness avails. You wait for the money, without which nothing at all is possible. And it is this extinguishing of possibilities, human possibilities, other ways of managing, that marks the modern poor. It is a closing-up rather than an expansion of life.

Mr McFarlane feels that he was deceived. He came here to work. And for a few years, it seemed all right. He worked as a steam fitter on the railways and was able to get married and start a family. With the change to diesels on the railway, he became an assistant fitter because he wasn't qualified. Then with railway closures, he became redundant, and moved on to factory work, semi-skilled machine operating. When that factory closed, he took a job labouring on buildings until he was made redundant again in 1979. During that time, he was able to buy his house, and bring up his four children, who are now twenty, eighteen, seventeen and fourteen. And for them, there is no prospect of work at all. His experience has symbolized the decay of labour – the declining sense of function and progressive de-skilling of working people. Mr McFarlane is fifty-six, and he sees hope dwindling, not only for himself, but for his children. His arrival in Britain coincided with the last dearth of labour in the 1950s, but this, – and he couldn't know it – was only a temporary phenomenon. His own motive for coming – the search for a better life – has been sabotaged by the fact that the brief shortage of labour was only an aberration which hid an accelerating long-term decline in working-class function, with the result that with time, instead of improvement and advance, his experience has been of decline and the extinction of opportunity. Thus the evolution of the employment structure contributes to the sense of personal discrimination which he has felt. Just as he came here to better himself as an individual, he now sees himself personally rejected. He feels shame, as though the changes in labour needs were his own fault. He still wakes up every morning at 4.30, because for the last years of his working life he was on the six o'clock shift. 'But now I wake up, and I sometimes think I must jump out of bed. But what for? I might as well be dead. How do I know I'm not dead? You feel worthless, nobody wants you. You come to work in this country so that the children get a good education, and get something better. I don't mind if my own job seems to go lower and lower; but they don't get no work at all, it worse for they . . . I don't think about Jamaica no more. It isn't home now; but home isn't here either.'

It was the week of the Brixton riots. In the little park behind Ladypool Road, the young black kids were tense and excited. 'It the best news we heard for years.' They said it made them want to be there, where the excitement is. Their experience is identical with that of Brixton – no work, police harassment, a sense of despair, the feeling that there is no longer anything to lose. It is this feeling that gives some measure of the sense of loss of many migrants. The generation which left the West Indies brought with it memories of dealing with primary poverty – very much as the old working class knew how to deal with the old urban poverty; but the transitional generation has given up all that for the sake of promises of what money can buy; and then the young discover that they are denied that money, and the promises have been false. It is the sudden and violent impact of the market relationships that has transformed the lives of the poor. The parents have adapted to this new culture where everything depends on money, and the young find that they have been shaped for that culture, and are then denied the chance to survive in it because they are to be the new poor, stigmatized by their lack of skills. When this coincides with black skins, it looks like even greater discrimination. The black young grow up separated from their white counterparts, and fail to see that they are all victims of the same processes. They haven't learnt any of the old skills either, the sharing, the coping, eking out, scratching a living on the margins of the city. In fact, the new skills which many black and white young people are beginning to learn are those to do with (mostly) petty crime: stealing, taking, robbing, nicking, lifting become a means of survival for an important minority of the young – all activities which are vain attempts to claim back the things that have been taken from them.

One of the boys, a lively and passionate eighteen-year-old, said, 'My parents came here in the 1950s. They didn't mind doing rough jobs. My Dad worked in a hospital, a porter, and my mother was in a plastics factory. My Dad was sick and he lost his job, and he went on invalidity benefit. My Mum was made redundant. You go to school, right. You get teachers, they say, "Oh you're marvellous, very well done, good." You take a report home to your parents, they think you're a genius. They believe it all. Then you get a bit older, you find you haven't learnt anything, you can't even do the exams, you just didn't learn. So then your parents say, "Why did they tell you you were so good?" It was a con, it was all a fucking load of lies. You're not stupid, you know what you can do and what you can't; it's just that taking exams, nobody wants to know you if you can't do them. So that's one big lost illusion for your parents. The next thing, there's not even the jobs they come here to do. Nothing. You go for interview, they see a black face, "Oh the job's gone." You don't even give them the pleasure of spitting in your face, you stop trying. Why should you? That's the next big disappointment. Your Mum and Dad, they come here to get a better life. Where is it? Then, you can't go anywhere, but you're stopped by the police. The next thing, you're accused of nicking something; they take you down the station, you get roughed about.

My mate, three cops jumped out of a car, it wasn't even marked, they said he spat at them. He was gobbing in the gutter, he didn't even know they was police. What you supposed to do? So that's the end of all their illusions for your parents. They see what's happened to their kids, and they lose hope. They realize no black people is going to get anywhere because they're black. You know the way your mates are treated by the police, but you're not so stupid as to think it's just the police. The police are there because they are what most white people want. They couldn't do what they do to innocent people if they didn't get all the support they need from white people. It means they can get away with anything, and that includes murder. They make you into criminals. People who don't have no hope and no illusions, they get desperate. They'll finish up doing everything they get accused of.'

He insists that the police are only symbols of racist society; that a vast tacit support permits them to treat black people as they do. Nobody who sees the damage done by unemployment and poverty on black and white alike can doubt that the origin of these things lies in the brutal impersonal mechanisms of a social and economic system: the fact that racism becomes the main issue has this great advantage for capitalism in that it keeps inviolate its deepest mysteries, however banal these may be. That the police are the guardians of society takes on another dimension: their real stewardship lies in cloaking the dynamic that brings people to such despair and impotence that they see nothing for it but to react in the way we have seen in the summer of 1981.

Dale and Karen Taylor are twenty. They have been married eighteen months, and have a baby just under a year old. Karen and the baby have been living with her mother, while Dale has been living with his mother. Neither of them works, and this, with their desperate housing need, means that they have no outlet for their anger but each other. When I met them they were thinking of getting a divorce because, at least, Dale would be free to go away and find work. He was thinking of emigrating. 'This country's finished,' he kept saying. Karen wears a coat of imitation leather, split at the seams, cork-heeled shoes. She has a pretty face, pale, with big brown eyes, and dark hair that falls like a curtain whenever she leans forward and lowers her head, which she does frequently: it is the pose of someone trying to withdraw from too many official questions, of someone unable to account for herself and her plight. She eats from a bag of sweets. Her mother talks for her. 'It's breaking up their marriage. What a start in life! Whenever they get together, they just start rowing, and it finishes up in tears. You can't blame them. They visit each other like friends. It isn't like being married at all. If he wants to come and see her, I have to go out. It's like being in prison, you know, what do they call it – conjugal visits.'

They were offered a maisonnette, part of an older house that had been reconditioned. They had no money at all when they moved. For a month, February 1981, they lived in the maisonnette with no heating or cooking facilities. The place had been badly neglected and had to be cleaned throughout: it was still full of rubbish from the previous tenants and builders' rubble. They were granted £105 by DHSS for a cooker and bedding. Even this was delayed because the postman, seeing no curtains at the window, assumed that the house was empty, and failed to deliver the money order. When this had happened twice Karen went with her mother to explain that they were indeed living there. Her mother complained that the bus fare for the two of them cost a pound each time. The DHSS official said 'Well there's no need for you to come with her, she can speak for herself can't she?' Whereupon Karen's mother lost her temper and had an emotional and inconclusive row with the man who was talking to her. What she wanted to say, but couldn't, was that Karen wasn't able to speak for herself, and that it isn't her fault. Like many others of her generation, Karen has had no experience of anything very much apart from the commercially created culture in which she has been nurtured, with its invitations to fantasy, inertia and unknowingness. It isn't her fault. She is an intelligent but shy girl; and there is something woefully stunted about her twenty years, wandering through the labyrinth of 'caring' agencies. There is fear and resentment in her eyes. 'It isn't fair,' she keeps saying. Somehow, as she has grown, only those needs that can be answered by buying things have been cultivated – and those not very effectively – whereas that deeper hunger, the requirements of the intelligence and the spirit have been smothered. All those old people who knew that their intelligence would never be allowed to develop properly, and their real personality never flower because they were claimed by factory or mill at the age of fourteen or fifteen, have their direct counterparts, intelligent and able people whose abilities are undermined by the manufactured temptations of a commercially determined culture, the buying of instant excitements, momentary consolations that destroy long-term purposes, and maintain hundreds of thousands of individuals in thrall. What Richard Hoggart[27] cautiously but presciently called 'the process of debilitation' has had a generation of unhindered development. It is as though the opposite of the repressive methods formerly used against the working class has been miraculously discovered to serve the same end – to destroy any understanding of and hence ability to cope with the forces that shape their lives.

Why is it that education seems to have done so little for many working-class children? Is it because a more direct medium of communication has interposed itself, the culture of the consumer economy – an alien implant in the decayed working-class culture that grew around the discipline of work and poverty, and which yet achieves the same result – the same subordination, the same incomprehension. In a way it is more subtly malevolent than the old poverty because the fact that it is not in the long-term interests of children is not so immediately apparent as the poverty of hardship and basic want. It seems to grant so much and to withhold nothing with its insistent seductions and compelling invitations. But whatever it is, Karen at twenty does not have the resources or the confidence to deal with the officials at the DHSS, the Housing Department, even the Social Services. She has been detached from a tradition of labour, and now lives in a shadowy unidentified terrain from where she can see nothing of the forces that mould her life. If an ability to understand and respond to the social institutions which determine her world is a prerequisite of democracy, Karen and many millions like her simply do not live there, but inhabit an eerie twilight created by others for her puzzlement and continuing subjection. The damaged spirit and the crushed intelligence are just as disabling as an absence of material sufficiency. It isn't enough to say that Karen won't starve. We accuse the mechanistic materialism of Marxist societies of denying everything that cannot be calculated in material terms; and yet here we are, using the same measure, suppressing everything that cannot be bought or sold or so distorting it until it can; and it is this that leads to the sense of impoverishment that hangs over these sad places that make up the inner city and its problems.

The Lane Neighbourhood Centre is a former shop on Ladypool

Road, a three-storey building, the ground floor of which has been divided into interviewing cubicles with lengths of hardboard; full of gunmetal filing cabinets, battered office desks, black plastic bags of second-hand clothing for the shop that is run from the top of the building. The shop window is crowded with notices about women's groups, a carpentry course for women called Do-It-Herself, CND meetings, tenants' associations, the local carnival, how to deal with harassment by landlords. In the area of the former shop is the reception desk, a long bench and some tubular metal and canvas chairs. Two mattresses stacked against a wall limit the space even further; there is a rack of dark-blue leaflets on how to claim special allowances, mobility, disability, special attendance allowances. It is more disordered and more lively than a doctor's waiting room. In the interviewing rooms which are cell-like and claustrophobic, it soon gets very warm, the cigarette smoke curls upwards, the atmosphere is stifling. Throughout the day there is a continuous press of people around the reception desk. Although the problems the people bring here often appear quite simple – a giro that has gone astray, an unexplained change in the DHSS assessment of their needs – it doesn't take much for the deeper anxieties to surface, the helplessness, the isolation, the bewilderment and despair. It is impossible not to be deeply moved and disturbed by all the people who have to spend so much time and energy trying to discover why their benefit has been altered, why it is impossible to get some essential repairs carried out in their property, or who are simply looking for someone to help them or even just listen to them.

There are people whose whole life seems to be spent in movement from one authority to another: Mr Beaumont from Trinidad in one week in March 1981 visited the Housing Department about a transfer from his fourth-floor flat because of his heart condition, the doctor to get a duplicate of a letter that had got lost stressing the urgency of his case, hospital for his three-monthly check-up, the solicitor about divorce proceedings between himself and his wife, the education welfare to see about continuing free dinners for the children, the social service department to talk to someone about his wife's threat to throw him out and install her boy-friend in the flat, the doctor again for the renewal of a prescription for tablets for depression, a second hospital for tests on his sickle-cell anaemia, the school about his youngest child's behaviour – an endless succession of officials, his only relationship with white society.

An Irishwoman, about fifty. She looks older; her hair is uncombed and greasy, streaked with grey. She is fat, and she sits in the green plastic office chair, her shoulders rounded, her legs apart, her hands playing with the rosary around her neck. She wears an old fur cape, a thick cream-coloured knitted cardigan of a black dress with brown spots and badly fitting boots. Her face is lined, and furrows of habitual misery run beside her downturned mouth. Her eyes are red with crying. Six weeks earlier her daughter died in a fire. She was eleven. Her mother speaks of her as 'my baby', and she rocks to and fro saying 'I've lost my baby, I've lost my baby', as though it were a prayer. The child was sleeping with relatives, as she usually did, because the flat where her parents live is damp and cold.

'They put her to bed in the little room, but they never told me they were having a party that night . . . There was a fire in the room, they always looked after her. They loved her. But they had the music on, you see, and they couldn't hear her screams. And when they found her, it had choked her, the smoke had got to her and choked her. If I had known they were going to have a party, I could have taken her home. Oh, I can't get it out of my thoughts, to think of my baby dying like that and nobody with her. I can't blame anybody. The woman of the house, she had a nervous breakdown over it. They all loved her. I hate to go home. I can still see her where we live, I think she's going to come round the door at any minute, and I'll see her darling face and find out it was all a dream. I can see her going off to school, oh, she loved school, and she was doing so well. I want to move right away from here because wherever I look I have memories of her; I can still see her doing all the things she used to do. There's just me and my husband now, he's been ill, he had only half an hour to live with a burst appendix, they only just got him to the hospital on time . . . But did it have to happen, that's what I'd like to know, could I have stopped it? If I'd fetched her home, would she still be here now? Did it have to happen?'

She plays with the pale-green and black beads of the rosary, and passes a black lace handkerchief across her face which does not touch the tears running down the deep grooves and falling onto the cardigan. 'The priest talks to me. It's a comfort. I can cry, and they tell me to cry is a blessing. I've done nothing but cry. He tells me there are some poor people with grief in their hearts who cannot even cry. For them it must be worse still. The priest said to me "God wanted her." And I say "Yes, and I wanted her too, she was my child." He says our Saviour's mother suffered when she lost her child, and she accepted it. You can accept it. With time. But how much time? I can't do anything, I can't eat. I can't even take the medicine the doctor gave me, nor the tablets. Sometimes, when I'm in company, I forget about her for a few minutes; and then suddenly I remember, and it might be in the middle of somebody talking, and I start to cry again. And then I feel guilty even that I've forgotten her for a few minutes. But nobody wants to be with you when you've nothing but tears and grief to offer them all the time. Sometimes, when I walk about the street, I'm in a daze. I don't know what I'm doing; I fall down in the street sometimes and forget where I am. I don't see that I'll ever get over it.'

There is no need for a response; her grief echoes inside her; and there is nothing to do but wait until she has finished. In the meantime, the centre becomes crowded; people sit silently in the shop, and her voice can be heard over the thin partition wall, a lonely cry of desolation and guilt.

A man of about thirty follows her with thinning fair hair and a red face, and several days' growth of beard. He doesn't look at anyone as he speaks, but fixes his eyes on the calendar on the wall, his fingers clutching the corner of the table obsessively. He isn't used to talking about himself, explaining. Whenever he has been in trouble he has either fought his way out of it or run away. He is in an alien world here. All his life he has been a labourer, and the energy in him has always expressed itself through heavy physical tasks. His fingers are scarred and calloused, his arms covered with scratches that haven't healed properly; his manner suggests a disregard of himself, indifference to his own safety, the recklessness of someone who is unloved. He was working for a building firm, and an accident on some clumsily-erected scaffold injured his foot. He had no national insurance card and had not been paying tax. He said the firm had assured him they were paying tax and insurance, and he had never bothered to find out. He lives alone, going from town to town, living in lodging-houses or sleeping rough. He wears the clothes he last worked in, still covered with dried mud and plaster. He has been able to make no claims since his accident, but has continued to do odd jobs, bits of casual work, and when the money run out, sleeping in the old houses. He says he once spent a few nights in a scrap-metal yard inside some clapped-out cars, and was wakened by the sound of a metal-crushing machine lifting up the vehicles one by one. He grins when he says he might have been a sardine by now if the crane had picked up the wrong car. The broken bones in his foot were not treated, and they healed badly, so that he now limps and is in constant pain. He is in his late thirties, already past his strongest, and finding work harder to find. He will not go to Social Security because he is afraid of trouble for all the money he has earned without declaring it, and his failure to pay insurance. He has led a casual, unsettled life, going from place to place, having perhaps £200 in his pocket one week and nothing the next; generous, living in the present, accepting. He says he has a horror of being closed in, hates the idea of working in a factory, above everything dreads prison. He goes away, saying he will go to Manchester.

I saw him a little later, waiting for the pub to open. He said he has never lived in a house since he came to this country; he lived one winter in a hut on some allotments and scavenged for food at night; a half-vagrant but not wretched existence. He said he was proud of the fact that he had never had a woman and never wanted one, but it was nothing for him to drink nineteen pints when he had the money.

A young woman from West Pakistan. She wears a dark blue head-dress, and a coat of the same colour; her hair is concealed, and her eyes dark brown and apprehensive. She has been in England for fourteen years, but she is too shy to speak English. Her son has been at college, and she was receiving child allowance for him; but after six months, it has been pointed out to her that the number of hours per week he is spending at college just fails to qualify him as a full-time student. The money she has been receiving in child benefit for six months has been wrongly paid, and she must now pay it back. She is terrified by the thought that she has been receiving money she is not entitled to, and she will do anything to pay it back. But she has no resources other than Social Security. Her husband is dead; he died two years ago on his way back to Pakistan to visit his sick father. Out of a crumpled plastic bag marked Safeways, she takes out a bundle of documents tied with string; many immigrants carry plastic bags crammed full of almost any piece of paper they have ever been given, as though they were always about to be accused of entering the country illegally, or of having failed to pay for something. She takes out her passport, communications from DHSS, receipts, photographs, a mass of papers, fingered and worn at the folds from having been passed round and puzzled over by friends and relatives.

The centre is open to anybody who wants to drop in; and many do, regularly, most of them lonely and without occupation. An elderly Welshman is there. He wears a red knitted hat, a gabardine raincoat, and holds a carrier-bag. The poor always seem to carry bags, a sad gesture, perhaps, to conformity in possessions they don't have. He takes out a packet of thin arrowroot biscuits, which he shares with the people in the shop. His eyes are pale blue and the water in them looks like tears; but the pointed red hat gives him a slightly mischievous air, an elderly sprite. He used to be a pharmacist, and once had his own pharmacy. 'But I used to help other people too much, and that was my undoing.' He doesn't elaborate; but he offers it as a kind of warning, so that his hearers may profit from his example. 'I had a job once,' he says elegiacally, 'I should never have given it up.' From his carrier-bag, he takes a little plastic flowerpot with three tiny eucalyptus plants which he has grown from seed. 'I've been a rolling stone. What is it they say? "Gathers no moss." Well what good is moss, only for plants.' He waters the ferns on the window-sill of the kitchen, and presses the earth down around the cactus plant with his thumb, shaking his head as he does so to indicate that none of the plants would survive if he didn't come to care for them. When he has watered each plant, he wipes the pot carefully – some of them only paper cups – and replaces it carefully on the window-ledge. He says 'People are so badly educated about diet. They are badly educated about many things of course, but diet is particularly important. Take fish for instance. That is very bad for you. It's dead flesh, you see, and when you eat it, it putrefies inside you, it rots. Well, who can say what poisons that releases into your body? Tell me what you think of this theory. I have a theory why children go dumb. It's through vaccination. When they stick a needle into a child, what does it do? It yells and yells. And that damages both the larynx and the pharynx. And that is why they cannot speak.'

He is always bringing biscuits and plants and medicinal herbs to the people in the centre, an exchange for the friendship he receives here. He drinks tea, gives advice, expounds his theories; a fragile and touching return for their welcome. He is an example of the lonely individuals these wasting streets still shelter, the misfits, the unregulated population who still find comfort away from the increasingly bleak and institutionalized world of those marble slabs on the other side of Moseley Road.

Lynn works as a volunteer on the reception desk once a week. She is in her thirties, dark eyes and hair, wide smile. She wears a black anorak and jeans. She has not worked for eight months. Although she belongs to several women's groups, is active in CND and does voluntary work, she says she frequently feels depressed and aimless. She says that she is in many ways characteristic of the generation formed by the 1960s. There was a feeling then that work, although subordinate to the real business of living, would always be there, to take up and set aside, to use to one's own advantage. There was a feeling that work was just a means to get the bread to go on a trip round the world, to go East, take off for another country for the summer, then spend the winter reading philosophy or studying Marx.

'It seemed the natural thing to do, because the atmosphere was so relaxed. Everybody seemed to spend a few months doing nothing, bumming around, taking casual work. I used to work as a cleaner, office cleaning, domestic cleaning. I found it quite satisfying because I knew I didn't have to do it for ever. I did community work, social work. I never bothered to get a qualification, it seemed there would always be that demand for people. The whole feeling was different then. It seemed as if life was going to become easier, more expansive; the only anxiety was about what new and exciting things were going to happen next.' Lynn feels that she and many like her were waylaid during the process of acquiring skills or qualifications by the sense of continuous carnival that was in the air through the sixties.

I met a number of people in their thirties who echoed Lynn's experience, although most of them were sufficiently prudent to play safe by taking a CQSW course, or a teacher training diploma, as a kind of insurance. They remain a significant group; those who feel that their abilities were undermined by their failure to apply them; those who dropped out into drugs and music and communal living, who thought life was going to be like that for ever. Some of them have been too damaged or demoralized to start again; others have gone into far-Left politics. In retrospect, all the relaxed, laid-back hedonism of the sixties looks very different: it had the same effect on the articulate young as all those processes which were at work in the lives of the majority of working-class people – the lure of redundancy money, the promise of leisure, the ready giving up of jobs without wondering where the work was going to come from for the next generation. When Lynn talks of the sixties, it is the same process, detaching people – at that time, a very sophisticated, young and often well-educated group – from the idea that work or function is important, a process which encouraged people to lose resources, fail to realize their own abilities. I can remember going to parties in the sixties and committing the greatest solecism of all – that of asking people what they did – and was always put down with the chill response 'I think what people are is so much more important.'

Upstairs in the centre, Kath runs a second-hand clothing shop. It looks down onto the streets adjacent to Ladypool Road from the top floor of the building. In the shop, there are racks of dresses, suits, skirts, hats, children's clothes and shoes, which Kath keeps in perfect order, even though she has to remind people that it's not a jumble sale when they start rummaging through the neatly packed boxes and the carefully hung rows of coats, each on its wire hanger from dry-cleaning shops. Kath is in her fifties, one of the few people who were actually born in the neighbourhood. She looks out at the post office opposite, with its glass panel advertising lodgings and articles for sale and services for a population of transients, and she says: 'It used to be lovely round here. All my people lived in the few streets you can see from this window. My uncle lived down there, and my grandma was just round the corner; you had somebody belonging to you wherever you went. Some of the houses were lovely. My auntie went into service when she was fourteen in a house just up the hill.'

Kath is a small energetic woman with greying hair and a thin face. She is committed to the neighbourhood still; she sees in it the ghost of the compact community it was when she was a girl, and she is determined to contribute to its stability by not moving out, as so many of her neighbours and relatives have done. Fred, her husband, is sick; he had a stroke four years ago and has not worked since then. This means that the time she can give to the community centre is limited.

Kath and Fred have been living on his invalidity benefit since he became ill. They had a lodger, who was paying £12 a week for his board, including food, light and heat. The DHSS disregard £4 of earnings, and so Kath was paid £4 for the work she did at the centre. When the DHSS discovered that there was a lodger – and the fact emerged quite naturally, there was no suggestion that Kath and Fred had been trying to conceal the fact – their income was re-assessed and it was decided that out of the £12 a week they had received from the lodger, they were making £4 a week 'profit', which they had, of course, failed to declare. Kath and Fred had no idea they could be assumed to be making a profit out of the friendly arrangement they had with the lodger. The DHSS official insisted that rules are rules, and that all the money that had been paid out by them above the limit would have to be paid back. The amount was assessed at £360. This was reduced to £240 after some negotiation between Yvonne from the Neighbourhood Centre and an official from the DHSS, and Kath agreed to pay £2 a week. But before this plan could be carried out the new regulations of November 1980 prompted the Department to alter the agreement, and it was decided by them to subtract £6.50 a week from the family income, £4.50 from long-term invalidity benefit and £2 from the disregarded earnings. Yvonne wrote to the local MP saying that she felt the decision was rather harsh, and that a loss of £6.50 a week was excessive, and she asked him if he could not get the amount lost reduced. The MP wrote to Fred's doctor, who confirmed that the reduction of £6.50 a week would result in severe hardship, because 'his medical condition causes additional unavoidable expenses'. The DHSS refused to modify its judgement, and insisted on the payment of the full £6.50 a week. The letter from the DHSS read 'I am sorry I am unable to be more helpful in the circumstances, but it is the Department's normal practice always to seek repayment, as a result of the requirement imposed by Parliament that the Department should safeguard public funds.'

The MP was unwilling to take the case any further when he was told that Kath and Fred had 'capital', a nest-egg of £753 in a building society account. This was money that Fred had set aside for Kath. It had always been properly declared, but he had never considered spending it because it was intended for his wife after his death.

A few days after this, Fred had a coronary and was rushed to the intensive care unit of the hospital. Kath telephoned the centre in tears. She had telephoned the DHSS, but their only response was to insist that she complete form A9 to enable them to reduce benefit while Fred is in hospital; there could of course be no question of the additional payment for heating which he would not require while away from home. Three days later Fred died. The workers at the centre felt that Kath had been insensitively and unjustly treated, doubly so because of all the work she had done for the community, all that she had offered of her time and her commitment.

One of the people who have been helped by Kath recently is Frances, a sad-faced nervous woman in her fifties, whose marriage has just broken down after thirty years. She has been helping Kath in the second-hand shop. She moved into the area only recently, and she hates it. She is disoriented and unhappy. Helping in the shop has been a comfort, and has meant the difference between coping with the shock of parting from her husband and giving way to absolute despair. Frances is still fragile and incredulous that such a thing could happen to her. 'I never knew how lonely it would be. All you think about is getting away, being free; it isn't until afterwards that you reflect that breaking away is always into something else as well as away from something you can't stand.

'I feel I'm trapped. I'm afraid to go out after dark. I'm in a flat I don't like. One evening, I only went out to get a pint of milk, I only had to walk a couple of hundred yards up the street, and the things that were said to me made me cringe. There are a lot of prostitutes in the area, and the way men spoke to me, it was shameful. They must have known I'm not like that. I said "Look, I've just come out to buy a pint of milk, leave me alone. Look, there are three women standing on the corner there, that's what they're waiting for, go and ask them." Well, if any white man treated their women like that, they'd be furious . . . When I get home in the evening, it's just knowing that you're not going to see anyone else all night, not unless somebody breaks in to where you're living . . . I read a lot, but reading when you're lonely is very different from reading when you've someone else's companionship. I don't feel safe, even when I've locked my door. I lie in bed in fear and trembling. Being on the ground floor, people come and knock on the door in the night . . . The young man who lives upstairs, he has parties, he plays music till all hours. I feel I can't trust him. I can't trust anybody.

'I know it's partly me; it's the frame of mind I'm in, prepared to see the worst everywhere. With my marriage breaking up, it predisposes me to see the worst. It's all so desperate, people seem so unhappy here. Each evening, I think "Well that's the end of another futile day." When I go home now, I'm unlikely to see anyone to talk to until after the weekend, except the people in the shops. I might see my son and his wife, but you can't ask too much of them. I only stayed with my husband all those years for my son's sake. I was brought up rough; I don't want him to go through what I did. I wanted him to get an education. That's why I put up with it. I was a doormat for thirty years. With my husband it was always My life, My plans, My house, My car, My social life. I never came into it. But there you are. I played the game for my boy's sake. And you can't ask them for gratitude; it isn't their fault. They don't even realize the torment you've been through.

'At first, just to get out of it, the relief is overwhelming. The sense of freedom. But that doesn't last long; the boredom soon sets in, the sense of futility. It's a different kind of loneliness from what you feel inside a lonely marriage. You achieve what you want, but when you achieve it, it seems so little. You only think of what you're escaping from, not what you're running to.'

Naseem, a tall quiet girl, with her hair swept back into a bun, comes into the centre to help with translations. She came from Kenya two years ago for an arranged marriage. She and her fiancé have undergone a civil ceremony, but they will not live together until the religious ceremony has taken place in six months' time. In the meantime, she does not see her husband. He lives with his parents a few streets away from her, and has just been made redundant from the factory where he was working. Naseem's parents are still in Kenya. She was very frightened when she first arrived in Birmingham.

'The middle is a bit like the middle of Nairobi; but the rest is nothing like the cities in Kenya. I didn't know what to expect. Coming to England was much more frightening than the idea of getting married. I know that my mother and father love me, and want to do what is best for me. People in this country think that an arranged marriage is wrong. But when you see how people hurt each other in marriages which they are supposed to have chosen freely – in this place I am always meeting wives who have been deserted, people who have parted from their children – how can this be better than the kind of marriage that is contracted by the people who love you best in the world, those dearest to you? They would never do anything to harm you. In our culture, a husband and wife know their duties to each other, they know their roles. This is more important if a marriage is to last than whether you share the same feelings of romantic love; that always fades in the end. You keep a bit of distance, and so you keep respect. It's the way you behave that makes you a good wife, a good husband, not whether your selfish wants are all answered. There has to be a balance. You must know what to expect before you start a life together. I'm afraid it is happening here now; some women are rejected by their husbands. That isn't something to be proud of. Sometimes, the men that girls come to marry have learnt to be selfish and don't keep their part of the bargain; they ill treat their wives or go off with other women, while the women are too frightened to stand alone; they get the worst of both worlds then.'

Later the same day, a woman came in who was in just the situation Naseem was describing. She was perhaps in her early thirties, hesitant and depressed, and she spoke scarcely above a whisper. She brought her son with her, a serious boy of twelve, who is part interpreter, part protector; and she speaks to him in a low and breathless voice. He is an intelligent but frail-looking child, and although he does all the talking, he has absorbed much of his mother's anxiety, and he doesn't find it easy. His voice is soft and polite; his manner suggests a childhood that is very different from that customary in Balsall Heath. He wears a green tie and blazer, the uniform of the local comprehensive school. His mother prompts him, and he speaks as though he scarcely understands what he is saying, in the emotionless voice of interpreters. His mother says that her husband has gone away and deserted them. She cannot afford the heating bills, the phone bill, so she will have to sell the house, but where will she live then? She talks of her disappointment and hopelessness through the child who only half understands, and who filters out all the bitterness and anger, leaving only a residue of sadness, his sadness. The shame and indignity are incalculable for her. Is this what it meant, her voice asks through the words that I don't understand, to come and look for a better life – desertion, isolation, money from the State to keep my children? This child, who ought to be sheltered and cared for by me and his father, finds himself having to face Social Security officials, housing officers, social workers. What will it do to him, she seems to ask, as her hand rests on his head, when he cannot look to his parents for guidance and moral instruction, a safe place in which to be a child, when all he has seen has been loss and inconstancy, defection and the breaking of bonds between people?

Mr and Mrs Kennedy are in their late forties. He is a thin man with short lank hair parted in the middle, pale-blue eyes that look out with an expression of hurt innocence. He wears a grey gabardine raincoat, grey flannels, a royal blue cardigan with the buttons fastened through the wrong holes. He walks very unsteadily. His wife is smaller and self-effacing. She has fair hair, and wears a pale-green coat. Mr Kennedy moves his hands all the time as he talks, the fingers separated so that they seem to spike out at different angles; his wife moves and gesticulates imitatively. This expresses something of their relationship: it isn't always clear with which one each characteristic originates. They both drink, and have been badly worn by years of alcohol; Mr Kennedy has occasional bursts of violence, and his wife is often beaten and hurt. But they cannot part from each other. She did once try to leave him. A new flat was arranged for her, but she never moved in. She couldn't exist apart from him. When they are together, she appears more timid, and acts as a mitigating influence on his aggression which, at least for the outside world, is not very coherent or convincing. He sits, stabbing the table with his finger, although he often misses the edge of the table and then stabs the air with such force that his whole body lurches forward and it looks as if he is going to fall out of the chair.

The couple have one son, a handicapped boy, who is in a hospital for the severely subnormal and who needs constant attention. Mr Kennedy has come in to say that he wants his son home – an ineffectual and wounded assertion of a power he doesn't have. 'I want him out of that place. He is my son. I don't care what you think, I don't care what anybody thinks.' Dave, the worker he is talking to, insists that he cannot make the hospital release his son, and in any case, even if he could, he doesn't think it would be a good idea for him to go home. Mr Kennedy makes no response to anything that is said, but continues with his lonely internal obsession. 'I want him home. You can get him out.' 'No, I can't. And even if I could, I wouldn't. Look what happened last time he came home. He only came for a holiday, but had to go back because you couldn't look after him properly.' 'You can't stop me having my son home. He is my son.' 'No, I'm not stopping you. You know where the hospital is. You go and ask them. That's the way to go about it.' 'You can't stop me. Nobody can stop me doing anything I want to.' His mouth sags open; he forgets for a moment what he is saying; and the tone falls from being aggressive and becomes plaintive, helpless. Mrs Kennedy pulls at his sleeve. 'We want to move. If we had a house with an indoor toilet and bath, he could come home then.' Mr Kennedy has a renewed rush of aggression. 'No. I'm not moving. I want an indoor toilet and bath when I am now.' Then he loses track of the argument again. 'I want him home. Now. This afternoon. I want my son home.'

It seems appropriate that in the pub at dinner-time, two women in their late sixties sitting on the torn leatherette bench should be talking about change and loss in the area where they have spent all their lives. They discover they are both war-widows, and the conversation that began as competitive anecdotes, develops a deeper and sadder tone. 'Of course, them as lost their husband earlier in the war, they got more of an acknowledgement, they got a scroll. My friend, she got a big parchment like, all embossed in gold; but he was killed in 1940. All I got was, well, a note really, saying "missing, presumed dead", and then a letter to say I'd go on getting paid for six months. Of course my friend, she made a shrine to her husband really in her living-room, photographs, mementos, everything. I couldn't do that. I carry his picture with me, I still do, wherever I go, but I couldn't bear to sit at home and look at it. I think that's morbid.'

'Aah.' Her companion is slightly older, she wears crystal earrings, her grey hair is tinted almost lilac beneath her felt hat. 'They were sad days, but people did treat each other decent. I loved my husband, there's only me knows how much. My Mam used to say every tear shed in grief shortens the time of a soul in purgatory; well the tears I've shed must have rescued millions. I haven't ever got over losing him. But you had people, you had your family, and all them as knew him. They could see you through your grief.' 'That's it. People wait now till you're lying dead, before they start to wonder if there's anything wrong with you.'

This kind of conversation is often heard; but it is seldom followed through. The women fall into a reflective silence, and their eyes glaze slightly as they look inwards, each to the memory of her husband; and in the pub the music from the jukebox is oppressively loud – Shakin' Stevens singing 'This Ole House'. You can only marvel that the War should continue to be evoked as a time of human solidarity after so many years. Surely this is a measure of the damage that has been done to us. The fact that people can think of the War, which robbed them of those they loved, and still remember the human warmth is the most cruel comment on the decay of shared values. The War is another of those working-class metaphors for what has been taken away. When they say 'The War kept us together,' they are actually recalling a time when what was common to all working-class communities seemed to take on a wider significance: it seemed as though the recognition of our shared humanity was to become the dominant response of the whole society. Certain truths – that we have nothing if not each other – are not just cosy sentiment engendered by an external threat, for there is always an external threat: time and loss and death are always there. The bitter thing has been that, instead of building a society which recognized these inescapable truths about ourselves, that spirit was so easily subverted, so swiftly overthrown, and that in its place the reverse was reasserted, a society re-established that actually exploits human insecurity and loneliness, and exults in the damage it does to the social and fraternal part of human beings.

The rejection of those values after the War and the substitution of something else is what the two old women are talking about, the older one setting down her Guinness and playing with the gold ring deep in the flesh of her finger, the other sitting with her elbow in one hand, and the other hand across her face, little finger in the corner of the mouth. The deep and seemingly irrecoverable losses they are talking about have been separated from any acknowledged social and political issues, so that they float as abstractions that only War could summon forth. As the women talk, they seem to accept that certain basic human needs have been separated from their own lives, which is what indeed has happened. Our common humanity has been consigned to an area of melancholy regret called nostalgia, while real life is about something else.

Two women, expelled from Uganda in 1973, sisters. The younger is distressed because this morning she received from DHSS a notice of revised assessment of benefit, which has been reduced from the £44 she and her two daughters were living on to nil. There was no explanation. She takes out all her documents from the ubiquitous carrier-bag, this one stamped 'Spar Supermarkets'. Among them, there is a void building society pass-book, phone, electricity and gas bills, a much-folded used ticket of Sudan Airlines, tv repair bills, a receipt for a suit, a delivery note for some furniture – every financial transaction for the last two years. Mrs Gupta has kept every piece of paper, many of them tattered and falling to pieces. The Department, it emerges, has insisted that she has capital in the bank, and has deliberately disposed of it, which automatically excludes her from benefit. What had happened was that her husband had been made redundant from his factory job, and with the money he had received he had opened a chip shop. But he lacked experience and expertise. There were already too many food shops in the area competing for too little money, and it failed. He had borrowed £1,000 to set himself up with the basic equipment, and this loan had been paid back when the chip shop closed. It had been paid in cash; so what appeared to be a withdrawal of all the family's remaining money was interpreted by the DHSS as a voluntary disposal of capital. Mr Gupta has gone to Mombasa, where his father is dying. The DHSS official had asked why he should insist on going on holiday when he was in such bad financial straits. His wife says bitterly that it is not of their choosing that her father-in-law should be in Kenya, nor even theirs that they should be in Birmingham. If they hadn't been thrown out of Uganda, the old man would not have gone to Kenya; if he had been allowed to join them here, his son would not have had the expense of going back to Kenya to be at his side when he dies.

Jabeen, eighteen, has long hair thick and dark, pushed back behind her ears, wears small crystal earrings, a dark-green gabardine coat with a fur collar over a flimsy chocolate and orange saree. She was born in Balsall Heath, and has a strong Birmingham accent. She has been working in a nursery school on a Youth Opportunity Programme. She is waiting for her fiancé to be allowed to join her here. Male fiancés find it harder than any other group to get permission to come into Britain. Jabeen has taken great care to ensure that she complies with all the conditions: she has been to Pakistan to meet him, they do intend to live together as husband and wife, her father has given an assurance that he will make no financial demands on the State. She applied for him to come here under the old rules; but from recent communication with the Home Office, it seems that her sponsorship of him will have to be re-processed under new and far more stringent rules.

Jabeen went to Pakistan for the first time last year. Although it seemed familiar from what she has heard from her parents, she could never imagine living there. 'In this country, you can get your parents to give you the things you ask for. My father buys me what I want. If I want a music centre, some new clothes, he will do everything he can to give them to me. That doesn't happen in Pakistan, where the children have to wait for the older generation to decide. There, the young don't have power over their parents.' She smiles. The observations of those who have adapted from one culture to another are sometimes simple and to the point. Jabeen has been at the centre of the process, the modification of the family relationships, the overturning of traditional values. For her it is a fact of life, morally neutral, the price of survival.

But for those who are too old to accommodate themselves, there is only the pain of the changed values, none of the advantages. For Mrs Mustapha, the experience has been one of continuing loss.

Monday afternoon. We are taking two chairs in red uncut moquette which have been stored in the cellar of the Lane Centre to where Mrs Mustapha lives, on her own, in a housing association flat. The house was once a substantial and ornate Victorian villa, but has been divided into flats, painted chocolate brown. The garden has been concreted over; six new metal dustbins with the number of a flat on each. Mrs Mustapha lives essentially in one room, although there is a small kitchen and bathroom. There is a plain carpet, a large low bed with a duvet. The walls are bare and painted cream. There is a calendar, two pieces of delicate embroidery on dark material, a motif in Gujarati, Mrs Mustapha's only language. A photograph of two grandchildren stands on a trunk draped with a piece of bright cloth. The curtains are pink nylon, with a design of lime-green leaves. In a coffee jar, stand three purple daffodils and a spray of pink blossom in plastic, and there is a white plastic portable television and one plain kitchen chair. The room is not uncomfortable, but there is a sense of desolation that is quite different from the usual plainness and frugality of an Asian interior. Mrs Mustapha is a big woman; her dark hair is greying, and her glasses magnify her eyes, so that what you see is an expression rather than the eyes themselves, a dark swimming sadness. She wears a saree in dark-brown material, with a navy-blue jumper, and a long piece of orange chiffon around her neck, which she flicks from time to time over her shoulder, but it is so light it always flutters back into position again. She wears open sandals and thick green socks. The newly installed gas-fire gives out tepid fumes smelling of metal. Mrs Mustapha crosses her arms over her breast, rubbing her shoulders from time to time, rocking gently as though seeking relief from pain. She is sixty-four, but looks older; an old woman alone. She lived in Kampala until eight years ago, in a one-storey white house shaded by eucalyptus and plantain, when she was expelled by Amin. Her husband had just died, so that she had not had time to mourn him when she was forced to leave. Her exile and sense of personal loss merged. When she arrived in England, she spent eight months in a disused army camp on Greenham Common, a proposed site of Cruise missiles. She had nothing when she arrived in this country, and was given £55 by Social Security. Her family is scattered. There is a nephew who lives not far away; sometimes he collects her and takes her to his house for a few hours at the weekend. She has brothers in Canada. She is visited by people from the mosque, who make sure that she is able to attend to her religious observances. She has just had an operation for cataract and she is diabetic.

When we arrive, the door is open. Mrs Mustapha is sitting on the bed, stoical, uncomplaining. She has a home help, even though she cannot understand what she says to her. This woman does the cleaning and the work which Mrs Mustapha cannot manage. But she does no shopping because she doesn't know what to buy; she doesn't cook because Mrs Mustapha is unused to English food; and she doesn't receive meals on wheels for the same reason. She cannot bath herself because it is impossible to get in and out of the bath without help. The silence and isolation of her life are bad enough, but they are made much worse by her loss of role and function. She has no one for whom her experience is of any relevance, no one to whom she can tell what she has been through and learnt from it, no one to consult her and honour her age. She is in fact learning to become like many old people in the host community: their children and grandchilden are also on a different kind of journey, to which the lives of the old offer no guide. Mrs Mustapha though, unlike many of the indigenous old people, has the strength of her religious belief to support her; and it is perhaps this that makes her seem slightly remote, abstracted and self-contained; she is a figure of dignity and endurance, a quiet reproach to the 'humanitarian' values of the society into which she has arrived.

The Asians are resented because they do not voluntarily give up those things that the old working class seem to have surrendered so easily. Mrs Mustapha feels that she has had the wisdom of her years stolen from her, that store of experience which is the most precious thing she has to offer to the next generation. It is these things that the extension of the market-place has so brutally interrupted in working-class life. The irony is that those who have clung more tenaciously to older cultural and religious forms, those who have resisted the process of divesting themselves of all values and traditions in favour of the cultivation of appetites that can be satisfied only by what can be bought, are those who are accused of taking away the consolations that formerly comforted the people in those poor places. We have indeed been robbed, and of things beyond price. If it is those people who try to hold to more human values who bear the blame for what has been done to us, perhaps it is because they are the ones who appear to delay the transition to the time when we shall all be subordinated to what must be one of the most tyrannical and destructive ideas ever set loose in the world, the idea that everything can be bought and sold for money.

6

Outside the Ghetto: Selly Oak

A mile or two outside the ghetto; a respectable late nineteenth- and early twentiety-century suburb. Colin Tivey, thirty, lives with his mother in an old-fashioned terraced house not far from the factory which used to be known as 'the blood tub' because of all the accidents which occurred there. Colin is not employed. He says there is too much work to be done to take paid employment. He works in a neighbourhood centre, in a health food co-operative; he works against racism and for the community. He gets £38.40 a fortnight. Because he lives with his mother, some of what he would otherwise receive is deducted for rent. He gives £10 a week to his mother for household expenses, and spends £3 a week on a travel pass so that he can travel anywhere in the West Midlands without extra expense. He almost never buys new clothes: he wears an ancient pair of almost indestructible workman's boots, jeans, a khaki jacket, a knitted jumper. It is easy to dress cheaply if you ignore fashion and use second-hand clothes' shops. The rest of his money goes on books, cups of tea, a Coke. He doesn't need money. He left school at fifteen; and says that he never spent much time there anyway. He says he was what would now be recognized as a school phobic, but was then simply a truant. He was apprenticed to a gunsmith when he left school, but gave that up after a few months. He was for some time a cinema projectionist, a great empty Odeon closed now and tinned up. Since then he hasn't taken any more jobs because they interfere with the work that so clearly needs to be done but for which there are no wages on offer. He is one of the most energetic and hard workers I know; and is always going to see somebody about the next edition of a community newspaper, organize an outing, interpreting the problems of the poor and inarticulate to the relevant authority. He says that most work currently available is anyway futile and unnecessary. He has no political affiliation. Periodically the unemployment review officer calls him for interview and asks what efforts he has made to find work; and he always reassures the officials that he is making an effort. But he never stops work; if the supply of things to do seems to run out, he can quite easily find something else.

Colin goes home for meals. His mother is a small woman, with short grey hair and a welcoming manner. The living-room is cluttered, mainly with Colin's books; there is a rocking-chair, and a dresser and a large table; a tiled scullery and a neatly kept back-garden. Mrs Tivey came here when she was fifteen; her mother was from Evesham where she started her working life as a parlourmaid, and her father from Chipping Norton. Of these streets she says 'They're not the same. People only come here as a first house when they get married; they don't care about the neighbourhood or the people in it; their eyes are fixed on where they're off to next. There's only one woman left of those I grew up with. She looked after her mother and father until they died, the same as I did. Everybody knew everybody else, and they all helped one another. My father was a builder. He pushed a handcart, and used to go round to the Cadbury's private residences, doing repairs. When I left school I had to go and work at Cadbury's, in the cocoa factory. I loathed it. I worry about Colin sometimes, but I let him do as he likes with his life because I had to go into Cadbury's as soon as I left school. I never had the chance to go on with my education. Nobody asked me, it never occurred to anybody it might not be what I wanted to do. That's why I've never interfered with Colin, I think he should lead the life he wants, when I think how unhappy it made me, all the years in the factory; those big cocoa machines. I worry when Colin goes on these demonstrations, CND and so on. It's always a relief to see him come home. When he's a bit late, I start to think "Where is he?" I depend on him such a lot, I suppose that's it. My sister used to go on about it, letting him live without a job. But I wouldn't want anybody's young life to be the same as mine was.'

Colin takes me to a house two streets away, built in the 1950s in pinkish-grey brick. It has rounded bay windows and a long front-garden. The front room is simply furnished: the wallpaper an unobtrusive motif of lemon and grey leaves; a glass cabinet with engraved panels, and a display of six glass tumblers and some white china cups patterned with blue cornflowers. Over the gas-fire, two pieces of embroidery in bright silk thread, one representing a mosque, another an Eastern city skyline.

The house overlooks a piece of parkland, a children's playground, tall plane trees, a concrete shelter and public lavatories. The lawn in the front garden is growing fast in the warm April sunshine. A 'For Sale' notice is fixed to the wrought-iron garden gate.

Mr Khan came from Pakistan in 1961. Two years ago he bought this house, moving away for the first time from Balsall Heath. Now he is leaving because it has been made impossible for him to live here any longer.

On the coffee table, Mr Khan lays out a newspaper, and from a carrier-bag he takes out some of the bricks that have been thrown through his window in recent months: two half-bricks, green with lichen, and two pieces of concrete studded with pebbles and stones. Mr Khan sits in the armchair, nursing his oldest daughter, a handicapped twelve-year-old, with her dark hair swept up into a cockade on top of her head and tied with a silver lurex ribbon. He rocks and kisses her, stroking her face as he speaks. Mr Khan is a man in early middle age, greying, anxious and bitter; this man who came from Pakistan to make cream eggs – Elizabeth's First, Henry's Eighth, Schubert's Unfinished as the posters all over the city say – and whose life has been made unbearable by the National Front. He looks down at the pieces of rock on the table. Two small spiders, disturbed by the pieces of concrete having been moved, run quickly across its surface onto the newspaper.

Since last autumn his house has been attacked frequently by groups of young people. They are, he insists, 'not kids'. They are young adults. Kids could not have thrown the bricks with such force that they went through the upstairs windows; but even if it had been kids, this would hardly have mitigated the horror of it. 'You hear the little ones chanting "Paki, Paki". Even children of eight or nine.'

The first time the windows were broken, Mr Khan rang the police. The first couple of times he dialled 999, but no one arrived at the house until two hours later. And even then, they asked 'What is your name, how long have you been in this country' before they asked anything about the incident Mr Khan was reporting. Then they asked which way the attackers went. 'After two hours, that was hardly a relevant question.' Then they said to him 'Well, what do you want us to do about it?' 'What did they want me to do? "Catch them", I said. The police wanted to know if I knew who they were. How could I? It was dark. They ran away over the park, it's the ideal place for them to melt away. The next time it happened, I dialled 999 again. The policeman who came sat on the sofa there where you are, and he said "Is this your own property?" I said "Yes." He said "Well you fucking well look after it then." And that was it. He went. I can honestly say that was the worst moment of all; worse even than waiting for the brick you knew was going to come through the window. You feel powerless; everything seems hostile, you feel you have no protection against anything people might do to you.

'I made a complaint to the Chief Constable, Sir Philip Knights. Then two inspectors came, and they said they would put a guard on my home. At the same time, they advised me to withdraw my complaint. And I did withdraw it, because I know a man in Small Heath who complained about the way his son had been treated, and he refused to withdraw his complaint when he was advised to. And now he can't go out anywhere, he can't even go in his car without being harassed, charged with driving dangerously or having something wrong with his car. Whenever there's any sort of crime, a robbery, a burglary, the police always call on him to find out where he was at the time the crime was committed, even if he was at work. They go straight to him, insult him. That was why I dropped my complaint. I have my wife and family to think of.

'But the attacks still carried on. I had fireworks through my letterbox. I had to seal the letterbox every night because I was afraid the house might catch fire. The worst was when a brick came through the bedroom window, and was within six inches of my wife. We began to sit up half the night. I would sit here in the dark, waiting for it to happen, hoping to catch sight of who it was. You have no idea what that can do to you, how badly it can affect you. My wife was pregnant at the time. She had a nervous breakdown and had to go to hospital; and as a result of that she had a miscarriage.'

Mr Khan's other children, a boy of ten and a girl eight, come into the room. Since the autumn, all the children have been sleeping in the same bed, clinging together each night in fear. Mr Khan said that even the handicapped child became unhappy and restless in the evenings, and started to cry if her father went to the front door to see if there was anyone around. The little boy had to be sent home from school; he was being sick every day.

'The people at the school were very understanding. So were my neighbours. The man next door came round and helped me to mend my windows. Every time it happened, he would be there; he was a great comfort. They are good people. But then they threw a brick through his window. We heard them shouting there, out on the green. You could hear their voices in the darkness, 'If you help a Wog, you get treated like a Wog.'

'After I'd withdrawn my complaint, they sent a policewoman to sit inside the house. She sat there in the dark by the window for six nights in succession, from six o'clock until 10.30. Nothing happened. Then on the seventh night, a brick came through the window again. After that, two detectives came, and they sat there every night for two weeks. Nothing. Then, on the very next night, a piece of concrete came through. What did that mean? That someone in the neighbourhood had watched, and when there was no one here, told the people who were attacking us? Do people want us out that badly? In the end, I had to say to my neighbour "No, John, I don't want you to come round here any more. You have to think of your own wife and family." His wife was also pregnant. I said to him that I didn't want him to risk their safety for my sake. There's no point in two of us suffering.

'But what kind of a world is it that our children are going to grow up into? I have always had the highest respect for the police, for British justice. What can I feel now? I've always worked; well, some people might be jealous of that now, but they weren't when they didn't want to do the jobs in the factories. Of course I'm bitter. I worked and worked to struggle out of the ghetto. I've tried to do my best for my family, give my children a good education.

'Now I'll have to go back. Back into the ghetto. Go and get a smaller house, Sparkhill, Balsall Heath, where nobody will notice me and I'll be left alone to lead my own life. I'll get a little house tucked away in a corner where I won't be conspicuous. But what kind of freedom is that? I'm not allowed to live where I want to. What kind of freedom do you think we stand for, if a basic right like that is impossible? Those are questions the politicians don't address themselves to.

'When the bricks come through the window now, they have National Front leaflets wrapped round them. What kind of people are they? Don't their parents know or care what they're doing, where they are at nights? Are they all drinking in the boozer until 11 o'clock at night? Doesn't it matter to them at all?

'I applied for a gun. I've handled guns in Pakistan. It's like America there, anybody can get hold of guns. Of course I've no chance of getting one, the application has to be heard by a magistrate. If I apply for a gun for "self-defence", what would they think? But if you feel there is no one to defend you, what are you to do? And anyway, if I put a slug into one of these hooligans, I'd only lose the sympathy of the people around here; and they've been very good. But how is it going to be stopped if they can get away with it? Where is the moral authority that will prevent them? They smash my car up, break the windows. Will people have to be killed before anyone takes any notice?

'My employers have been very good. I work programming the computer for the chocolate eggs. My employers have even driven me home in the middle of the night if anything has happened at home. They even offered me their private guards to help look after my home. They couldn't have been better to me.'

In the early evening the sunlight comes through the still bare trees opposite the house. 'Thank God the lighter evenings are coming. I've had nobody enquire about the house yet, even though I'm willing to sell at a loss for the sake of getting out. I don't want to spend another winter here.'

The grass in the park has been cut for the first time this spring, and the air is full of the scent of fresh grass and narcissi; the blossom is on the viburnum and the fruit trees in the gardens. A warm spring evening; a day, if ever there was one, on which to express a love of England. But surely not in that way; not like that.

The three boys are in the park, sitting on the roundabout in the children's playground. A few younger children look at the roundabout from a distance, but dare not approach. One of the boys kicks the ground idly as the roundabout moves, and a little cloud of dust rises from the gravel. They are sixteen or seventeen, two of them wearing white T-shirts, one with a union jack on it, blue jeans, khaki-drill trousers, black boots. Two of them have had their hair shaved almost to the skull; the sun shines almost silver on the stubble; there is a glint of gold from an ear-stud. One has a tattoo on his neck in dark-blue and red of two swallows in flight; all have tattooed arms which are bare: a dagger, a swan, a hooked cross. One of them has the traces of a hare-lip operation, a healed cleft and epithelial shine. They are not the boys who attacked Mr Khan's house, but they do support the National Front. This country is becoming the dustbin of the world, all the shit of Pakistan that's not wanted comes over here, sucking our life-blood, bringing the plague back and taking our jobs.

Two of them left school last summer; the other says he doesn't know whether he's left or not – he hasn't been there recently to find out. None has yet worked. 'My Dad used to say I was a layabout, then he got redundant, so I said "Now you know what it feels like."' The style of skinheads is as basic as it can be. It is almost an emblem of their most fundamental characteristic, their whiteness: a racist statement. While many of the other groups embellish themselves, elaborately dependent on fashion, there is a puritanical simplicity about skinheads which these boys recognize. There's nothing behind the other styles, they're empty.

'You should be proud of being white. What we've done, we went round the world and gave them civilization, but they don't know what to do with it. All they can do is beat each other's brains out.' 'What brains?' 'They're from the Stone Age.' He assumed a West Indian accent 'Stoned out me mind man.' 'They want to take over this country. Nobody knows how many there is, they can't count them.' 'There's more black people already than there is white. We shall have a black king on the throne and black government. King Godzilla.' 'I've got nothing against blacks, everybody should own one.' 'Power to the Wogs,' says the boy with the hare-lip, 'forty thousand volts.'

They are waiting for the big fight, the civil war. 'It's got to come. There's going to be a big scrap. Look at Northern Ireland, even white people can't live together, so how can black and white? You've got a duty to keep fit, look after your body, so you're ready for when the showdown comes. You'll have to be on one side or the other; the whites against the blacks and the race-traitors.'

'Where do you get the idea of being a race-traitor?' I ask.

'It's common sense. You've got your country and you've got your race. It's what people have always fought for isn't it?'

'They say the National Front is like the Nazis. It's not the same.

The National Front is going to win.'

One of them thought we had been fighting the Russians in the last War. The others turn on him 'You stupid cunt.' 'He thinks white power is a powder for washing-machines.' One says that his teacher was a communist, and they sent him some shit through the post. 'Who did it?' 'What?' 'The shit?' 'We found it. Dogshit.' 'You should've asked him, he'd've done you a special, Britain's secret weapon, poison gas.'

The boy with the hare-lip says 'I don't want the nigs to suffer. I want to put them out of their misery.'

'The trouble with the world is that it's overpopulated. You need to get rid of about three-quarters of the people in the world. Just keep the white races, then we could all live decent.' 'What do you mean decent?' I ask him. 'All have plenty of money, live good, cunt and booze, booze and cunt.' They say they hate the Asians, but they have respect for the West Indian kids because they are fighters. The Asians are pansy. 'They aren't even allowed to choose their own wives, it has to be done for them; they have to be told where to stick their greasy little tools.'

But beneath the hardness, they are uncertain individuals. When they had finished expressing their beliefs, their personal stories came spilling out, unbidden. They call the boy with the hare-lip Scarface; he had deep cuts and bruises on his arms and hands as well as his face. He is always doing crazy things which damage him, and he ends up in hospital: a fist through the window of a bus shelter had to have eighteen stitches; competitive weaving through the moving traffic on Bristol Road cost him another spell in hospital; and he once clenched his hand over some barbed wire 'because I got depressed one night'. He is the youngest of five children, badly treated by a stepfather when his mother married again.

The toughest of the three lives alone with his mother. 'I get on all right with her. She does what I ask her.' He never knew his father; his parents never married. His mother had a succession of men, 'But now she's too old and ugly, she hasn't got anybody.' She is now thirty-seven. He told a touching story about a young man he admired on the estate where he lives. When he was about fourteen, he was befriended by this man, an eighteen-year-old. He used to take him to football matches; they went fishing occasionally; sometimes they went out on his motorbike; but most of the time, the young man came to the house for meals, to watch television. 'He was always there. I used to want to go out all the time with him; but I thought "Why does he like sitting round here, with my old lady going on and talking a load of rubbish?" I must have been stupid. He was only really coming round because he was poking her. I thought he was my mate; I really did. I thought he liked me, I used to boast about it, tell everybody. I looked up to him. Never again, you won't catch me like that again. I wouldn't trust anybody now. It really choked me up when I found out.'

It is tempting to think that their personal vulnerability – the obvious self-hate of the boy with the scarred lip, the sense of betrayal of the older one – are the cause of their allegiance to the National Front. But these things aren't causal; it's rather that the personal weaknesses are submerged in the commitment to something wider. This is what has been wrong with their lives: detached from any alternative Labourist or working tradition, the personal has been lived in a social vacuum, in the pretence that there are no wider issues, but simply individuals. They are beginning to demand what they have been cheated of – the right to feel that they are part of society; even though the way they return to that consciousness is damaged, sad and frightening. All the diversions of style, the teenage-manufactured culture, the prisms of music and fashion through which social issues have been filtered and blurred, no longer work for them. They have been wounded in the social part of themselves; and this, especially allied to the individual pain, is a threatening combination.

The growing resonance of far-Right rhetoric in working-class areas in recent years is the price being paid for the inability of the Left to keep pace with what has happened to its own 'natural' supporters. Racist feeling has flourished in the vacant space created by the failure of the Labour movement to acknowledge or confront that pain which has accompanied the changes which the movement cherishes as its most positive and undisputed achievement – the vast improvement in material living conditions within the last thirty years. Almost unobserved, in the shadow of this overwhelming development, other, more negative forces have also been at work, and these have led to an epic shift in what E. P. Thompson calls 'the sub-political attitudes of the people'.[28]

For a long time this change in working-class sensibility has taken place at a level that has scarcely expressed itself through voting patterns. It has not been visible to those who work by opinion poll, or even through the political processes as they are narrowly defined by those who conduct them. It is not that racist organizations have become mass movements, but rather that they have grown with far more tacit support than has been recognized. The sentiment of which they are the outcrop is a direct expression of the pain and dislocation felt within large sections of the working class, the people whom the Left continues to regard as its own rightful adherents. There is a tendency to believe that racism is only an aberration; they're only kids; somehow it isn't real. The Left continues to interpret the unhappiness and bewilderment within the working class exclusively in terms determined by capitalism itself, that is, as though it could be cured by money, while money is the root cause of it.

The Labour movement has failed to take account of the systematic impoverishment of the working class, which has never let up for a moment, even during the period of apparently greatest affluence. It would find it difficult to do so because the concessions which capitalism so ostentatiously yielded looked like lasting victories, the reward of long brave struggles. However, throughout this whole time – the 'golden age' of the fifties and sixties – the cry of anguish from traditional working-class areas was consistent and sustained. But it was disregarded, played down, denied. It was consigned to 'non-political' aspects of experience; something to do with 'social change', as though this were quite separate from economics or politics, which are, it was felt, the real concern of the Labour movement.

The experience of impoverishment and loss was most keenly felt in the inner-city areas and the council estates; and it has been intensified in recent years by the accelerating decay of the old industries and the dispersal of the communities that depended on them. During this same period, all those who could buy their way out of these traditionally poor places have done so – through education, the acquisition of skills, the opportunity to start again in a new town – with the result that the old neighbourhoods become places of punishment and deterrence to those who can't or won't comply with the pressure to self-advancement. The migrants who fill the space recently occupied by family, neighbours and workmates are seen as usurpers. Because the suffering caused by this sustained impoverishment has been disregarded by the Left, the resentment grows, and what eventually surfaces as racism is charged also with a sense of the violence that has been done to people through processes over which they have no influence. In this way, the blacks have to bear a symbolic role, as well as all the other burdens of being poor and migrant; they become associated with all the distraints, losses and forfeits exacted from the communities, as well as with the deeper losses incurred by the working class as a whole. While these changes were taking place, the Left was silent, and the obscure pain was not expressed politically. But below the level of conscious debate, a shift occurred – 'a subterranean alteration of mood', to borrow another phrase of E. P. Thompson's[20] – which was not considered to fall within the area of politics, that increasingly arid and unfruitful terrain defined by those who believe themselves to be politicians.

Of course it is easier to see now: at that time the sufferings of working people were easily drowned by the clamour of the consumer economy; and, indeed, to submerge them seems to have been its greatest achievement. The losses seemed, if not inconsiderable, at least tolerable. It seemed then that there would always be enough money to buy consolations for what was being given up. It is only now that some of the factitious excitement engendered by the convulsive extension of the market-place to the working class has subsided in the more sober conditions of the eighties and that the vanity of its promises is beginning to appear. The shrillness and the glitter fade; and we find ourselves in a new and blighted landscape, in which the working class have been, as always, the losers. The spectacle of abundance was a diversion and a trap. The material comforts wear thin, but the losses sustained by the working class become more achingly real: not only the loss of community and the supports of neighbourhood, but also the growth of violence, mental disturbance, indifference and cruelty; not only the setting aside of skills, social and human as well as industrial, but the decay of knowledge won through struggle. Even more important than all this is the end of that deeper meaning of working-class experience, which consoled and bore people up through even the worst privations: the feeling that here, in these poor, proud and stoical places, would be forged values and practices that offered an alternative to those imposed by capitalism. Instead, we have seen the working class shrink through a loss of its substance, brought down from offering the basis for an alternative to capitalism to become simply another interest group. The model is not difficult to discern: it follows the pattern of the Labour movement in the United States: a strong influence, capable of exacting what capitalism has to offer – money, able to inflict damage upon its workings, but no longer capable of generating the vision of an alternative to its cold and continuing destructive processes.

The experience we have lived through, is something as epic and disturbing as an attempt by capital at the undoing of the working class. When E. P. Thompson wrote of the opacity of working-class culture, its dense and guarded richness, its well-defended complexity and secrecy in the face of capitalist oppression, he might well have been writing about the reverse of what confronts us now. It is the hallucinating display of capitalism that offers an appearance of opaque richness, and the drained working class, transparent as crystal now, gives back increasingly only the reflection of that alien and manufactured diversity. The young see their own reflection in shop windows, and they haunt the malls and precincts of the Arndale and Grosvenor Centres. They express the hunger and disinheritance of the working class, but they have been nurtured on a promise of capitalist plenty and no longer know what it is they have been dispossessed of. And they believe that money can restore it – if only you can get enough. The old have a keener awareness of what it was, the unspoken surrender of that which gave them hope and meaning, but the young have little such direct experience. For them, everything has been pared away – the disciplines of work and the constraints of family, and with these also the knowledge and the wisdom, the values won through adversity with such effort and struggle. Their deliverance from that old defensive working-class culture has been a kind of liberation; but beyond the shallow masquerade of the market-place, they find they are denuded, robbed of everything but the colour of their skin.

In this way, racialism – as if it were not hard and cruel enough in itself – has become a metaphor for all those other unacknowledged things, the stripping away, the dissolution of so many skills and competences and abilities, and the worthlessness of what has been substituted for them. It is a commonplace that the extreme Right makes headway at times of absolute economic decline. But even when it is at its most 'healthy', capitalism depends on a growth that is at the expense of one form of human substance or another, and as such is always cancerous. The success of capitalism in the fifties and sixties derived to a considerable extent from the process of wrenching away from working-class people needs and satisfactions they had learned to answer for each other, and selling them back, in another form, as commodities.

The development of the National Front, an underground, semi-secret, unrespectable popular movement is a grim caricature of the early experience of the Labour movement. It occupies that space evacuated by the decayed working-class alternative, and in many ways, is shaped by it. But its feeling is cynical, hard and brutal, amoral. The vacuum has been invaded by ghosts – the phantoms of all the old oppressions in opposition to which the working class originally formed its brave resisting response; not only the spectre of colonialism and racial superiority pervade the gutted working-class communities, but the values of the poor law also have their echo there, the harshness of the early nineteenth-century penal code, even the death-worshipping imagery of Methodism has its counterpart in the graveyard fantasies of much popular culture, fiction and film. And these ugly resurrections come upon the young with the force of a revelation, and through them a deformed version of the extinguished revolutionary role of the working class begins to shape itself.

It is, of course, as easy to be apocalyptic as it is for the Left to be defiantly optimistic in the face of those changes it prefers not to acknowledge. It is true that the more humanizing aspects of the old working-class experience could have provided an alternative model for us to live by; but as direct experience they are now almost extinct and the circumstances which gave rise to them won't ever come again. But the values which they represented don't die. Even though the old industries vanish, and the function of the working class has been changed or impaired, the example it furnished survives. As a model of sharing and co-operation it is as perishable only as humanity itself. Even if they have to be rediscovered all over again in quite different circumstances, those values will not be lost. 'As long as men are men, a poor society cannot be too poor to find a right order of life, nor a rich society too rich to have need to seek it,' as Tawney put it.[30]

It is sad that those values do not grow organically out of the way we live now. The transition to socialism will not come as a natural evolution of that stoicism and sharing; and to impose it would be a mockery of them. It is impossible not to feel a profound melancholy and regret at the blighting of those things within the working class; but it may be that sooner or later the demonstrable need for some version of them if we are to survive will ensure them an even wider spread than when they were confined simply to the working-class experience. In a world of increasing population and shrinking resources, something of these values has to inform a search for a way of life that doesn't damage further the world's poor. But the effort and struggle to reach for such a way of life are the greater for the loss of the practical embodiment of it. What seems to be a loss to the working class alone in the end impoverishes everybody. Far from rejecting that example, it is something we should never cease to affirm and to remember. We need it now, and for far more urgent reasons than preserving the profits of the rich.

7

Sunderland

Sunderland. The river opens the town, a deep wound in its granite base, and the cliffs glitter like silver beneath the grass that partly covers them. In the old docks area, some reminders of the old seaport: the orphanage for the children of men drowned at sea; an abandoned warehouse that used to hold stores of the woods from tropical Africa, teak and sapele; some gutted pubs with the weathered figurehead of the bows of a ship; the shops that incorporate the remains of a chandler's business; a compass manufacturer. But the streets where the dockers and shipworkers lived have gone, even though there are still red-brick chasms of warehouses, rusting hoists still hanging from third-floor windows. Some of the area was cleared in the thirties, and there are monumental blocks of flats – themselves a little like the shell of a great sea-going vessel – called Wear Garth and Covent Garden. But most of the buildings are from the fifties; hastily assembled flats and houses which display all the flaws of the beginning of an age of instant consumption. The future has already caught up with them – stained concrete and rusty metal, broken glass, leaky pipes and graffiti.

The houses of the shipowners and the tradespeople who provisioned them stand in elegant late-Georgian terraces, many of them now occupied by solicitors and estate agents and small workshops, their red brick ingrained with the soot from chimneys long demolished, but their pillars painted cream and white, and the street names etched on ornamental plaster scrolls on the street corner. In this part of the town, there is that sense of exhaustion which pervades those places where human beings have worked for generations, have expended their life energy in making and creating things, which for the most part they never enjoyed the use of. It isn't really the place that seems exhausted so much as some of the people, those who have continued to pay for the privation and harshness of those years when they or their parents stood begging at the shipyard gates.

Not far from the river were the pits. Sky and sea seem to offer false freedoms to the dark single-storey cottages that still cluster round some of the pitheads. In the same way, the red shells of churches and Victorian pubs offered possibly more real freedoms. In Southwick, the terraces are still full of smoke blown through them like a funnel by the cold wind off the North Sea. The lights from the shipyard in midwinter are brighter than the sun that lingers on the green hilltops to the north of the town; the harsh beauty of a place where epic struggles have occurred. The Miners' Hall, now a car showroom, with its bas-relief of lions, rams and boars, its foliate fresco and the Italianate tower with constellations of iron stars in the metalwork, was once a place where children whose fathers were not miners used to plead with their friends to take them inside for the warmth and the company. The Primitive Methodist chapel is now the Majestic furniture store, offering another kind of comfort to the recently poor, while on the opposite side of the ring road Genevieve's Discotheque lights the night sky above the great iron bridge over the Wear, with its spikes to prevent people climbing it, and 'Nil Desperandum Auspice Deo' worked into the metal panel in the centre. In a brick-and-glass old people's rest centre – a sort of bus shelter with doors – the old men with white stubble and coal-grained skin play dominoes and remember the magnificence and harshness of their childhood, when they walked to school barefoot in the snow, feet so calloused they could slide like hooves over the frozen surfaces.

In a big Victorian pub on the corner of a main road, a man of about fifty-five sits with a single pint of beer which he makes last the whole evening. He smokes Players No. 6, smokes them until his fingers are burned by the heat, and still he manages to draw some smoke from what is left before crushing the end between his thumb and forefinger and placing the few shreds of tobacco that remain into a leather pouch. He says 'That's how to make twenty cigarettes into twenty-two.' He wears a sports jacket, flannel trousers, black shoes elasticated at the side, an open-neck shirt with a frayed collar; clothes that had been his best until he lost his job two years ago. He had been a cabinet maker, and he had been in his last place for sixteen years.

There is a snooker table and a dartboard. The younger men come in, put 20p in the slot to release the balls for a game of snooker. They scarcely speak to each other, and they acknowledge each other only by a nod or a brief touch on the arm as they leave. There is no conversation. The music of Boney M singing 'Ra-Ra-Rasputin' recurs frequently, filling the space between the high pillars with their Corinthian capitals and the space between the men who do not speak. An old man comes in. A gust of wind accompanies him, and some dust and waste-paper from the street. He sits at one of the round glass-topped tables. The girl behind the bar brings him a pint; he acknowledges a man at the dartboard who has bought it for him. If people do not say much, it is because little has happened since they last saw each other that is worthy of the telling.

The man who has been a cabinet maker says: 'The same things happen every day. Bugger-all.' He has thinning hair, straight and brown, through which the skull shines pink. His eyes are deep and bright blue, although the face is lined and heavy, with two parallel furrows like scars at the side of the mouth. 'The firm just closed down. We didn't hear about it till the day we finished. He went bust. That was it. I'd got eight hundred pounds in my last wage packet. You can't believe it you know. We were raised on work up here. I find myself even now thinking it's time to get up, and I put my feet out of bed, grab my trousers before I remember I don't have to go. Then you get back into bed, and you're glad you're not late; till it dawns on you you'll never have to get up early ever again. I miss the early mornings. In winter I used to love it. I used to walk to work from where we lived. I saw the sun rise over the cranes and the shipyards; the snow made everything look different; and in summer the sky was open and clear, you never minded going to work. You don't realize what it means to you. I worked with three good blokes over ten years. You get to know them, you respect them, you know all about their families. You talk about the football or the horses or the telly; you know exactly where they stand, what they think. But if I see them now, there's none of them working, we haven't anything to say to each other.

'When I lost my job, the family was grown up, the boy married, the girl courting; she's married now. It was all right for a few weeks, you think "Well, I deserve a holiday." I used to go shopping with the wife; it was all right. We went to the Lake District for a fortnight, that was an ambition we'd always had. That was beautiful. But then you start to look for work. There's nothing doing, and you start to resent it. The wife is still doing what she has to do, what she's always done over the years. But she's got it all worked out, she doesn't even want you to help her. That's the first thing. I irritated her. I'd got nothing to tell her. I used to go to the betting shop, I never won much. But then I felt I had to stay out all day, otherwise she might think I wasn't really looking for work. She did think that. She didn't know it's not very clever trying to find work at fifty-four.

'After a year, things between me and her started getting really bad. We rowed. I felt I didn't want to be with her. We stopped having much of a sex life – oh, years ago. It didn't bother me, not really. I've always made things. I'd got a shed where I'd make models out of wood, metal; I like modelling things, planes, boats. I'd like to have been a sculptor; I chip away at stones, anything; I feel I can get a shape out of almost anything; I can see something waiting to get out.

'I felt restless. I used to walk; I'd wander round the town. I couldn't stay in, but there was nowhere I wanted to go. I found myself looking at women, girls. And I even used to sit on a bench where I could see the girls coming out of school. I don't know why. It was on my way home in the afternoon. And it came to me that I was deliberately getting there at about four o'clock, so I could watch them. Girls, not more than thirteen or fourteen some of them. I found I was getting all sexed up watching them, you know what I mean?

'Of course I was upset. I told myself I must never go back there again; but I did. I kept on going back. I thought somebody'll report me for hanging around. I never did anything. I never spoke to any of them. I felt I wanted something. I wanted something I couldn't have. Oh, I thought about it, the ignorance we grew up in, I'd never had a woman when I met my wife . . .

'I got scared. It was sitting and having all that time to think about yourself. All the years you'd never really bothered; you'd done what you had to do. I think I never knew what was going on in my own mind till I started to have time on my hands.

'Then I thought I'd better stop going out. I felt I was somebody else, I wasn't myself any more. I felt like Jekyll and Hyde; there was this other man inside me. I saw a film on telly where this man changed into a monster at night; it was a horror film. I thought, Christ that's me. I felt so ashamed. I went to see the minister at the church, but I couldn't tell him.

'I mean, with the blokes at work, you joke, you talk about sex. But it's open; pictures in the paper, you look at it, but you don't think of it for yourself. Nothing like this. I thought I was ill. I went to my doctor in the end. He was a very good bloke. I talked to him. He gave me some tablets for depression. I said, "But I'm not depressed, I'm frightened." I even found myself looking at my own daughter, God forgive me. I used to leave the bathroom door open and hope she'd come in to see me with nothing on. I used to pick her dirty bits of washing out, it fascinated me. When she left to live with her bloke I was glad. The missis said it was wrong not getting married straight away, but I was pleased when she went.

'I've never done anything, don't get me wrong. I can control myself. I wouldn't. It was like a great gap in your life, and all the things you've never thought about – they get through the gap and come into your conscious mind. Idleness. My mother always said the devil finds work for idle hands. It's true of idle minds, I can tell you.

'It's funny. I've always been broadminded. At work, when they used to go on about queers or prostitutes, I've always defended them. I've always stuck up for those who people have a down on, I never knew why.

'But I do know of people's lives that's been smashed apart by having nowt to do. Time. It can be a funny thing. There's times of the day that definitely go slower than others, did you know that? There is definitely times when the hands move slower on the clock. I hate the middle of the day. And the long summer evenings. I go for walks sometimes, to Hebburn, along the beach, in the wind. It helps block things out. You walk twelve to fifteen miles on an afternoon, come back tired out. That reminds me of coming home from work, when I felt tired but knowing you'd given a good day's work. That was satisfying; something I haven't known since. You feel now you've got nothing to give, nothing to offer. You feel ashamed of yourself.'

Many people mentioned the sense that work and the structure it imposes on life offers a bulwark against chaos. Marie Jahoda,[31] in the C. S. Myers lecture 1979, quotes Hebb as saying 'the psychological function of the social environment is to protect man through institutional arrangements against being swamped by extreme emotionality.' Most people who are without work for a long period are aware of this; but generally it is described as depression, a feeling, as one man said, 'of being swallowed up by time, so you don't bother to do anything today, because you know tomorrow's going to be the same.' Several people said they had had more time to think; and that the results of this were not always welcome. 'You get to know yourself better; but what you get to know you don't always like.'

It is not only from talking with unemployed people that I have such a strong sense of the bruised intelligence of people, the wounded talent, the rejected abilities; even many of those in work feel that only a small part of themselves is involved in what they do. The richness of perceptions, the skills and capacities that have never been summoned forth, suggest an enormous reservoir of energy that we haven't begun to use. One of the great advantages to capitalism of the present high level of unemployment, with the sense of futility that attends it, is that it prepares people to accept any kind of work, because anything is better than staying idle. Jobs in themselves come to seem desirable, no matter what indignities their creation heaps on people, no matter how demeaning they are. The young, who have never had a proper job, come to feel it is a privilege to do anything; and this is a way of preparing the working class for an even more de-energized and fragmented application of their powers and possibilities than that which has engaged them until now.

Janet is nineteen. She is a lively and intelligent girl who worked in shops in Sunderland when she left school; then she went to a big store as a window-dresser, but she felt that she had no real scope for what she felt she was capable of. She went to London, and took a job in the Piccadilly Hotel as a chambermaid. She was offered £51 a week, out of which she was to pay £10 for a bed at a hostel in Earl's Court. 'When I got to the hostel, I couldn't believe it. It's not that I was shocked, but the place was full of these Filippino girls who couldn't speak a word of English. I shared a tiny room with a black girl. She was the first black person I'd ever met, but that was the least of my worries. I don't know what it is, you think living up here in Sunderland, it's the back of beyond; you feel you're missing out on life, nothing ever happens. You feel you've got to go where you can spread your wings a bit, discover yourself. I don't know what it is. The job was horrible. There was this incredible luxury in the public part of the hotel, while the kitchens were crawling. It was disgusting. If any of the guests could have seen what was going on out of their view, they'd have run a mile. I lasted a week there. My boy-friend was a porter in the kitchens. He didn't mind it, he would have stayed on. I couldn't bear it. I couldn't wait to get home. They tell you that the hotel and catering industry is the thing of the future. If it is, God help the people who work in it; it'll be a bloody future of slave labour. It was horrible.

'You know, living in the North, something makes you feel, not inferior exactly, but everything tells you London is where all the action is. There's a pressure on you, a feeling that only where the big money is can there be glamour and excitement.'

Something compelling and insistent goads the young. Those who are in their last years at school can't wait to leave; those who have left, if they find there is no work or only some kind of occupational therapy, wish they could go back. I've never heard so many seventeen- and eighteen-year-olds talk like old men, saying they wish they had paid more attention, made more effort when they were at school. But it isn't really their fault. And it certainly isn't the old poverty and hunger that prevent the working-class young from achieving. An excitement emanates from the market-place that tells them that getting and having are the most important things, that the development of their tastes and appetites, the search for sensations are the only things that count. And the easy gratification, the momentary consolation become a permanent substitute for any long-term aims. Their abilities are smothered, their intelligence is undermined just as effectively as they were when the cold and want of primary poverty kept them from self-realization. And the same effects are achieved by what appear to be completely different circumstances.

A group of boys, seventeen and eighteen. Zit, Tim, Scruff. A skinhead with a red T-shirt, jeans and Dr Marten boots is known as Knobhead because the short hair accentuates the contours of his forehead. The boy with dark hair is called Zit because he has acne, and Scruff has big miners' safety pins holding his tattered suede jacket together; he wears wellington boots and mud-splashed trousers. They live on Pennywell Estate, a vast spreading estate on the north-west of Sunderland, a place of austere concrete geometry to house so many people whose redundancy stares them in the face from their earliest years – people no longer shaped by mine or shipyard or factory, but simply by the monstrous images of material wealth that are thrust at them from the moment they are born, which, as they grow up, look increasingly like taunting and mockery. Their impoverishment seems to increase as the power and wealth of the rich grow, power and wealth that no longer even seem to have been achieved at the expense of their labour, but, mysteriously, at the expense of their enforced idleness and absence of resources. Their lives depend on money that will buy them excitement, sensation, escape; and failing that, they have to make do with the most meagre consolations; a quick fuck in some girl's front-room while her Mam's out shopping; sleep until midday in the grimy unchanged sheets, with the faded pictures of yesterday's heroes on the bedroom wall, and the litter of broken toys in the boxes under the bed; the ride in the car nicked from behind the barbed wire under Genevieve's disco on Saturday night; drinking from the bottles of beer taken from the workingmen's club; buying new clothes with the money taken from a woman's shopping basket in the supermarket down town.

The exuberance and energy of these young people is diffused and lost in their aimless fantasies that grow in the space that has developed from their wasted sense of function. They are full of bravado and cynicism, a crust of hardness hides the sense of being unwanted, the hurt that the society in which they have grown despises and humiliates them. 'When you don't have anything to do, you sit in the house all day, back horses, watch television, wait for time to pass. You feel like killing yourself; perhaps somebody'd notice you then.' The references to suicide are frequent among the young unemployed. They are not serious threats for the most part, but another of those metaphors for the generalized feeling of a lack of worth. The sense of futility cannot express itself against the shining panoply of the consumer-spectacle, so it turns inwards and corrodes their self-esteem, and then re-emerges as a desperate kind of violence, vandalism or racism. Their health and youth are mocked by the lack of any use to which they can be put, by the missing social purpose, the repressed impulse to idealism or change. 'We gang down the town, hang about, wait for something to happen.' They have had jobs with the Youth Opportunities Programme, fence erecting, building, in a butcher's shop; but when these have finished, going back to doing nothing is even harder.

'I had one job that lasted ten minutes. And it only lasted that long because I wasn't there. They said "Where you been?" I said "I overslept." They said "Well your job's gone."'

'I had a job digging graves in the cemetery. All the coffins were rotted, and all water came out of them.'

'Didn't you open them up? Take all the rings off the fingers and the jewellery?'

'That's the only job I had. It lasted two weeks. Then nothing. I used to get up in time to watch Play School, then have me dinner, watch the school programmes, have me tea, watch telly again, then go out with my mates.'

'It was the same as when we were at school. We used to doll off every day, go to each other's houses if your Ma and Da were working.'

'I gang into town every day now. I go shoplifting. Me Mam says "Get a job"; I say I've got one. She says "What is it?" I say "Signing on". I've been caught lifting things, I've been away for it. I take anything. Clothes, sweets, fags. A lot of kids hang round and break in houses round the estate. I wouldn't do that. You shouldn't shit in your own backyard. Sometimes we break into clubs, get a load of drink, crisps, sweets. What I really want is to be rich. Buy a house, have adventures. Get other people to do what you want them to because if you got money, you got power, you can get people to lick your arse. I know a bloke in this town, and some kids nicked his car; he offered a contract to anybody who'd get the lads that did it; a contract to break their arms and legs. He offered £75 for each arm or leg.'

'If I had a lot of money I'd buy a big house on an island, guard dogs, barbed wire. Get myself a beautiful woman.'

'Be better than what you got now. He goes round sniffing women's bike saddles.'

'Better than you, you go round licking old grannies' sofas.'

'I wouldn't mind a contract to kill Mrs Thatcher.'

'I hate her.'

'She's not in charge. It's the blackies.'

'Who'd you rather be ruled by, Thatcher or blackies?'

'Thatcher.'

'I wouldn't. They should be shipped out, all the blackies, then there'd be jobs for our own people.'

'Who's your own people then?'

'British.'

'English. I hate people from Scotland.'

'Scotland! I hate 'em from Newcastle. We got this gang of Maggies when they were playing Sunderland. This kid threw a dart at this lad from Newcastle, and he ducked, and the copper got it straight in the face.'

'Did they get him?'

'I'm doing community service now because I took a car and I was being chased by this police car at about eighty miles an hour; they followed me up a dead-end; I tried to turn round and went smack into it. I got a £50 fine and seven hours a week community service.'

'If you want things you have to go roguing. If you're breaking in somewhere, you're shitting yourself while you're doing it; but after, you feel good, real good. You like talking about it. We went into the Conservative Club, through the cellar window. There was all this money in a bottle for charity, we got a load of whisky as well, gin, beer. It gets you all excited while you're doing it, then afterwards, you feel relaxed, it feels good. You feel you've achieved something. I wouldn't do anything bad. I wouldn't hit anybody for money. You might kill them. It wouldn't be worth it. There's no need; there's enough old grannies who carry their bags where you can get at 'em easy.'

'That's the difference between a rogue and a villain. A villain'll do anything, but roguing, well, it's just an ordinary way of carrying on.'

The simple account of these conversations makes them sound much bleaker than they are. The hardness is ritual and formalized; the only social manner permitted in the competitive group of age-mates, tough, defensive. It is the old ethos of heavy manual labour, but the need for endurance in grim working and living conditions which created it has gone for these young people; and with it, also, to some extent the vision of a more human alternative which that toughness sheltered.

And even while we spoke, the hardness wasn't sustained; warmth and spontaneity constantly broke through. Mur, the skinhead, told this story.

'There was this hunchback and this woman with a big nose, and she was his girl-friend. They were walking home late one night, and they had to gang through the cemetery to get home. The woman said "Oh I'm not going through there at this time of night, the devil might get us. Let's walk round the outside of the cemetery, I'm afraid of the devil." But the hunchback says "I'm not scared of the devil, I'm ganging straight through." So she said "Well, I'll see you when you get to the other side." So the hunchback is walking through the graveyard, and when he's gone half way through, suddenly the devil appears. The devil says to him "What's that you've got on your back?" He says "It's a hump." "Right," says the devil, "I'll have that." And he takes the hump off the hunchback. The hunchback is really happy. When he gets to the other side of the cemetery, there's the woman with the big nose, and she says to him "What's happened to your hump?" He says "Well, the devil jumped out and took it away from me." She says "Oh, I wish I'd been with you. Do you think if I walk through the cemetery he'll take my big nose?" So she walks through the cemetery, and when she gets half way through, out jumps the devil, from behind a gravestone. He says to her "What's that you've got on your back?" She says "On my back? Nothing." The devil says "Well you have now," and when she comes out the other side, she finds she's a hunchback.'

When Mur finishes telling the story, everybody laughs; a great gust of uninhibited amusement; and they are transformed. All the tough postures vanish, and they seem artless, almost child-like. It is as though they are finding a childhood that has been stifled by the packaged excitements and manufactured stimuli of their early years. What he is doing, this great tough-looking kid, is telling a folk story, a fairy tale. And it delights them because it is the kind of experience that has been crowded out by all the things that have been sold to them or promised by the fantasies of the market. All the premature knowingness, the shaping of children's needs so that they conform to what will profit others, whatever damage it has caused, it hasn't quite crushed the simple need to tell stories. It is a moment of rare warmth and deeply moving.

'Have you heard the one about these two policewomen? They're on duty on a street corner, and it's a very windy day. One of them has forgotten to put her knickers on, and the wind's blowing terrible; it keeps lifting her skirt up and she's freezing there. She says "I wish I'd got my knickers here, I've left them on my locker at the police station." So the other policewoman says "Tell you what to do." They'd got a police dog with them, so she says "Let the dog have a good sniff, put its snout up your fanny, then send him back to the police station, and then he'll find your knickers and bring them back here." "Oo, that's a good idea." So she lets this dog put its nose up her skirt, and when it's had a good old root around, she sends it off, back to the station. Ten minutes later, it comes trotting back, and in its mouth it's got the sergeant's finger.'

'There was this woman in a wheelchair, she's a spastic, and her boy-friend is wheeling her along the beach. He wheels her a little way and she says "If you wheel me a bit further, I'll let you feel me tits." So he wheels her a bit further and she lets him put his hand inside her blouse and feel her tits. She says "Nobody's ever felt me tits before." She says "Wheel me a bit further, and I'll let you put your hand up me skirt." So he wheels her on and she lets him feel her fanny. She says "Nobody's ever felt me fanny before." She says "Wheel me a bit further and I'll let you fuck me. I've never been fucked before." So he tips her out of the wheelchair onto the beach and he says "You're fucked now."'

The harshness returns; the laughter that follows is not the same. It is as though they sense a mood has been broken, and try to return to the earlier feeling. Zit tells the story of two tortoises who went on a picnic. They're sitting on the grass about to start eating these two oranges, when they suddenly remember that they forgot to bring the tea with them. So one of them says "Oh I'll go back and get it. Don't start on the oranges till I get back." So off he goes, slow as slow. The other one sits there, and he looks at these oranges, and he thinks "Oh I'd love one of them oranges, but I'd better not start till he gets back." And time goes by, a couple of months pass. Still he doesn't start on the oranges, and his friend doesn't come back. Then in the end, he thinks "Well I wonder what's keeping him. Perhaps I'd better go and look for him." So he waits another week or two, then he sets out to look for him. But he only gets as far as the first tree, and there, behind it, he sees his friend just sitting there. "Oh there you are," he says, "I thought you were never coming back.

Where's the tea?" The other one says "I haven't gone yet. I was just waiting to see if you'd start on them bloody oranges without me."

But the moment of warmth has been broken; and the conversation drifts towards the preoccupation of the healthy young with sickness and horror. They talk about what happens to you when you die; whether you go into other forms, other bodies. Where you go, what you do: 'If you can't fuck I'm not going.' Then they talk about accidents they've seen or heard of, what you feel when you're dying; but the wondering is soon sidetracked into specific instances: people crashing in the jungle and eating each other; a film in which somebody shipwrecked got a taste for human flesh, and once they'd started they couldn't stop, and they used to murder people and eat their flesh at parties once a week. Then car crashes they've seen; dwelling on the blood and the remains that had to be collected in a plastic bag; bodies that couldn't be identified, mutilated beyond recognition; murders – how you would dispose of a corpse if you had to. And somehow all the spiritual and moral questions which they asked at the beginning of the discussion become locked into images of violence and horror which they have absorbed from tv and films; and the most real and perplexing spiritual experiences become tangled, can't leave the earth except in metaphors about man-made robots, journeys into space, beings from other worlds. The materialism of their lives holds captive even the capacity for spiritual experience; minds and spirits shackled, tethered to all those industries that exploit their credulity and awe. All the search and questing, their sense of wonder at human mortality, is diverted into channels that will make money for others. And it hurts to see their captivity, the new subordination that has detached them from the tradition of labour, and found other ways than hunger and relentless work to keep them in their place.

Harry King worked for a telecommunications company for twenty years. During the last seven or eight years of his time there, the numbers of people employed by them in Sunderland slowly declined. Harry had seen the original firm, Erikson's, taken over and grow to 4,500 by the early seventies. 'You could tell what was happening, if you knew how to interpret all the official jargon.' 'Natural wastage' gave way to 'trim-backs', but with a promise of no redundancies. Then it became voluntary redundancies; then early retirement. Then, as the post office cut back on its investment in equipment, the company closed the factory.

'The word "redundancy" in the early days didn't sound like a threat. A lot of the men thought it was going to be all roses. They saw the promise of a fistful of dollars, a lot of them had personal problems. In debt, they needed instant cash, so redundancy payments seemed like an answer to all their prayers. They thought they'd have a little holiday, pay off the money on the tv or the carpet, then start looking round for another job in a few months. But when you see them in a year's time they're different people, demoralized, unhappy, shabby. We have a moral obligation to fight to retain jobs. This is what they don't see. They are selling work, not just for themselves, but for their children.

'You hear a lot of people talk in a big way about what they have done for their children, the things they've bought for them or are going to do for them. People talk as if they would lay down their life for their kids – you know "if anybody lays a finger on my kid, I'll rip his heart out, I'll swing for it"; that kind of bravado.' Harry suggests what they are doing is damaging their children's future by going along with the killing off of future jobs. They are actually conspiring with capitalism against their own children. This is the ultimate individualist philosophy; have it all now, sod tomorrow. And the loud over-protectiveness of parents towards their children, the talk of giving them all the things they never had, the ostentatious self-sacrifice conceals their guilt, the suppressed feeling that they are in fact betraying the next generation because they are feeding them to a system which may or may not have any use for them.

Harry King feels that the defection of a generation of working-class people towards their children is because they have had no clear leadership; no one offered sufficiently convincing warnings, when all the propaganda emanating from the capitalist machine was about modernizing, rationalizing, preparing for the space-age future.

'Out of the dozen shop stewards who left the company when I did, there is only one working now,' Harry said. 'I had no job for fifteen months. I'd go for jobs and be offered them; then they check your background and find you've been an active trade unionist, so they say "Sorry" and give some trivial excuse why they can't take you on.

'I was chairman of the stewards' action committee. We achieved equal pay in the company two years before it became law. Several times I was told by management "Harry, you're wasted on the opposite side." I was offered four or five times the chance to go over to management. It's very easy for dissent to be swallowed up; once you cross the divide, if you're a bit smart you easily float to the top.

'But if you are an activist, you get a reputation. You can easily get smirched, a hint of communism, however untrue it is. So when I tried to warn about what the redundancies meant, and what was happening, I was accused of crying wolf. Only eleven out of 100 stewards supported me. They said the company had orders for three years, they employed 4,500 men; they said there was no chance the company could close the factory. They said "You're wrong, Harry." Then the next thing it was lay-offs and closures. There was no will to resist. The factory was run down; a lot of the blokes apparently went away happy, even though they lived to regret it.

'My job was working on the electrical test repair section on the telephone equipment. The factory assembled the structures for the automatic equipment. The electrical inspection was very stringent; all the pieces that were faulty came to the section where I worked. I enjoyed my job; and I enjoyed my trade union work.

'I had no job for fifteen months. And then I did get taken on by an old company that made switch gear, switch boxes for dynamos and electric motors and so on. Every ounce of steel they used came from abroad. They said Consett couldn't deliver on time, but that wasn't the real reason of course. The company was one of a group which didn't all trade under the same name, and of course they were buying their materials from other companies in the same group – South Africa, Rhodesia, Australia. It's now been taken over by Delta Metals. I was there for a year. They distrusted anyone who'd been an active trade unionist. I refused to take any official position in the union; but it was so poorly organized there that I got involved. If it's in you, you can't help yourself. Anyway, we were made redundant from there a year later.

'My home life suffered as a result of it all. The tensions built up, my marriage broke down. It was my fault. I got involved with a woman at work. And being an open sort of person, I didn't hide it. My wife divorced me. My woman friend and I both talked it over, and in the end we both agreed that we didn't want to break up our marriages; but by that time my wife had already found someone else so it was no longer in my control. It was my own fault. I'd always been strong; you have to accept the consequences of your actions. But all this blew up at the time of the disintegration of my work.

'I suffered for my TU background. While I was out of work, I was divorced, and I spent over a year doing nothing. We had two daughters, both grown up and married. For two years I stayed away from them; I felt I had to wait for them to get in touch, which in the end they did. But everything came together. You feel as if your whole life is crumbling. You feel devalued out of work; you feel your age, you feel you have less and less to offer. Instead of feeling you're getting richer in experience, you feel something is being taken away from you. I was very lonely at times. But I have a very stubborn streak. I'm very hard with myself. Self-discipline. You learn to be very tough. I think what I went through would have brought a lot of men to their knees. But we were brought up to be strong: you knew that life was hard. I don't think the younger people have the same resistance. You've worked, brought up a family, you've no real savings, no chance of saving anything for your old age, you know you'll have to depend on charity. You'll be another lonely old person, whereas now, I'm fifty-one; at my age I should be enjoying the fullness of life.

'When I left work I had £1900 redundancy money; and with the few hundred I cashed from my pension scheme, it came to £2400. Even though you've no security later on, you feel you want to amass as much as you can at the time. I should think ninety-nine per cent of blokes made redundant cash in their pension money.

'When you first see all that money, you have a feeling of security; it's more than most people have ever seen all at once in their whole lives. I think that dazzles people. You feel almost rich. But you're amazed at how soon it goes.

'I felt like a millionaire. At first, great, you don't have to get up in the morning. That goes on for a few weeks. Then you have a twinge of anxiety. You think "Next week I'll look for a job." You put it off a week or two. Then you have a casual look round, and the thing that strikes you is the shortage of work. You get more anxious; you see your money dwindle. You have grave thoughts about economizing.

'The car is nearly always the first thing to go. You stop buying any new clothes; you don't renew your suit and it gets shiny and shabby. Then you have to economize on necessities. It's out of the question that you can replace furniture.

'Then you come to the final stage, when you find there's next to nothing left in the bank. You get your first giro cheque; you think

"I'll cash it next week. Then as time goes by, you cash it the minute you receive it; and in the end you sit there wondering how the hell you'll survive until it arrives.

'And then, no matter how self-disciplined you are, you have the problem of time; how to fill time. You don't realize just how much your life has been parcelled out to fit the needs of the company you worked for. You're not used to constructing it for yourself; and when you get to a certain age, it becomes harder. First of all, you start improving your home, painting, decorating; but even then you come to the point when you can't afford to do anything more to it; the expense is too much.

'You improvise, you find you're looking for something to do. You go to the library, spend time reading. For a while you try to learn something, improve your mind. But then the feeling of being useless gets to you to such a point that you only read to forget the problem, all your efforts go into escaping your situation. You read fiction, war stories, something exciting.

'You have to divorce yourself from your own feelings all the time; otherwise it would be too painful. You lead a sort of double life: the pointlessness of the reduced daily round, and the knowledge that you are still a feeling, thinking human being whose skills and talents are lying unused for the time being. I'm lucky. I have nerves like steel. But with people of a more nervous or introverted nature it's different. They lock themselves away, they're ashamed. There have been one or two suicides; people jump off the bridge. The police play these things down, naturally. They say there is no connection between being out of work and doing away with yourself. Those who are out of work know better.

'A lot of people are afraid to lead a full life; it prevents people marrying, having children: you feel you're not a whole person.

'When I look at what is happening in this town, I see the loss of skills, Plessey, Bridon Fibres, the shipyards – there is a loss of priceless skills just for a few thousand pounds. For a multinational company a couple of hundred thousand pounds is nothing; but the couple of thousand an individual receives seems a fortune to him. He's dazzled by it; and he doesn't see that it's a very unfair transaction – he's given up something that will never come back – not just a job, a whole experience of life. Our lives become narrower through the loss of work.

'I think this time the depression came on us very quickly. People were committed to new cars, a new freezer, the mortgage. They hadn't really thought it could happen, and they were devastated by it. Even in a town like this, a town that knows all about unemployment, we'd been lulled into believing it would never be like the thirties again. The transition was so sudden, it was emotionally disturbing. People find it harder to adjust to the loss of things they're used to. You can get used to easy times in the twinkling of an eye; but to get used to hardship again is long and painful.

'Of course, when a company is closing down, the way it works to divide its workpeople never shows up in any of the reports of workers' reactions. The company uses whispers, uneasiness, rumours. Not knowing where you stand is soul-destroying. People anticipate the worst; and this was the atmosphere we lived in for months.

'People get tired of not knowing, and you get some who leave because of that, with no thought of the redundancy money. They went, and most of them got jobs before they left, before the situation had deteriorated. They were the wise ones really. Those with foresight got out – they didn't over-calculate their redundancy pay, which is what a lot of people do. Those who stay on often believe they're going to get more than they do.

'Then there were those who rushed to ask for voluntary redundancy. They tend to be the ones who think only for the moment, getting a new car; they are obsessed with something they want, a music centre, a trip to Canada to see their children. So when the company announced there would be a few voluntary redundancies, a lot applied. The idea of getting a lump sum festers in people's minds. They've already spent it before they know how much it'll be. Even some of the shop stewards asked for it. That's the dirty part of the whole thing. The company create the uneasiness, then make it look as if people are begging to be made redundant, confirming all the stereotypes that working people are venal and money-grubbing. It was because they had been brainwashed. They feel trapped. It turns into a rat race to see who can go first. Then, in the end, all your union work goes by the board. You spend all your time trying to negotiate the best possible deal. We did have meetings, there was talk of work-ins, locking the machinery, sit-ins; but as soon as the redundancy money is dangled there you find your supporters have melted like snow on the dykes.

'I was born in Shields in 1929. My father went through the

Depression, and he was out of work for ten years. He came home from the First War – he'd been with the army of occupation in Germany; and he came home to ten years on the dole, only casual labour now and again. And it stayed that way until the next war came. When he did get work it was as a quarryman at the Marsden limestone quarries. It left a scar on him, but I think it scarred our mother even more deeply. I don't know that what is called male dominance was necessarily insensitivity. When you think of what working men could expect in their lifetime – poverty, unemployment, hunger, war, being wounded – there was no space for the more gentle emotions. It wasn't that people didn't feel them, they just couldn't show them; they wouldn't have survived.

'My father still feels bitter about "the land fit for heroes" he was supposed to come back to after the First War. Our mother was more cruelly affected because she was the one who had to see the children going without. I think the scars of my parents, they're imprinted on me. The point about working-class life is you go on paying, even after the hardship and the suffering is past. People say "things are better, why have you got a chip on your shoulder?" But the effects of the traumas of that generation – you can't just spirit them away. And now it's starting all over again. When you hear people say "Why can't the workers be more reasonable?" it's the fears and anxieties that have been bred in us, the distrust and resentment. It smoulders on through time. You can't abolish all the influences that made you what you are, and which you didn't exactly ask for in the first place.

'I think people are having their pride taken from them. You'll need O-levels to go on the dole next. Over the past thirty years people have been told the bad days will never come again. You hear it all the time. That's progress. But, of course, here we are, going through it all over again, and nobody can prevent it. There isn't any progress in human affairs.

'When things are easy, it isn't such a tragedy to be out of work. There are all kinds of fiddles, little jobs you can do; but as the level of unemployment rises, these avenues close down, you can't get the little jobs window-cleaning, car-repairing. On my estate, in the little road where I live, there were eight out of fourteen households that had cars; there's one now.

'The one thing I do know is that people should fight redundancy tooth and nail. Money is no compensation for having nothing to do.

Nothing evaporates like money.

'Once you've got a pool of unemployed – I dunno about a pool, it's more like an ocean up here – employers jump on the waggon and offer lower and lower wages. I went for a job as a hearse driver. The wages were £47.50 a week for forty hours. They said you have to make up the balance of a decent living in tips. That's no way for a man to make a decent wage. I toyed with the idea of going away. But my father is eighty-two, I'm all he's got.

'When I was a boy, I had a feeling for writing stories. I loved that. But it was never developed. There seemed no way to. The last thing there seemed any market for in the early forties was working-class kids who liked writing stories. And then I love cars. I've got engine oil instead of blood, I think. I had a garage as a hobby when I was working. I spent about twenty hours a week repairing cars. I loved engines so much I used to do jobs for people, not to make money out of it, just for the love of the work. I lost it all one night. It was cleared out, all my materials, all my tools, the lot. Somebody must have come in the night with a lorry or something; the next day it was all gone. I'd built it up over years. Well, it didn't break me, but it bent me. Those three things happened all within a short time, the job, the relationship with the wife, the garage.

'There's nothing special about me. I've not been particularly good or virtuous. I'm not proud of letting my marriage go to ruin. But you learn from it. Steel is tempered by its impurities. Perhaps that is true of people as well.

'There's a story I heard tell of Fyffe, the banana king. When he was very rich and successful, somebody went to interview him, to try and find out the secret of his success. He told the reporter, "When I was a young man, I went to apply for a job in a gents' toilet. I didn't get that job because I could neither read nor write. But then I went on to import bananas, and that was how I built up my fortune." "Good Lord," says the reporter, "I suppose you learned to read and write then?" "No," says Fyffe, "never." "Whyever not?" asks the reporter. "To think you've built up this enormous business, you've done all this, completely illiterate. Do you ever wonder where you'd have been if you'd been better educated?" And old Fyffe says "I know where I'd 've been. I'd 've been a toilet attendant."'

Jake is eighteen, a slight youth in tight black jeans above Dr Marten boots, a red T-shirt. His hair is fair and spiked into a crest, blond one side, auburn the other. On a leather cord around his neck he wears a silver boar's head; in his left ear a small gilt razor-blade. He left school at sixteen; did nothing for six months, then a basic skills course in metalwork, woodwork, maths and English; and then a year on the dole.

'Having nothing to do is boring. You stand on corners, you gang in pubs. You get persecuted if you're a punk. The pigs hate punks. If you're on your own, they'll clobber you. I used to have a "Who Killed Liddle Towers?" badge, and they'd always give you a couple of clips as you went past them, as long as you were where nobody could see them.

'I'd rather work. I've done nothing for two years. I've been to hundreds of places looking for jobs. They have a prejudice against you if you're a punk. I used to be a skinhead, but I didn't agree with what they stood for. They were all British Movement; I found I was in the wrong place. They thought if we got rid of the blacks there'd be no unemployment. There's no blacks up here, so how could they cause unemployment? So I became a punk.

'You have a lot of trouble with your parents. My Mam used to burn all my gear at first. They don't know what you're trying to say. My Dad doesn't mind; he's on invalidity benefit, he can't work. There's nine of us in our family. My older brother has been on the dole three and a half years.

'People think we're mad when they see the way we dress. It looks funny to them; the only conclusion they can draw is that we can't be right in the head. But you only have to look at the way people live; there's no question who's right in the head and who isn't. They think we are just being awkward. We are. There's plenty to be awkward about.

'All I really want is to be myself. I'm not bothered with money. I'd like a job where I'm valued for myself. Living on the dole is demoralizing. I get up between ten and eleven, then I gang up to my mate's or gang down the shops; have a drink in the pub, come home between one and two, listen to records in the afternoon, Clash, Sex Pistols. Then I have me tea, then gang up me mate's again. If we've got money, we might gang back to the pub for a drink.

'I get £12.95 a week. I've been in trouble. I got done for GBH. It was a snowy day, and there was a kid I was having a fight with; he was on the floor, and I was kicking snow at him. He sort of went to get up and I caught him with my boot. I've got a brother in detention centre for GBH. There's a lot of fighting between people from the different estates. Gangs have to get their revenge on each other. It's the natural thing to do, you have to hate somebody, so you hate the gang from the next estate. You're brought up tough. You have to show you're not afraid of anything.

'I could've stayed at school to do O-levels, but I wanted to get out. Now I wish I was back there. You can't wait to get into the big world; you soon find it's not very big; it's petty and it doesn't want to know anything about you.

'The biggest influence in my life this year was going on the Right to Work march. I found that there was people from Wolverhampton, Leeds, Liverpool. If I'd met them at football, I'd 've been fighting them. I'd 've regarded them as my enemies. That's the way you look at people, as if they're a different tribe. It's so futile. But there we were. I was amazed to find all kinds of people who were just like me; they'd all left school, got no jobs, and we were all in the same situation. It was something I'd never thought of – you think you're just one individual, and nobody is going through what you're suffering. You know that a lot of people are out of work, but you think sod them, I've got myself to worry about. The trouble is that gangs and football are the only collective ventures young people ever go on. It keeps you away from any understanding of what a political force you could be if you all got together.

'I joined the skinheads when I left school. It was a natural thing to do because my mates did. But what you're doing there, you're trying to find a way of belonging. I'd nothing against the blacks personally because as a matter of fact I didn't know any. The skinheads were all scared that the blacks were going to invade Pennywell; and they would sit around talking of defending their territory, you know, defending an estate as if it was a country that was going to be overrun. It got everybody worked up and excited.

'Money is what people worry about all the time up here. How to get some. Some kids are trained in shoplifting by their parents. I saw this woman passing things from the counters to her kids to put under their coats, little kids so small they can't be prosecuted. Most kids pinch out of their Ma and Da's pockets. Everybody fiddles. I was working on the rifles down the fair at the seafront last summer. A lad I was working with there, he had an argument with his neighbour about their cat; so this neighbour went and shopped him to

Social Security, that he was working for a few quid down the fair. We were there one day, and there's this bloke hanging round; he comes and uses the rifles, then tells us who he is. My mate had to pay back all the money he'd had from Social Security.

'People want excitement in life. That's why so many young kids are bloodthirsty; always talking about who got knifed, who got kicked in the nuts, who got his brains bashed out, who got killed in a crash. That's because people need to express themselves, and they've got no positive way of doing it.

'I'm lucky. I'm in a group. I'm a singer, and I'm learing to play bass guitar. I think more than anything else I want to make my feelings heard in music. I've written a lot of songs, poetry really. To express myself is the most important thing in life, it's everybody's right. And being denied that right is what is wrong with a lot of young people.'

Late afternoon. The November light is almost indigo in the shopping precinct; the girls are emptying the windows of the bakery, and collecting the wire trolleys that are scattered around the entrance of the supermarket. The job centre is closing; a young man of about twenty takes a last look at the cards on the orange frame in the window; exasperated, he kicks the window; not hard, it only vibrates a little. His shoes are lopsided where the built-up heels have worn down on the outside. He has dark hair and two or three days' growth of beard. He wears a greasy imitation-suede jacket, split at the seams, and flared jeans that were in fashion a few years ago. It's cold and windy in the street. He isn't going anywhere: the pubs aren't open, and anyway he's only got 15p in his pocket. We go to the buffet on Sunderland station, which has one entrance onto the street. At the end of the afternoon, the paper cups and spilt tea and chips seem to be winning against the inadequate staffing. As we stand at the counter waiting for a coffee, an old man with matted grey hair, a gabardine coat tied with string and odd shoes, picks up a packet of half-a-dozen biscuits wrapped in cellophane. 'Twelve pence,' says the woman behind the counter. He has ten and a half pence which he offers her. 'It's not enough.' She is herself elderly, has dark rings round her eyes, and looks tired at the end of the day. 'Go on love.' 'Twelve pence.' He puts them back. Then, when she has turned round to the coffee machine, he picks them up and puts them in his pocket. He looks at us and grins. 'Silly bugger. I would have give her what I had.' He walks quickly out of the buffet.

The young man wants to talk, but not about being unemployed. That seems to be the least of his problems. He talks about himself; he lives at home with his mother. He is an only child. He never knew his father and suspects his mother didn't either. The man she married hated him. 'She was so jealous of him, she used to follow him to work, because she thought he had another woman. She wouldn't let him go out on his own because she always thought he was going after some bint. She used to follow him around and take me with her. When they were building the new flats, we went onto the building site where he was working. She came and took me out of school one day, and then we went onto this site where he was working, putting all the kitchen units in, and she accused him of having a woman there on the site. And he gave her a bloody good hiding, and I had to go and fetch one of the blokes working there to help me rescue her.

'Then one night she took me to wait outside the pictures for him. She said somebody told her he was taking a girl to the pictures. So we stood outside, bottom of the steps, from about half eight until the pictures finished. It was freezing. And there he was, and he'd got some girl in tow. She couldn't have been more than fifteen. My Mam went for her and started knocking her about in front of all the people. And he was shit scared he'd get done for unlawful sexual intercourse because it turned out she was still at school.

'They used to have these arguments. He used to say she didn't care about him, and she said she was crazy about him; and he said if she loved him she wouldn't be so suspicious. My Mam couldn't give him the affection he wanted, and he thought she didn't love him, so he went for this girl who gave him all he wanted.

'I wished he would go. He was always threatening her. When I used to come home from school I used to think that perhaps he'd gone. She loved him a fucking sight more than she did me. She used me to get at him. Christ, he hated me. When I got older, he used to say she was using me to spy on him. He did leave her in the end, when I was about ten. But he gave me the worst pasting I'll ever have before he went. He knocked me out.

'Then she had it in for me. Nothing I did was ever right for her after that. She fucked up her own life and mine as well. You should see her now, she's only forty, she's got nothing. She drinks, she's been on drugs, everything. She goes to bingo, she studies the horses. She looks sixty.

'What a shithouse my life is. I can't trust women. I think they're getting at me all the time. The only good women are prossies; it's honest, you pay them and that's that.

'Work? I'd do anything. I have done, but I can't stick at it. If I think somebody's getting at me, I just walk out. It's me, I'm that thin-skinned, I lose my rag over nothing. I imagine people are getting at me. I don't like myself very much. I'm intelligent though. I don't know why. It don't come from her, it must have been my Da. I only know one thing about him, and that's he's intelligent – he pissed off the minute he screwed her.'

There is something frightening in the way people's lives boil over in this way, indiscriminately. In the absence of any demands placed on people, they turn inwards, and burrow into the pain, division and isolation which can never be remedied that way. It is only by a sense of shared venture, of joint struggle that those things can be assuaged, not by being plunged deeper and deeper into them. This young man wears his pain as casually as he wears his shabby clothing. It would be naïve to think that work could *cure* the damage that has been done to him; but in the enforced vacancy of such lives, self-disgust and introspection only make that pain more unbearable. Many young people, instead of being liberated from the cruel constraints of back-breaking labour, have inherited only a sense of broken purpose, the experience of ruined relationships and associations. It is that wretchedness which we seem unable to come to terms with, that violence which the changing needs of capitalism have visited upon the working class. Just as the forfeits of the old working class cannot be priced, so this kind of suffering exceeds the measures we use; and both make only partial truths of the crude money assessments of improvements in living standards, which mock human lives wrecked by violence and loss.

Mr and Mrs Anstey were shaped for that other era, the time of work. In their late seventies now, they still bear the values of that experience of Sunderland of shipyard and mine, streets and pubs, discipline and labour. Mr Anstey left school at thirteen. His first job was in the Institute for the Blind: his job was to take the canes out of the water in which they had been steeping, take them to the blind workers, splice the ends so they were ready to be made into the baskets that would be used for heaving coal or wood. His first week's wage was 1*s* 11*d*.

'My father was out of work for a long time. My mother didn't work; in this part of the world the only jobs for women were actresses and prostitutes, and there wasn't much call for either of them.

'I soon left my first job, and then went to Hutchinson & Jackson, compass makers. I got 4*s* a week there. I have a compass I made there.' He takes from the hearth a brass cylinder, only slightly tarnished after sixty-five years. The needle trembles before coming to rest at North. 'I worked there for a year. All the talk was of war, and of course all the boys were excited. The company made compasses, sextants, leads for measuring the depths of the water. I used to go with Hutchinson on a tarrant ship to test various instruments.

'My grandfather came from Yorkshire. He had been the skipper of a tea-vessel; but he sold his ship and left the sea when I was about four, and with the money bought some hotels in Sunderland, the Turk's Head, where we lived, and the Forester's Arms. I can remember the men coming in from the tugboats, paying 3*d* for a glass of whisky. It was my job to crush a lump of sugar into the whisky for them. We were lucky for a time; we had good food, clothing, and it was fun living in the hotel; you saw all kinds of people. Outside there were people starving. The kiddies would come in and beg a drop of tea, and grown men and women would beg for scraps.

'It came to an abrupt end. My father was a gambler and he had bad luck. There was some connection between my grandmother and the Lambton family; and my father and Uncle Jack decided they would contest some money in the Lambton estate, see if there wasn't some claim on it. They seemed to think there might be something in it; but after they'd been through Chancery, they ruined their father, lost all his money in the process, and the hotels had to be sold.

'We were all left penniless. We left the hotel and moved into a fish-and-chip shop. They got the premises just to live in, but they thought they might as well sell fish and chips; they had no other income. But it wasn't a living. From when I was ten until fourteen, it was misery, misery, misery. Coming from relative wellbeing, I don't know if that made it worse; we were living like everybody else –

poverty was everybody's close companion. We used to go barefoot. You hear people talk about the blacks going barefoot, saying it proves they can't be civilized; well it's only half a lifetime ago that a lot of the children in this town ran round unshod. Did that make us uncivilized then? My Uncle Jack was hired to help make the road, the Newcastle road there; it was just being made up into a proper road. Rocks were dumped on both sides of the road, and the men had to sit there with a heavy hammer, and they had to smash all these rocks into stones to roll the road out, make a base for the road. And they were paid a shilling a day. Sometimes I used to walk to Boldon with his bait in a handkerchief: it would take me two and a half hours to walk there, the same back, and all his bait would be some bread and margarine and a little bit of cheese if he was lucky.

'I joined up under age. I was seventeen. A lot of young men went in the army; for every one that went out of patriotism there was two went for the sake of getting regular food. Thousands of them gave the wrong age.

'But in spite of the poverty, the stealing wasn't so bad as it is now; there wasn't the vandalism, not the brutality. Men did bash their wives sometimes, but not the children. They were strict with children. If you went home and told your Da that the teacher had thrashed you, you'd get another thrashing. But they loved you, they formed your character. You grew up to endure suffering in silence.

'And then, when you started work, your boss, he would continue to train your character. When I was working for Hutchinson, I was standing outside the works one fine morning waiting to go in, and there was an old ragman with a horse and cart – you know, collected all bits of rubbish, lived by scavenging. He stopped his cart where I was standing, and he had a cigarette in his mouth. He asked me for a light. I lit the cigarette for him, and he went on his way. At that moment, the boss was coming down the street. He'd seen what I'd done. He said to me "Why did you do that?" I didn't think I'd done anything wrong. He said "Don't you ever be a servant to a man like that." That's how they were, severe; hard perhaps, but straightforward. Life was hard; they were only bringing you up to what you had to expect.

'One day I was driving with Hutchinson all the way back from Newcastle. It was a hot day, and he said to me "Would you like a drink?" I said, "I don't mind." Well, we drove along, we went through Boldon. There were three pubs there, because I took particular notice; but we didn't stop. Then we got to the next colliery village; two pubs there, but we still didn't stop. Well, we got back to Sunderland, back to the premises. He didn't say anything till we drew up outside. Then he said "I asked you if you wanted a drink. You said you didn't mind. Well, neither did I. If anybody asks you anything in future, answer 'yes' or 'no'."

'He was very subtle. If you, or any boy, went with a message for him, he'd take the message; and if the boy moved away as soon as he'd delivered the message without hesitating, he'd say "Wait a minute." And the boy would get something, a small tip. But if you didn't shift the minute you'd delivered whatever it was, if you hesitated just a fraction of a second, he'd say "What are you waiting for?" And the boy got nothing. He would never give a tip if anybody expected it or behaved as though he expected it.

'You see, when you think about the fate of all those men, those who went to the War and perished, those who came back, the poverty, the finish of work, men wasting away with idleness and despair, you had to be hard. When I came back, I got a job with a provision merchant, I thought that would be safe, provisioning the ships. I'd been there four weeks, and a notice went up on the wall "As from Monday, wages will be reduced by the rate of so much per cent a week." And underneath, it said "If any man does not want to work under these conditions, he may tender his notice at once." Some of those who didn't want to accept it never worked again.

'Now people haven't got the grit in them; the men up here were made of granite. You never squealed or hollered, whatever you had to bear.' When Mr Anstey regrets the loss of that stoicism and hardness, it isn't only that he is lamenting the passing of his youth and vigour, although that is there too; but there is something else. Out of that toughness was to have grown that 'steady intensification of the role of the working class . . . a class which is disciplined, unified and organized by the very mechanism of the capitalist method of production which has flourished with it and under it.' He wouldn't articulate it in that way of course; and he is preoccupied now with his own failing strength and his wife's growing disability. But he smiles at her, on the other side of the hearth, the woman he met in 1917. 'I was home on leave, and I met her at the wedding of a pal of mine. She was a bridesmaid. The moment I saw her, I knew she was my girl, and that we would go through life together. Even then, she was wearing a ribbon for arthritis, a yellow ribbon on her wrist. She's almost crippled by it now. But if you'd seen her then, oh she was beautiful. To me she still is, even though she can hardly move without help.' As he speaks, she nods assent to his account of their life. If she agrees with him, it isn't because she is subordinate to him and echoes his ideas; it is because the conditions under which they have lived excluded any other than a shared response of stoicism and endurance.

A new development in Southwick: cubes of flats and maisonnettes, three storeys high. On one side is the main road, demolished streets, only a few Victorian pubs standing on the old street corners; a view over the valley of the Austin Pickersgill shipyard, and beyond, the hills that separate the Tyne from the Wear. On the other side there is the Romanesque Victorian church of St Columba dominating the closely packed terraces with their cobbled back-ways, with the bricked-up openings in the walls through which within living memory the night-soil used to be emptied once a week.

Mr Keach is forty-two; his wife a year or two younger. They have five children. The flat is warm and comfortable. There is a view over the smoking chimney-pots towards the town on one side and over the river to the sea on the other. In Sunderland you are always conscious of the sky and the sea; it doesn't have the claustrophobic feeling of many inland cities.

Mr Keach is one of those people who have not been diminished by unemployment, but have grown through it. He was a joiner. He did an apprenticeship when he left school, and worked on building sites all over the North-east. He worked for the big contractors – Wimpey, McAlpine – but didn't take work that would take him more than a day's travel from his family. Both Mr and Mrs Keach were brought up in poor families in the old docks area of Sunderland. Moving into the new flat at first seemed the answer to all the family's problems. But like thousands of other families, they found that the new place imposes its own expenses; and this increases the pressure to work more in order to keep pace with the demands that are placed on them. Mrs Keach developed angina and had to give up work, and her husband had a nervous breakdown and could no longer keep pace with the expense. The quarterly bill for heating the flat in winter was over £200. One day, he felt he could no longer go to work. 'Suddenly, without any warning. It just seemed hopeless and futile.'

Both Mr Keach and his wife had been active in the tenants' association from the time they moved in. It was a deliberate effort on their part to try to foster some of the closeness and support they had known in the older neighbourhoods. After a spell in hospital, Mr Keach went to the Poly to do a course in community studies. After a year he had to give this up. In the tenants' association he found the troubles and anxieties of people in the area too overwhelming. He was so upset and angry at the way people were suffering that he became depressed and had to withdraw a little. Since June 1979 he has been unemployed.

'Socially, not having work is upsetting, especially if you've been a fairly tough sort of bloke. You do lose something of your self-respect in the company of people who are working. You go into a pub, people look at you critically. They say "I'd die of boredom if I was at home all day," or "How can you afford to drink ale in your position?" There is a stigma, even where a lot of people are out of work. You're almost an affront to people who are working. They feel guilty because they don't care enough; perhaps you remind them it could happen to them, and that's the last thing they want to think of because they're still living up to the last penny they earn.

'I've learned that the old spirit isn't there any more. The community no longer stays together and unites in the face of the outside world; there's division and mistrust within. People remain strangers to each other, and the worst thing they can imagine is getting involved with other people's problems. When we were poor, we had common cause; and this is what's lacking. There's this division between workers and non-workers. You hear them say "He gets all that help from Social Security and we don't get any help because my man's working." They feel you're getting something for nothing.

'I'm lucky. Financially, I don't find it degrading. I get the money from Social Security each week, minus a direct payment for the electricity. Two of my daughters have just started work, so that's a help.

'I'd worked fifteen, twenty years on the buildings. I should have tried to break away earlier, but when you've a family, you can't think of the luxury of getting yourself educated or whatever. I'd been with a squad of blokes who moved from place to place; they didn't seem to care, the money was the only thing that mattered. You do feel that earning a living has got nothing to do with you as a person. That's why I can bear unemployment.

'My relationship with the family has always been my greatest support. Some of the blokes you worked with, they spoke of their wives as if they were millstones round their neck. They didn't respect them. With my wife being ill, some days she can't do anything, it's given me a purpose. I can take some of the burden from her, and I don't feel useless. We've always got on well together. We share everything. We've always been the best of friends as well as being married, and it's not everybody who can say that. People say to you "We don't know why you stay together", as though they don't believe you can still enjoy each other's company after all these years. Well it's true, a lot of people don't – they're out drinking or they look on the home as somewhere to escape from. And it's true that a lot of people I know who've lost their job, it's their wife or their husband they start on first. I couldn't imagine us falling out. The experiences we've had have drawn us closer together.'

'A lot of men used to be tyrants at home,' Mrs Keach said. 'My father was. They had a hard life, and they took it out on their families. I was ruled with a rod of iron when I was a girl. If I wanted to go to a dance, my mother always said "Well make sure you're back home before he is." He drank; he was tough with us. I was dumb when I went into marriage, I knew nothing. I want to make sure my daughters don't go into it as ignorant as I was. My husband was as strictly brought up as I was; so what happens, you temper the excesses of each other. You come to a compromise. We've been a good influence on each other. A lot of men see their role as being attacked, and they can't cope with it. Being out of work, it finds them. If a man is used to being his own man, he doesn't believe in equality, he has been the master really, so when he falls out of work it can be traumatic. They're the ones who fall apart, get violent, just go on the tramp.'

Mr Keach took up the theme: 'Well I'm not a brute, and then I'm not one of those who are under the wife's thumb, I mean, I like my ale, but I've always given her good money. I don't mean I tip my wages up, but create a fair partnership, that's what counts.

'I don't feel I've been destroyed by not having a job. I've had a set-back yes; time hangs heavy sometimes. But my purpose now is the same as it's ever been – to look after the kids; and now I've got the added job of looking after my wife as well. That isn't unworthy of a man. Quite the opposite. Being out of work is an attack on dignity and self-respect, but maybe that's because we set too much store on things that don't matter – dignity and self-respect should come through your relationships.

'Our eldest daughter, she got married too young. She thought all marriages were going to be like ours. Her husband came from a rough family – no mother, a lot of boys, there was a lot of fighting and violence. And he took that into his marriage. She wasn't used to it. She's back here now, so that gives us plenty to do, as if we hadn't enough. She lives here with the baby. They split up because she couldn't take it. Well, when you're faced with your own daughter, you couldn't let her go off and live in some flat on her own with a baby.'

Anita comes in. She is twenty-one, a shy dark-haired girl, wearing a yellow-check nylon overall with the name of a local supermarket on it. This is her first complete day at work: until now she has never had a full-time job. She was at a special school. She works sorting and wrapping the different cuts of meat in the butcher's department. When she has gone, her mother says 'She's always been very introverted. We were worried about her. They said she would always be four years below her age; when she was fourteen, she was like a child of ten. She used to come home and beg me to teach her more than she was learning at school; but she couldn't learn fast enough. It made her very unhappy. She would like to work with children, but she has no chance while they demand so many qualifications. All children love her, you can see how they take to her. She worries about our children. If they come home a bit late, she wants to go out looking for them. She's always wanted to mother them. She would have taken my place if I'd let her. That's where her skill lies, there's no doubt about it. It seems a shame she should be humping meat about when she could be caring for children.'

Mr Keach feels he has been shielded against some of the effects of losing his job 'because I have my priorities right'. For many people, the experience brings a moment of a different sort of truth. Ron Carey, former steelman from Consett, now living with his sister and her family in Sunderland: 'What it's taught me? You can't trust a soul. I found out my wife married me, not for love but security. She said as much. Not till she'd spent the best part of the money I got for leaving work. Then she could see herself settling down on Social Security. She poisoned the kids against me. As if it was my fault. Things were all right as long as she'd got the money to buy clothes, pay the Avon lady, go on holidays. She was always such a fidget, she couldn't be still. She got jilted just before she was going to get married. She'd got it all prepared. That's why she married me, so she could wear a bloody wedding dress. I lost my job and my family at the same time.'

At a takeaway stall near the centre of town, an old man wearing a scarf tied round his head, with a knot of iron grey hair, unshaven chin, trousers tied at the ankles to keep the warmth in, a pair of plimsolls, threadbare greasy coat too short for him, buys a sandwich and a plastic cup of hot tea. He sits on a wall with his back to the strong wind and joins his fingers round the white plastic cup. Then he sets it down on the wall and opens the sandwich. With a sudden outburst of anger, he says 'Do they think I'm a fucking animal?' He throws out the wilting yellow lettuce and the thin piece of tomato into the road. Then he looks at the pale smear of margarine on the soft bread, and he throws that after the filling. He hurls the plastic cup with the hot tea, and it bursts on the tarmac in a dark blot. 'Do they think I'm a fucking beast? Am I not fit to eat food?' He sits, sullen and angry, as the cars drive over his discarded meal. Tears at his self-inflicted punishment stand in his eyes.

It isn't easy to say what draws you to the streets of these poor towns and cities; the unrecorded heroism of people who spent a lifetime of labour without ever earning enough to keep themselves and their families adequately clings to the decaying streets in which to live was to struggle. The attempt to eliminate all traces of them through changing the appearance of things is certainly cynical: even the new shopping mall, surely no more than ten or fifteen years old, is in danger of collapse, and is being shored up with a metal sculpture of scaffolding. Something of the tragic expenditure of lives haunts the dismantled scenery of their living places; the bitterness and regret linger. But that isn't all. It is that the chance to release people from that kind of indignity has not been seized; but instead a different kind of indignity has been substituted for it. That old epic of labour is surely finished as far as the young are concerned, but so is the resistance to it. Why, then, should the indignity and abjection remain for so many people, their lives feeling to them ingrown and functionless? In the *Collapse of Work*,[32] Jenkins and Sherman say:

> We do not believe that work *per se* is necessary to human survival or self-esteem. The fact that it appears to be so is a function of two centuries of propaganda, and an educational system which maintained the idea of work as its main objective, but which singularly failed to teach about leisure and how to use it. This is not to say that a lack of work, even with a reasonable amount of money attached to it, would be acceptable to society as it stands at the moment; indeed this would be patently untrue. . . . The old notions underlying the work ethic are outmoded. The wheel has turned full circle, and it is now in the interests of capitalists to disemploy people if profits are to be made.

It is significant that all those who dwell lovingly on the possibilities of leisure are in no danger of having their own function destroyed. Jenkins and Sherman concede that it is in the interests of capitalism to keep increasing numbers of people in idleness; and then insist that social attitudes need to change drastically. But if the imposition of the kind of work traditionally associated with the labouring poor failed to cause them to change the structure of society, it is difficult to see how those unemployed or underemployed will achieve it. And any society which promises people a diminishing function and dwindling contribution of their skills and abilities doesn't seem especially desirable, no matter into whose benevolent hands the 'education for leisure' may be delivered. Indeed, even those without work now who might be thought most able, by virtue of their education, to come to terms with long periods of leisure, seem to express very much the same ideas as those who haven't had the privilege of long cultivation of their inner resources before joining the dole queue.

Mid-afternoon on Pennywell estate. A low red sun gilds the windows and throws long shadows of the houses across the muddy green. The whole estate seems to shine briefly, as though illuminated from within; but then the sun is hidden and the lights go out, leaving the dark brick and the concrete hardness of roads and houses.

Steve Caswell is twenty-one. He is reading in the front room. The television is on: a woman from Age Concern is talking about keeping the elderly warm in winter. The room is warm and untidy. There are two dogs and two cats. Steve was at York University for two years. He left in July 1979, before finishing his course in physics. He lost interest in work and failed his exams. Since then he has been unable to find work. Leaving university without a degree has pursued him, and left with him the aura of someone unable to finish whatever he undertakes. What doesn't show in his record is that during his second year at university his father died after a long and slow decline: he had a brain tumour, and went from being an alert and hard-working man to a fat and lethargic stranger, who became increasingly incoherent as the tumour developed. Under the strain, Steve's mother became ill and needed psychiatric help. Steve came home for a week at the time of the funeral, and he stayed – at least in part to look after the family. This is what has jeopardized his chances of work; and it adds a dimension of bitterness and resentment to the sadness of seeing his father die at the age of forty-two.

Steve went to the local comprehensive school. He got two A-levels. He was pressurized by teachers – nobody suggested anything but university. He was in part a victim of the desperate need of comprehensive schools to show that they can compete with the old grammar schools in getting people through to university. Anyone with the slightest talent is pushed and encouraged, no matter how unsuitable his or her temperament.

'Of course my parents were overjoyed when I was offered a place at university. I was the first one from my family, and one of the first from this estate. They were proud of me. It's hard not to feel guilty, and my Mam tries not to be disappointed. It isn't easy to study in a working-class home. There were five children at home while I was doing A-levels, there was no privacy. You can't ask for special consideration. The house is overcrowded, it's not exactly conducive to learning. When I got to university I felt impatient with a lot of middle-class socialists – there seemed to be no flesh on the political bones.

'I think I made a mistake to drop out; but at the time it seemed the right thing to do. After eighteen months, boredom, resignation, it gets to you. In the first couple of months, you're quite buoyant, you're keen, you think you'll get a job easily. But having been at university worked against me: kids straight out of school with A-levels were competing for the same jobs. You pay the penalty for not going through the machine in the orthodox way.

'When I was younger, I'd dreamed of being a big scientist. I went through O- and A-levels without any difficulty. But one of the things that happens when you drop out is that you get detached from the people you go through university with. Most of my friends now are people I knew at school. Most of them are working, local government, civil service.

'It's easy to fall into acceptance of being out of work in Sunderland. Being unemployed is part of the psyche. I get up about twelve, I have my dinner, watch the one o'clock news. I have the tv on practically all the time, half watching, half reading the paper. It's easy to do nothing. I read a lot – philosophy; but I also sit around a lot. It needs a great effort of will-power to do anything. If you have something to do, it's easy to put it off till the next day because as far as you can see all the days to come are going to be the same. You get lethargic, a couldn't-care-less attitude. It creeps up on you: no matter how intelligent you are; it's the *feeling* that gets you, a sense of being useless. Being at university, it hasn't benefited me materially, but I think I'm a better person for it.

'I don't enjoy the enforced idleness. I'd rather do anything than nothing, empty dustbins, sweep the streets. It's not that I've got big ideas. I've applied to be a lab. technician at Sunderland Poly.

'I go out drinking two or three nights a week with my mates; and going to football, that's the highlight of the week. I get £16.35 a week, and I give £7 to my Mam; that leaves under £10 to spend. Being out of work is a lonely experience. Even though many others are the same, you only live through your own particular way of being out of work. Work is collective; unemployment is solitary. I feel I'm accumulating a lot of wasted time behind me. I've achieved nothing. The majority of my spending money goes on booze. You feel you're living from one pint to the next. I might drink six pints on a night out, that's enough to make me feel okay for a few hours.

'I don't have fits of anger at being unemployed. It operates at a different level altogether: I'm a victim of processes that are at work. It doesn't stop you feeling useless. You feel the want of that respect which employment gives people. I feel I've a right to work. It is the duty of society to provide a function for people, which in turn will earn them a decent standard of living. And if society can't do that, it's society that's wrong, not me. That's what it tries to make you feel – that it's your fault.

'Having stayed on at school and been a student, at least I've not been spoiled by having a lot of money that has suddenly dried up. That must be the worst thing. In the thirties, they were used to it. But now you sit and look through the media, they're your window on the world. All the things that are good and desirable are associated with people who have money.

'When I go out at night, the topics of conversation are football, politics and girls, in that order. Football is the highlight of the week. That gives you a sense of elation, the speed and the movement, you soar with it. If it's a good game, you get a sense of exhilaration. If it's lousy, you feel disappointed, and it sharpens your frustration. Football gives you a sense of belonging to something greater than yourself.

'Having a project, something to do; it seems to be something the trade union movement doesn't offer to young people. I think work disciplines you. You don't just take, you have to give – work provides a balance in people's lives. I feel that I've a right to a job. It isn't a privilege that society confers on you. I've a right to employment, and if society doesn't provide it, then society has got to be changed.'

Many people spoke of the media, and the way they reinforce your sense of futility if you have no work. A man in his forties said that it had been the television that had made him politically aware, but not quite in the way that the programmers might have anticipated. 'If you have no work, everything seems to mock you: the television, the adverts, you feel it. The papers are full of the lives of millionaires, the shops are full of things you can't afford. It makes you feel humiliated, it destroys your self-respect. Your kids can't have what the others have; it makes you feel a failure. You start to listen to the tone of the tv commercials, and you realize they're not just inviting you to buy, they're orders: it's "Get this, have that, buy the other." You start to hate yourself because you feel out of step, shabby, unworthy. You can't afford to go out on a Saturday night, so you stay in; me and the wife, we play cards for pennies, share one bottle of Brown. Then you turn the tv on, and there's Parkinson, chatting up all the rich and successful and self-satisfied. You can't get away from it. It follows you everywhere, makes you feel like a criminal.'

The young are always ready to talk. There seem to be no reticence, no silences, as there would have been with their counterparts two generations ago. It is as if the young have no secrets. Everything is showing. Perhaps this is the meaning of the lopsided insistence on style and fashion. The need of the young for display has been exaggerated and distorted because so much of the inner substance has been suppressed, and externalized in objects and commodities which fascinate them in the shop windows. Much of what belongs to them as of right is on sale to them if they can afford it – their own senses, sight and hearing, memory itself seem to depend on the videos, music centres, cameras. I spoke to the mother of a seventeen-year-old, who spends all day playing an electronic tv game which his parents bought him. She said 'When I get home from work at night, there's nothing shifted its position, not even him sometimes. He has the house to himself from eight o'clock in the morning till half past five. I'm ashamed of what people'd think if they knew. I find the washing up in the sink, all the breakfast things. It seems he's not capable of doing a thing. He's all we've got. We're lucky. We've got good money coming in. We were such poor bairns, his Da and me; just after the War I was always cold and hungry as a kid, fetching coal in an old pram before we could have a stick of fire. My mother was disabled, she walked with a big built-up shoe, she was old before her time. We've given our lad everything. But he doesn't show any recognition. He just says he never asked to be born. I said to him, neither does anybody.

'I don't want him to suffer the way we did. My Dad was funny; when he came back from the War, he was restless, he used to go on the tramp. I wanted it to be different for our lad. He goes out soon after me and his Dad get home. I give him money. I buy him clothes. But I don't know where he goes. A neighbour might say "Oh, I saw your lad hanging round the bus station last night." The bus station, when we've given him everything at home. It hurts.'

You can feel how the love of parents has actually prompted them to deliver their children to the economic machine that so recently robbed and deprived them; and they have done it in good faith, as though everything really had changed. And it isn't until too late that they become aware of the deception: the good start in life, the best of everything have done something to their children which they never anticipated. As the parents discover that the jobs have disappeared, they also find that the strengths which they derived from struggle have also evaporated, the comfort they took in a sense of shared predicament has been obscured. But the guilt and disappointment at their defection from their own children's best interests cannot find a social or political target, and so they turn on the children themselves, or on each other; or they project their anger onto other helpless social groups – immigrants, other workers. They find they have lost the dignity and stoicism with which earlier generations confronted the cruelties of capitalism, and have gained nothing in its stead but the inability to live without the things on which they have been nurtured, and which belong absolutely to the global capitalist productive processes; and they see their children become little starvelings, helpless shrunken dependants, with no power over those processes, because they no longer have any significant role in them.

Late evening outside the Leisure Centre. An ambulance draws up and a man in his forties, who had collapsed while swimming, is rushed down the ramp on a stretcher. A group of kids quickly gathers out of nowhere. Some boys jump on the tailboard of the ambulance to get a better view. Two of them have Mohican haircuts, one a crimson coxcomb, some have Nazi insignia, studs and eagles on the back of their jackets. The ambulancemen have difficulty in getting them off the ambulance before it drives off. It goes with its siren sounding, and leaves a little eddy of excitement in the crowd. 'Did you see his face? It was blue. Was he dead? He lives near us. Let's go and tell his wife before the cops get there. See her face. Be a laugh.' The excitement dies away. A stinging wind from the sea, the cloud illuminated from below by the sodium lamps. Everything closed, bleak, empty. By the bus station there is a hot-dog stall, with a silver slatted shutter half closed against the cold; the smell of onions in big soft baps. Four of them share one hot dog. The boy who shares it out is criticized. 'You gave him too much.' 'That's 'cause he fancies him. He follows him round like a dog.' He starts yapping. The boy who has been insulted hits him. Half the bap falls on the oily concrete. They stop fighting and pause while they eat.

Della is twenty-five. She has two children, four and five. As a single parent, she finds it impossible to get a job. She knows many women who fail to register for employment because they feel it's hopeless. They just give up.

Della left her husband two years ago. She stayed with friends at first, and later, in a women's refuge. 'I loved it there. I felt really safe and protected for the first time. Occasionally there would be trouble from various husbands. The most usual approach was to say they were social workers; but you could always tell – if they were ringing from a call-box, you knew they weren't social workers. In the end, we got re-housed by the council.

'I didn't register for work till I'd been looking for work over a year. When I left my husband I had a breakdown. I went to the emergency Social Services. The social worker said to me I should go back to my husband, my little boy needed a father. I mean, what an insult. Do they think any woman leaves a man because it's easier to survive on her own with two kids? They should try it.

'It puts you in a very different relation to society as a single parent. People look at you quite differently. The neighbours resent it. Maybe the part of every woman that wants to get out of her marriage feels threatened. But then when I got Kevin into a day nursery, a neighbour said I was getting preferential treatment. Everybody seems scared that someone is getting an extra advantage. My friend was reported for cohabiting.

'My marriage deteriorated very quickly. My husband was odd. He took an overdose three times. He was very jealous of me. He thought I was having affairs with everybody under the sun – my friend's husband, the husband of the woman next door, even my mate's kid brother I was supposed to be jumping into bed with. He started to go round threatening people, trying to follow me, keep track of my every move.

'The first time I left, I stayed with my mother for three weeks. He went crying to everybody so I went back to him. On my first night back he made me sleep on the settee. That was supposed to be a punishment. But nothing was any different. So the next time I left him, I didn't tell my mother because she put all the pressure on me to go back. My mother was widowed when I was one year old, so she knew all about the problem of bringing up two children on her own. She didn't want me to go through it.

'The second time I left him, I stayed with friends. It took him two days to find out where I was – there was only me Mam or two lots of friends where I could have been. He was tearful again – "Come back, all is forgiven" sort of thing. But that doesn't work twice; not with me anyway. That was it. I wasn't going back again.

'It's a funny thing, being on your own. People don't know how to react to you. It shows you how people's lives are governed by doing the expected thing. It may sound obvious, but with a husband you're never on your own. And you go from that to being entirely alone. I liked the refuge because you could share experiences there.

But then I went straight into a flat: no furniture, no fire. It was a no-coal house, so I had to buy two bags of smokeless fuel a day. I got a cooker from Social Security and the money for three single beds. I got a double-bed from some neighbours and I bought bunk-beds for the children. I had no bedding so we had to borrow sleeping bags. I applied to DHSS for bedding, lino and curtains. For all that I was offered £30. On appeal, it was increased to £63.

'Everything is an obstacle; everything deters you from trying to be independent. It's like the system defies you: "Go on, you try and see if you can, we'll make it hard as possible."

'My husband and I used to have arguments. His health was bad. He was subject to dizzy spells, vertigo. He was a shipwright, but for the last two years we were together, he only worked about six months. And with him being ill, you see more of each other. He followed me about. He was always criticizing the way I looked after the house. I'm not very tidy. I don't happen to think things like that are very important. He hadn't had a very happy childhood. His mother's health was bad; she was forty-five when he was born, and she already had a son in his twenties; it was her second marriage. She got TB when he was six months old; from the age of four, he stayed with his aunt, his mother couldn't cope. It's funny how your childhood follows you when you grow up.

'My mother's mother was also widowed. In 1926. My grandfather died during the General Strike. He'd been in the army in the First War, and was always ill. My nana married again. And her mother had also left her husband in 1914 – he was the local poacher; they lived in a chip shop and he drank a lot. She left him periodically, but there was nowhere in those days for a woman to go. But when war broke out that gave her a chance. She went to Wales and got a job as a nurse. She took my grandmother with her, who was then fourteen. So there's four generations that I know of who've left their husbands. Sometimes it feels spooky – doing the same thing. But people's lives do repeat themselves through the generations. With my husband, there was a big age difference between his father and his brothers and sisters: his father was brought up by one of his older sisters, him and his niece were brought up as brother and sister; just like my husband was with his niece.

'I stayed on at school to do A-levels: Art and English. Then when I left school I did a foundation course in Art and Design at the Poly. I was accepted to do the Diploma in Art at Leeds; but I was engaged by the time I was seventeen, and I decided I wouldn't go. I think that was a mistake.

'He was six years older than me. We got on well together. There seemed no reason why we shouldn't be happy. But after we were married, I got more mature and he didn't. I was still immature, I had further to develop than he did; and that's something no nineteen-year-old can foresee. I got a job at Binn's, in the display department. It only lasted three months. They took on twelve people, then sacked six of them: they kept on the sixteen-year-olds because that's cheaper than paying the older ones. I got some temporary jobs, filing clerk, nothing I wanted really, but in the early stages of being married you're not that bothered.

'As a single parent, it took me a hell of a time to get a flat. And the one I took has a reputation for being in a rough area of town, near the town centre. It's the kind of block of flats where the kids nick the outside doors for Guy Fawkes bonfires. You get a lot of drunks coming along, you find them sleeping in the passage ways in the morning. It's nothing to have someone banging on your door in the middle of the night.

'Being alone you realize how closely people watch you. You get accused of things you're not doing. I was talking to somebody from the block of flats opposite; I told her where I lived and she said "Oh you'll be in the flats where there's a woman living with a black man." She meant me. And that was because one night, my baby-sitter was an Indian student from the Poly. He only came once; but somebody must have seen him come, so after that I was the woman living with a black man. But your immediate neighbours can be very protective. If anybody knocks on anybody's door and asks does so-and-so live here, they've never heard of you.

'My income is just a bit over £50 a week: £17 maintenance, £21 supplementary benefit, £12.50 family allowance. That has to cover everything. The rent is £11.05; upstairs you pay slightly less than on the ground floor. They attached a proportion of my husband's wages for maintenance. He's working at Pickersgill's. But he won't see the children now, which is sad. His girl-friend left her husband to move in with him. She'd like him to come and see his children because her husband comes to see his little girl. My little boy, to him, every man who's got a beard and glasses and curly hair is Daddy. My new boy-friend, he has glasses and a beard, and even though his hair is straight, Kevin still thinks he is Daddy.

'I think what ruined our marriage was when he was on the sick and we were together all the time, twenty-four hours a day. It's different when you're both working and you see each other only a few hours a day. You value your time together more. You can bring each other greater variety and richness in your life than if you've been cooped up together all the time. Then he went on the night shift. He got good money then; when they'd done their work quota they used to hop over the wall, leave one bloke behind to sign the board for the rest of them; and then he'd get home at four in the morning most days, that wasn't too bad. I was getting £40 a week housekeeping then. You get used to the money coming in: that happens to a lot of women; they stay with their men even if there's nothing between them; they say they're doing it for the sake of the children, but for a lot of them it's for the sake of the money.'

The Wheatsheaf, Monday evening. Dave, thirty-eight, fair hair, hazel eyes, deep cheeks with prominent cheekbones, eyes creased at corners. On his right hand a silver ring with an amethyst, amateur tattoos on his hands, LOVE and HATE smudgily across his fingers. A blue coachman-style coat, a three-piece suit with a silver chain across the waistcoat.

'I can't complain. I've had a good life. Only trouble is, I can't settle. I don't depend on anybody, and nobody depends on me. If they do, it's tough shit on them.

'I've done everything, I've been everywhere. You wouldn't believe how many people in this town have never been out of it. Even young blokes. I've been living in a commune up the coast, big house on the cliff. I've been there a year now; it's too long, time to be moving on.

'The secret of life is be flexible, adapt. I've been a dustman, I've worked on the pier at Scarborough, the fair at Blackpool, I've done the grape harvest in France, been potboy in hotels in Spain. But it's not so easy now. Times have changed. The sixties were the best time.

'I'm the oldest person in the place where I live. I can give them advice, the youngsters. Believe me, I've been a junkie, I've been a crook. Only one thing I hate, that's pettiness. I was brought up in a poor family, we were so poor the fucking mice were on Social Security. I went in the army to get away from it, five years, Greece, Cyprus. That was all right, it helps you grow up.

'I didn't start roguing till I was twenty-nine; late in life really. I wasn't a juvenile delinquent, I was a late starter. I got in with a load of villains. I used to dress up classy, and go round these firms, applying for jobs; I'd look round, sus out the weak spots – the alarms, the windows, the dogs – then report back with a plan how to break into the place. But some of the lads ripped me off. They used to wait for me to report to them, then they'd go and do the job and tell me somebody else had done it before they got there. So they wouldn't have to pay out, see? I was being used, I was a right sucker.

'So I stopped doing it with them, I went freelance. I nicked a load of copper and nickel one night; I was all night carrying this stuff out of the yard where it was kept, £10,000 worth. It was the hardest night's work I ever did. Then the fuzz jumps me the minute I'm through. I said to them "Why did you let me do all that fucking graft for nowt?"

'Next time I got nicked, they sent me to a nut doctor, see why I'd done it. I told him, it was just easy money. The last thing I wanted was this funny farm man. He said "Why did you do it?" I said "I wanted the money." He couldn't understand. Then he asked me about my relationships with women. These people can't take a simple answer. But I went along with it; the last thing I want is to spend years in a cell with my own shit for company.

'I've been through the drug scene: oh boy, have I been on some trips! A lot of my mates, they went on trips so fucking long, they never came back. There's four or five people I knew, six foot under now. One of them, he was a bit of a mystic, he said he knew a way of coming back from the other side. I haven't seen him yet.

'This chick in the commune, only last week, she was out for five days, Tuinal, Secconal. She was a mess. What bit of brain she got had been affected. I tell you, somebody on smack is a rose compared with somebody on downers. But they're young, you can't tell 'em.

'The only thing I'd like is a lass to settle down with, some chick to be a companion. We'd be all right. I know a lot of things. I know all sorts of herbs, in the commune, we go and get mushrooms from the fields, boil them up, then make tea or coffee with the water they've cooked in; that is something. You don't need all this stuff that eats your brain. Glue – I ask you, they must be warped.

'If I had one woman, I could be faithful to her. There's one girl, when her boy-friend is away, she starts ringing up people, asking them to come and sleep with her. If she was mine and she did that to me, I'd spin her fucking head round.

'I did live with a lass for three years. Trouble is, you get too involved, you can't out when you want to. You have to carry it right to the end. And it fucking hurts. So since then, it's a poke and a promise. It's a trap. You want somebody you can trust, somebody to spend the rest of your life with; but you can't let yourself go because they'll only shit on you again.

'I'm very right-wing. There's too many people in the nick who ought to be at the end of a rope. You go and do a bank, spill blood like it was milk, only eight or ten years. It's ridiculous. I've got no time for worrying about mankind, I'm too busy worrying about myself. I think everybody is selfish, everybody is out for himself. All our brothers! What brothers? I don't believe it. What happens in Asia, Africa, that's their fucking bad luck. And when they come here, give them hand-outs, offer them houses. It's asking for trouble if you can't house your own people. I don't believe in unions – the only union I believe in is a guy and a chick coming together for a good fuck; I don't worry about the bomb either; the only big bang I'm concerned with is the one I might get tonight.'

8
Southwick

A day with the Southwick Neighbourhood Action Project, November 1980. Most of the people who come for advice are unemployed. It is as though the forced inaction uncovers all sorts of other things they were less keenly aware of while they were working. They come here because they need someone to intercede for them with the agencies that are supposed to serve them. The atmosphere of the DHSS makes it unthinkable that you should try to tell the full story of your circumstances; the gas and electricity boards are too remote and indifferent, and in any case, you can never find anyone to take responsibility for anything; even Social Services seem too pressed unless you go and tell them you'll batter your child if they don't listen. There is a sad contrast between the people who come here – the bleak absence of resources, the sense of dispossession, the basic simplicity of their needs – and the cumbersome organizations which have evolved to 'help' them. It seems unbelievable that what is wrong with their lives should require such elaborate structures of intervention, such a complicated chain of communication before anything can be done. As the lives of the poor become more shorn and empty, it seems that the official labyrinths become more impenetrable. In the submissive patience of people waiting for the SNAP shop to open before 9.30 in the morning, you can see the effects of the stripping away of human resources: people who don't have to face the demands of purposive activity very swiftly become unable to cope: and anyone in

Sunderland will tell you that coping was what the old poor knew all about.

What I remember most about the people who came to SNAP that day are the strong physical impressions: the bruised look beneath sleepless eyes, the pallor of the skin, the indifference to dress – shabby coats over discarded fashions – bitten nails, nervous gestures, the air of defeat.

A woman of about fifty is there with her son, perhaps thirty. With short fair hair, she is anxious and combative. Her son is tall with long dark hair, moustache, worn royal-blue cords, short tartan jacket. He worked in the pits until eighteen months ago, but gave up work when he began spitting blood. He was found to have ulcers, and has been in and out of hospital since then. He went on a government training scheme, but gave that up because of his illness and problems with his marriage. He eventually got work four months ago; but has just been laid off.

'Ten weeks ago I moved into a new council flat on my own. It has two bedrooms, but I've no furniture. Nothing. I can't even live there. I spent all the money I had decorating it, anaglypta, it looks really good. I didn't know I was going to lose my job; otherwise I would have bought some furniture first. I was only getting just over £60 a week anyway, that's including overtime, fifty-one hours a week. I have to pay £5 a week maintenance for my little boy. She had everything when we split up. I had to start off with nothing.'

His mother says that is one of the longest speeches she's ever heard him make. She explains: 'If they'd moved away from her mother, perhaps it would have been all right. They might have made a go of it. But her family, well, they didn't like him. They weren't too bad at the start; but somebody belonging to her mother knew my sister, and my sister had been a bit of a lass when she was younger. She like to enjoy herself and was a bit carefree. Anyway, that made them take against Brian. They said they didn't want anything to do with anybody from our family. It was ridiculous because my sister is settled down now. She's perfectly respectable, and anyway, that's got nowt to do with Brian. Well, he came back living with me, but he's a young man, he's got to be on his own. He wants to find somebody else and see if he can start again. I mean, I know he didn't have a very good example. I've been married twice and divorced twice. His father, to hear him, you'd have thought what a wonderful man he was. He spoke beautifully, to hear him talk you'd think he was a clergyman. But you should have tried living with him. We might go out occasionally on an evening, he'd say "We'll go up the club"; and we'd go and have a drink; then about half-past eight, he'd look round and say "I think that's enough, we'll be off home now." Well. His idea of a day out for the family was to go out visiting old ruins and castles, walking round old buildings. Who wants to do that on a day out? So we split up and I found somebody else. Trouble was, the next one seemed to be the opposite, only it turned out he was ten times worse. If I couldn't get the first one to come down to the club for a drink, this one couldn't get there fast enough; he practically lived there. So you see, Bri hasn't really had the best experience of what marriage should be.'

Brian said he didn't speak to his wife's mother for three years. 'Then, when I did, it was to have a row. I can't really say what I feel, I just lose my temper, and it shows. I had a visitor come from Social Security, but I couldn't tell them all the details of my life like. I couldn't tell her I'd left the pit because I was sick, and that I'd split up from my wife and she had everything so there was nothing. So the Social Security never gave me anything.

'I had to give up everything I'd bought for the flat when we separated. There was about £1500 worth of furniture. I'd tried to make a decent home. I haven't even seen my kid for two years. Now I'm getting Social Security, £29 a week; I wasn't working long enough to get the dole. Out of that I'm still paying maintenance, and I can't buy anything I need to live. What gets me is that my wife is back living with her mother. That was the trouble, she couldn't really leave her. And her brother and his girl-friend are living in our flat. So she's not even living there, all the stuff I paid for, what we built up the years we were together. But the building society doesn't care about that, as long as the mortgage is being paid in her name. She got custody of the little boy, and if she's going to live in the matrimonial home with the bairn it means she's entitled to keep everything. But she's not even there. I mean, it isn't fair that her brother should be using all my stuff.

'I've been back living with my Mam, but that's no good. Then when I got this flat, I fell out of work. All I've got is a bed.'

A young couple in their late twenties; he is wearing a threadbare grey suit. She has a thin pale face, is wearing an old leather coat, a green polo-neck jumper, and long platform boots creased with wear. Her fair hair is scraped back behind her ears, which makes her look small and waiflike. They are both in an emotionally volatile state; a kind of defeated anger in the man, while she breaks into tears as she talks. He nervously rolls cigarettes, one for himself and one for her from an old Three Castles tobacco tin.

While she was in hospital undergoing a major operation, he took their two children, six and four, to the house of a friend, where they could be properly fed and looked after. During that time their house was broken into and the gas meter robbed. It wasn't the first time the meter has been done; and the meter had been specially calibrated to take some of the arrears. Denise had had a gall bladder operation; and then a second operation to deal with recurring jaundice, which has still not cleared in spite of extensive surgery.

'I don't feel any better; and it's been five weeks since I came out of hospital,' she said. 'This afternoon I have to go back again to have a smear, and tests to see if it's cancer. Then last Friday they came and turned the gas off, so I've no heating, no hot water, nothing to cook with. They came without any proper warning, and there's nothing we can do. I've been walking the streets all day yesterday, trying to look for help. I came here on Monday and Tuesday, but there was such a long queue, I didn't think they'd ever get to my turn.

'I was cut all down here when they operated on me; all I want to do is get well so I can look after the bairns properly. I can't stand them looking at me and asking why they can't have a cup of tea or something warm to eat. We reported the gas break-in to the police; they came and took finger-prints. The Gas Board believe we did it you see, even though the police agree there was a break-in from outside. The police said there's been lot a meters done in our street; they've got this lad; they found him with a hundred quidsworth of 50p pieces in his pocket.

'I don't even blame the kids for breaking into places. They're so desperate; it's the only way they've ever got of making money. Whose fault is it they've nothing? No work, nothing to do. I'm sorry for them that they should have to come this low.

'I wouldn't go anywhere else but to this place. It's the only place where you get listened to. If it hadn't been for them before, I can tell you I would've done away with myself. I'm tret like a criminal just for going into hospital and having an operation. When I first went in to have the operation, I was so thin and run down they wouldn't let me have the operation. Not till I'd built myself up a bit, they said. I wasn't fit enough. What am I to build myself up on, when there's not even enough to feed my bairns properly?'

Her husband takes her hand in his; it looks pale and fragile against his. He takes over from her. 'I can't work with her being in and out of hospital; somebody's got to look after the children. What do they want us to do, let them go into care? Why can't they give us enough to pay our bills so we can at least keep warm? She's got to be kept warm, she feels the cold terrible with being ill. Why should she have to go to bed in the evening because that's the only place in the house she can get warm? That's why I don't blame these kids who've got no hope but roguing and thieving. The only trouble is, they do it to poor people, them who've got nothing anyway.

'It isn't the first time. The last time they messed all over the carpet and weed all over the chairs. It was disgusting. It was a horrible thing to come back to. Perhaps they thought we did that as well. As if I'd be sitting here now if I'd done it myself. The fellow who came to cut the gas off – even he said how sorry he was. He said we should try to get in touch with somebody from the Gas Board to have it stopped; but by the time we got through, it was three o'clock, and they said they couldn't do anything till after the weekend. Then we waited in all day Monday and nobody came.'

She holds a crumpled paper tissue in her hand and wipes it across her cheek. 'Since it happened, I've been with a friend. But the trouble is, they don't eat at regular hours so my bairns haven't been getting fed till seven or eight at night. Usually they go to bed at half-past six. So I've been doing all the cooking myself, for her family as well as my own. On Sunday I cooked dinner for sixteen people; there was twelve of them and us four. It's too much for me; only I feel I've got to offer to do it, to thank her for letting us use her stove. But I can't wash the bairns; they haven't been clean since before the weekend.'

After repeated calls to the Gas Board, the Gas Consumer Council and a solicitor, it appears that there may have been a breach of the code of practice, and there may be a case for suing the Gas Board. An appointment is made for them to see a solicitor that same afternoon. And the next morning they are promised that the gas will be turned on again.

'I can't go to the solicitor, I have to go to hospital. And then, we've left the children, they'll be worried. And then do you know what I did? Yesterday I thought "I'm never going to use gas again", I was that mad, I thought I'd use electricity; so I went to the second-hand shop and sold my cooker. I got £20 for it. But then when I went to buy a second-hand electric cooker, the cheapest there was £40. I've still got the £20, but they'll never sell me back my old cooker at the price they gave me for it.

'It's not fair. Why should they treat us like criminals when all you want to do is bring up your family a bit decent. Then they wonder why people can't bear it any longer, they end it all. Everything I've tried to do, there's always been something that's ruined it. I took a little job before Christmas last year, just for a few weeks in a restaurant, to give the kids a decent Christmas. But somebody must have shopped me. It must have been somebody who knew me, who saw me go out at the same time every morning. I noticed there was a bloke following me on the bus; he got off at the same stop that I did every day. He was always there. It gives you the creeps. Then they told me at the restaurant that somebody had been asking questions so I gave up the job; but they came and told me they knew I'd been working, and I had to give back every penny I'd had. I was only getting £6 a week above what I was allowed to, but I had to pay it all back. It's a good thing, isn't it, when they employ touts to spy on you; and you don't know which one of your friends or neighbours ditched you. I've found that the neighbours haven't been all they might have been since we've had this trouble. It makes you bitter. It makes you wonder what you have to do to be tret like a human being and not like some sort of delinquent. Do they think you don't suffer enough, not being able to give your children what they need, having to fight against illness, wondering if they're going to tell you you've got cancer? What's it all for? You have rows, you quarrel, you get bad-tempered with the bairns. Is that what they want to do – drive us apart, because that's what I've seen it come to with hundreds of families.'

Two women, one perhaps in her early thirties, and her sister, several years older. The younger is pale with long fair hair. She is seven months pregnant. Her sister is smarter with a close-fitting grey coat, and a ring on every finger. Both smoke nervously.

Mrs Harris, the younger one, has seven children; her eighth is due in the new year. There are so many things she needs from Social

Security, and she doesn't know what she is entitled to. She needs blankets. Social Security allow only two for each bed, even though it is a freezing day, and the house in which she lives is in a mouldering terrace, condemned, but roughly refurbished to prolong its use. It is a ruinous and ramshackle building; the draught comes through every window; there is no heating upstairs at all. Mrs Harris receives £30 a week from Social Security and £28.50 family allowance. She has been making 'voluntary savings' because the Social Security visitor advised her this was the best way to avoid debt for fuel, heating and tv licence. She cannot read or write. 'I thought I had to make voluntary savings. I thought it meant you had to.' This means that £4.50 are deducted at source, as well as the rent that is paid direct to the council. She says that the social worker no longer comes to see her now that she has managed to keep the house straight for some months. She is proud of this achievement, a sign of growing self-respect. She smiles shyly, a radiant smile that illuminates her face quite beautifully, and the girl she was not so long ago shines through the heavy flesh and pallor. 'It's terrible though where I live. I've had my window out nine times, with break-ins, kids playing football. Social Security paid twice, but after that they refused. I have to pay for it out of my own money. Some people do it with a bit of card or wood, but it looks terrible; and anyway, I'm afraid of being there on my own with just the kids. There's been a lot of break-ins.

'My husband left me. After ten years. He found another woman. After all that time I never dreamed he'd go and find somebody else. I have got five of his kids . . . I couldn't believe it. And he's not even bothered about seeing them. And then I've lived with this other bloke for five years, and he's done the same thing. Well, near enough – I told him to clear out. He was only coming home late at night, using the place as somewhere to sleep. I know it isn't easy for a man if there's seven kids at home, but he knew what he was taking on; and two of them are his and another in the new year.

'I don't like being on my own. It hurts me that I can't give the children all the things I'd like to. While they're at school, it's all right; they stay at school for their dinners. I only have to get their tea. But in the holidays, I dread it. It's the time you should look forward to, but it's an uphill struggle just to feed them.

'I go to bingo once a fortnight; that's my only outing. I leave the oldest boy to look after the little ones. My sister lives next door;

she's the only one I bother with. I don't have much to do with anybody else. She'll come in sometimes and keep me company in the evenings. It's a nightmare in winter, keeping warm.

'They've none of them ever had a holiday, my kids. Seaburn, that's as far as they've been. I don't hope for anything for myself. My life, well, that's it as far as I'm concerned, but I do hope for better things for my kids. I don't want them to grow up poor. I worry about their future. I lay awake, wondering if it'll be a struggle for them as well. Will there be work, what kind of a world will it be for them to grow up into?'

Just as there is something immediately recognizable in the clothing of the long-term unemployed, so there is about their homes – a subtly corrosive quality. Mr Grice has been out of work for three years. The hall of his flat is cavernous and empty. There is no light bulb in the hall because they use as little electricity as possible. As you open the front door, it strikes colder than the street. The recent milder weather hasn't reached the inside of the house, and your breath condenses. The walls, painted chocolate brown, look damp and sticky. In the living-room, four children sit round a gas-fire, which is never turned quite as high as it should be for them to keep warm; and they all wear a thick jersey or a coat so that they look as if they're all about to go out. A little girl clutches a bottle of cherry-coloured cough syrup, which she shows proudly to visitors, because having a cough distinguishes her from the others. The walls of the flat are dingy: the cheapest council wallpaper, marked and greasy to the level which the youngest two can reach; the faint pattern of sedges and rushes is half effaced. The light bulb is only forty watts; and its shade of a brownish parchment is dusty and limits the light even further. The curtains are of a threadbare pinkish material, not quite meeting across the windows, and the sodium street-lamp can be seen through them. The metal window-frames are rusty with condensation, which stains the cream paint and runs in rust-coloured channels onto the window-ledge.

The children are reading a pile of comics which have fallen apart, passed round so often that it is impossible to find the continuation of any story; the detached cover of one of the comics lies on the floor – a picture of a green and red ape-like figure with an eye gouged out. The three-piece is covered in red Rexine, but it is scratched and dingy, and the buttons have come off the back; the dark-red cushions are discoloured and their threads loose. The little girl, as she reads her comic, plucks at the nylon threads with a half-bitten finger-nail.

There is a second-hand carpet, perhaps thirty years old, with a faded ricrac pattern in dark-green and orange, almost effaced in places. The television, which is also very old, with a faintly blackened screen, is heavy and bulky, and it has stopped working. This makes life more difficult; Mrs Grice says she didn't realize how much she depends on the television. The hardest thing for her is to decide what they shall do without each day, and whose turn it is to make some kind of rotating sacrifice – clothes, food, warmth. Not everything is available for all the family at the same time.

The sense of shabbiness in the houses of today's poor is different from the shabbiness of the houses of the old poor, those interiors of long-term poverty where things outlasted the people who used them. Those houses – and there are still some to be found in Sunderland – have been subject to a different kind of wear – the brass can still be cleaned, the Windsor chairs are solid, the rag-rug doesn't wear out; the chenille fades and grows dusty, but the great metal Victorian ornaments keep their dignity somehow. But in the newer places, the Rexine splits and the bright ornaments of only two or three years ago look worn – the opalescent punch set, with its coral plastic cups hanging round the bowl, the dyed dried grasses, the glass fish, the storm lamp with its panels of frosted plastic. The gauzy runner along the sideboard becomes inexplicably dingy; the picture of the Creation with Adam and Eve looking like Tarzan and Jane, she standing up to her navel in water, seems to lose its colour; the electronic game from Texas doesn't work; the instrument assembled in Taiwan has fallen to pieces; the bright-blue carpet is splashed with tea and coffee stains and has been walked almost black by the front door; the plastic chairs sway when you sit down on them, the metal is stained and corroded, the artificial flowers have lost their colour. It is so different from the old glass-fronted cabinets with their arrangement of Coronation and Jubilee china, the hearthrug made by Mam one long winter out of patches of wornout clothes, the stylized pictures in their dusty gilt frames – 'After the Battle' or the 'Stag at Bay'. The very setting in which poverty is lived through has changed: there is a feeling of impermanence, an absence of continuity which makes it worse, in which everything swiftly gets used up and needs to be replaced; and if it cannot be replaced becomes repelling and oppressive, whereas those old living-places, stuffy parlours or chaotic back-kitchens, were not comfortless in quite the same way. Even the food was different – the stew with its neck of lamb and three penn'orth of pot-herbs was not the same as the Colonel Sanders chicken in its red cardboard box and the saffron gravy in the tinfoil from the takeaway. The open fire was a living comfort, the old boots warming in the hearth and the lore and pictures in the flames had a consoling influence which the underfloor heating which cannot be regulated does not. Everything about these poor homes now is provisional and impermanent; not homes at all, many of them, but places of brief sojourn in which everybody seems to be on a list waiting for a transfer. Places, it seems, into which violence and cruelty can gain easy admittance; where parents, helpless and impotent, can so easily strike the screaming child; where the fragility of relationships between adults seems to mirror the lack of durability of all the used-up objects in the house; and people wear out their love for each other as readily as they do last year's fashions. And the story they tell is all about who moved in with some woman in the next block, whose husband pissed off with some tart he picked up down the club, who left her old man because he was having it off with some bint where he worked, who followed her husband to his girl-friend's flat one night and stabbed her with a carving knife, and whose kids had to go into care till she could get somewhere to live with some bloke she picked up who came down from Scotland. Through it all runs a thread of despair for which people see no remedy; a shaming, a disgracing of our deepest human attachments. Husbands and wives, parents and children, brothers and sisters fall apart in their discovery that there are no shared purposes, no collective projects – just individual destinies pursuing their lonely trajectory through time. This is where you can feel the pain of what has been taken away from people and see the scars of the relationships that have been broken; the amputated capacity to care is as obvious as the stump of a severed limb.

9

From the Thirties to the Eighties 3: Lancashire

Parts of Lancashire have lived with the decline of their basic industries through most of the twentieth century. Orwell's rage at the conditions in which people lived and worked contrasts sharply with the rather melancholy calm with which those same people look back on those times. And although there is almost no trace of the circumstances Orwell was recording, many people seem not to rejoice in the changes that have taken place.

Mr Cansdale is sixty-nine; a small white-haired man with deep-brown eyes. He lives in the centre of Wigan, alone since his wife died. He has kept the house just as it was while his wife was living, with their collection of teapots in the kitchen, and the marital bed turned down just as it was all the years they were together.

In the hearth he places an old piece of Donkey Brand whitestone, with which they used to clean the floor, and his mining clogs, hard leather with metal caps and metal around the sole, rusty now from twenty years' lack of use. Mr Cansdale is partly incapacitated now and seldom goes out. A few years ago he bought some sugar that had been poisoned by a workman who had a grudge against the sugar company. He remembered finding bluish grains in the sugar, but having been brought up frugally he didn't think this was sufficient reason to throw it away. It was cyanide. He was taken ill, rushed to hospital, and it was found that his bowel had rotted and had to be removed. 'I was given up for dead. They told my wife I'd only a week or two left. I was fourteen months in hospital. My wife died when I was convalescent. She was all right when she came to visit me on the Sunday afternoon; by the Monday evening she was dead. I don't know how I survived. It must have been the way we were brought up.

'I was born in July 1914; my father was killed when I was three. I can just remember him; I can remember these big strong arms round me in bed, and him leaning over me. I was the youngest of four. My father was a fine man; he was regimental sergeant-major; and stood 6 ft 4 in. My brother Walt took after him. Our Walt was the strongest man in Wigan. He once beat the champion Hackenschmidt in a weight-lifting contest. In 1928. Hackenschmidt lifted 370 lbs, our Walt lifted 375 lbs.

'When my father was killed, my mother married again. My stepfather was out of work, so mother had to give her little house up and went to live with my grandmother in a back-to-back house on the Billinge Road, on top of a stone quarry, number 8 Schofield's Houses. Them days, they called the houses after their owners. There was one up and one down; and in that house there was our Willy – he was my first stepbrother, me, Maggie, Walt, Joe, mother, stepfather, grandmother, Auntie Nellie, Auntie Maggie and Uncle Bill. Next door was the Gilligan family. Gilligan was crippled with arthritis through working in the pit up to his knees in water. There were twelve of them. They were the first family in Wigan to get a council house; they beat us by half an hour.

'I enjoyed every minute we lived in that one-up, one-down house. The stones had to be done with whitestone then sanded down. In the bedroom there were four beds; in one bed there was me, Walt, Joe and Willy; then grandma and Auntie Nellie in another; our Bill had a little bed in the corner – and he used to read in bed and had a small table completely covered in candle grease; and then Maggie had a little single-bed up the other corner. You could just squeeze between the beds. My mother and stepfather had a bed on the landing. There was no gas or electricity in the house. We had an oil-lamp hanging from the ceiling. We had no bedclothes, just jackets and old army coats. My grandmother had a patchwork quilt that she'd made. There was a tap and a sink in the living-room. Under the stairs was the coal-place. My grandma had a great big witch's pan that she used as a washpan; she used to boil the water in it for the dolly-tub. Where we lived, a lot of people had pens at the back of the houses, where they kept a pig. When I got a bit older, I found out you didn't get a penny for the pictures by skriking for it, so I went round collecting potato pillings for these pigs, and I'd get a penny.

'My mother couldn't pay her doctor's bills. There was a chap – they called him Johnny Blood – came round collecting for the doctor. They called him Johnny Blood because it was his job to get blood out of a stone. He collected sixpence a week; but he didn't often get it. One week he was sick, and the doctor came himself. Of course mother had no money. He spied a book *Culpeper's Herbal.*' Mr Cansdale reaches down a first edition of Culpeper, pale-coloured drawings of herbs and wild flowers, a bit specked with mould, but in good condition. 'Here it is. It had been in the family I dunno how long; and she wouldn't let him have it. It was one of two valuable things she had; I'll tell you about the other later. She wouldn't part with it. Anyway, time went on, and the doctor's bill got bigger and she got poorer. The bill stood at £32. Well, she knew she was never going to be able to pay; it was at the time of the '26 strike. So the doctor told her he'd straighten out all she owed him for this book. So she let him have it. And do you know, when the doctor died, it was about fourteen years later, a chap came round from the solicitor's office and he told my mother that the doctor had left instructions in his will for that book to be returned to her.

'Well, the other valuable thing was a picture. It was called 'The Light of the World', and it now hangs in the National Gallery. During the unemployment, my mother borrowed some money from a relative; but she was only allowed the money on condition that they'd get this picture when mother died. Now where my mother got this and that Culpeper book I don't know; whether it was through being in service, or whether they'd been well-to-do at one time o'er, I'm not sure. Anyway, Auntie Nellie had this picture when my mother died. She had a chip shop; it was through what they made in this shop that they started lending money. She's supposed to have sold this picture for £20,000, and with the money she set herself up in a big boarding-house in Blackpool. Of course, it passed through many hands before it finished up where it is now.

'My grandma was a washerwoman. She used to wash for the two biggest butchers in Wigan, all the blood-stained aprons and everything. The laundry couldn't get the stains out, but she could. She washed for them every day of the week until she was eighty-five. My grandma and Auntie Nellie used to walk arm in arm every night down to the pub to get a bottle of Guinness; and Auntie Nellie looked older than grandma. Auntie Nellie had started work down the pit when she was twelve, drawing a basket of coal on her hands and knees.

'I've come home from school many a time, and my mother's been sat in the chair with her head in her hands, crying because she'd nothing to give us for our tea. I've known her cut a single piece of dry bread in four pieces, one for each of us. She used to go round the big houses, "Can I mop your steps?" She'd keep them clean for 2*d* a week. She suffered from the years of self-neglect, going days without anything to eat herself. She died at forty-two, still worrying over her bills and expenses, wondering how she was going to pay them. In the 1921 strike, we lived on treacle butties, breakfast, dinner, and tea. I've skriked all morning on Saturday for a penny to go to the pictures; but you can't take a stocking off a bare leg.

'I started pony-driving down the pit when I were thirteen, Pemberton Colliery. Then I went to Owd Nat's colliery; called after Nathaniel Eckersley who owned it. But that colliery finished in 1929 when I was fifteen. They closed the pit at a moment's notice. They were working on a day-to-day contract; and on the Friday night they just said "That's it"; they just cut the cable, let the cage fall to the bottom, left all the machinery inside and left it to ruin. Just like that.

'My father, Walt, Joe and me, we all worked together at first. Father got the wages; the collier got paid for everything. The under-manager took you on; after that you belonged to the collier. Joe went in the army; Walt went away in what they called "the gold rush". The new pits in Yorkshire were paying £4 a week, twice what you could get here, no matter how hard you worked. When Walt came home, he had a £5 note in his pocket. Nobody in Wigan had ever seen one of them. But there was a big explosion at the pit, Maltby Mesnes in 1931, and Walt came home; I started with him at the Victoria pit. We got on champion there. A new coal seam had started. When they started, the fireman and the under-manager came to watch you get the coal, find out the conditions, see how hard it was, then they'd fix your price.

'Well, it was very hard coal, so they fixed it at 4*s* 5¾*d* a ton. After about two weeks, ten yards in, it went as soft as anything, and we were filling fifty or sixty tubs a day and making £6 or £7 a week. That lasted a tidy while. But we were sacked. A new under-manager came. He thought "Get baht these two and get some of my lads in their place." He got us sacked. They used to blow the kench, that's the roof of the tunnel, to make it higher; and one day, they'd done this, the night-shift had blown the kench, and left ten or fifteen ton of dirt in the road we had to go through to get the coal. The fireman said "You'll have to shift it." Well, we were on piece-work, according to the weight of the coal. "It'll tek all day to shift that." "Well you can do it or go whoam." The fireman gave us two envelopes. That was our dismissal note and cards.

'They said at the pit we'd sacked ourselves. The chaps they put in our place, they dropped the price to 2*s* 3*d* a ton. I worked at one time over in every pit in Wigan. At that time you got 17*s* on the dole, 9*s* for a single man. If you wanted work, you had to go and wait in the queue at the pit-head. The under-manager used to come and look at you, and if he wanted somebody, he'd say "You, you and you". They inspected you. I was little; I got took on when there was low tunnels. In one place I worked there was a lad, he blew his own head off. He had worries, work and money. He put some powder in his mouth, and the detonator and set it off.

'My great-grandfather was a sheep-farmer at Coniston. But his son, my grandfather, there wasn't work for him; he came with his six sons and two daughters to the pits in Wigan. That was in 1885. They lived in Peter's Yard. All the lads went working in the pit. Two of them, including my father, died in the War.

'I'll tell you how we survived the thirties. Walt married an Irish girl, and he lived in the same row where I was with my wife. Every Sunday after breakfast me and my wife, Walt and Greta – they called her Greta because she looked like Greta Garbo – we got ready and went for a walk round these fields. Walt used to take his dog, Spot. One Sunday, Spot just vanished as we were going along. Walt shouted "Spot, Spot". But there was no sign of him. We looked; we couldn't see anything, but then we heard this faint yapping. Walt got down on his hands and knees and said "Oh, he'll be down a rabbit hole." Then we could hear a lot of scratching and this dog barking. Then Walt said "Come and look at this, there's coal down here." I don't know if you know, but coal goes reddish if it's been standing donkey's years, and there was this surface; but underneath the coal was shining. So Walt gets down and he finds it's an old pit-tunnel. He says we must come back with some pit-lamps and have a look. So later on, we go back. And there's coal on both sides. We walk towards Orrell, and there's a big heap of dirt from a roof fall. Walter lights this rag, and he throws it into the dirt and it burns champion. He throws one the other side, and that burns as well, so we know there's no gas to be feared of. I goes towards the fall, and there's a bucket standing there. I shouts "There's a bucket here", but as I go to pick it up it falls to dust; it had rotted all away with standing there all those years.

'We examine the tunnel. One side goes to Orrell, the other towards Standish. All the roof is pure coal as well. So me and Walt decide to fetch our tools and get some coal out. We got our picks and started picking at the coal. We filled two bags straight away. The first night we filled six bags. We went back; then we kept on going back, every night.

'We had an arrangement with the landlord of the White Lion; we sold him coal for 8*d* a bag, and he sold it for a shilling. It lasted three years. We used to work this coal at night. We would fill the bags, and at the price we could sell them for, we couldn't get enough. Of course, we soon came to a snag. We got to a place where the layer of coal that we left on top as a roof all caved in, and it left our little mine open to the sky. The first thing we needed was props to stop the rest of it falling in. In those days, everybody had wireless poles in the gardens for the aerials, big tall ones they were. So we went round at night, pinching these wireless masts, and sawing them up to make props for our pit. Everybody round the district was talking about all these wireless poles that had been pinched; nobody could figure out why anybody'd want to take things like that.

'We knew that a bobby on a bike went by at ten o'clock; then he never came again until five in the morning; so we had seven hours to work in. And we did work. We put some pieces of plywood covering the hole where the roof had fallen; and on top of it we arranged all the sods as a camouflage so it looked like part of the field, just leaving a hole big enough for us to get in and out of. Every night, after we'd finished, we covered up where we'd been working, we didn't leave a trace. And so it went on for three years. Till one night, we go to this pit, I think we took nine bags of coal out that night. But while we were in the pit, there was a big snowstorm. We put back our camouflage all right, but what we never thought of was that our bikes were leaving tracks in the snow. I expect the farmers had been wondering why their fences had been disappearing – we needed more pit-props as we advanced underground; and one of them must have followed the cycle tracks in the snow back to where we'd been working. We didn't go back for a day or two because of the weather; and when we did we found that whoever had discovered our pit had been to Orrell council, and the council had filled it up with rubbish. It was all destroyed, all broken down and filled in.

'The Heinz factory covers the site where our little pit was. But it served us well for three years. It helped us get on our feet in those terrible times. We made a small fortune.'

It is only now that the old working-class way of life is almost extinct that the feelings of those who lived it begin to emerge. Orwell, for all the power of his observation of the social and working conditions, came nowhere near the relationships and affections of the poor. Indeed, this was not his intention, and neither would it have been possible. The deeper feelings, the anguish and private pain were part of the great reservoir of secrets which the working class kept, and which made it appear slightly less than human and very threatening to the rich. That these secrets can now all be told is a measure of the change that has taken place in working-class life. It is part of the process of emptying the rich cistern of working-class experience. Mr Cansdale spoke of his life in a way that opens up more of that closed past, which, after all, has become the stuff of much oral and Labour history. But we shouldn't delude ourselves. The reason why it can be disclosed now is because of the broken continuity, because it is no longer transmitted to children and grandchildren as part of living experience. It can still inspire and move the Labour movement, but not in an organic and living way. It is a precipitate of experience, which has an almost religious function in the present. All the rhetoric about keeping faith indicates as much, the homage to those 'learning from their experience and leaving others to distil that experience and to use it again to advance the cause.' (Tony Benn, *Arguments for Socialism*.)[29] It can't be used again; but it can inspire, which is at the same time the tragedy and the hope of the Labour movement.

Mr Cansdale continued: 'My father was killed on the Marne in 1917 when he was forty. He was shot by his own men. The way it happened was this. There was a big battle, a big attack coming off. The commanding officer wanted volunteers to put on the uniforms of captured German officers and go behind the German lines and listen and get to know all they could about the attack. The various companies were asked for men who could speak German. Well, in the Manchesters, my father was the only man who could understand German. There had been an old man where he lived who'd married an English girl and they kept a shop in our street; and my father had taken the trouble to learn German and talk to this man.

'So it was agreed my father should go and pick up any information he could, wearing this uniform. He had arranged a password for when he came back, so he should be recognized and not thought to be a real German officer. And the password was "Hände hoch". If he was challenged, he was to say this, and they would know who he was.

'He went into the German lines; what information he got was never discovered. When he comes back, he reaches his own trenches without being challenged, and as he approaches his own company, there's a piece of open ground he has to cross. There was a sergeant there, named Mick Brennan. He had been sleeping while the conference had been going on about penetrating the German lines. And when my father said the password "Hände hoch", he thought he was a German. And he ordered the men who were with him to fire. There were seventeen of them. And that was how my father was killed. He got seventeen bullets from his own men.

'Of course I grew up knowing nothing of this. One day, I'm working down the pit, I'm twenty-nine or thirty, and I'm working overtime, and one afternoon we miss the bus home. I'm walking it home with the lampman who lived not far from me. And he said "I've heard my fayther talk about thi' fayther. I don't know if tha knows or not, but his own men shot him." I said "I didn't know till thee told me." I knew that my father had been buried with full military honours, but nothing of what this lampman told me was in the cutting my mother had kept from the *Wigan Observer*. So when this man told me, I went to my Auntie Cissie and asked her, and she said it was all true.

'Well time goes on; then I'm about forty, my son is seven or eight. My wife had a job in the hospital, and she was friendly with a woman who she worked with, and me and her and her friend and her husband – Toff we called him – used to go and have a drink on Saturday night. One weekend we'd been with them to Swinley Labour Club, and at turning out time they said would we come round their house the next night, the Sunday. "Our Bill has his birthday on Monday, and the same day him and his wife are flitting from Wigan, so we're making a night of it." So we said we'd go.

They lived down Wigan Lane, Toff and his wife, Bill, that was his son and his wife Ann. So we came out of Swinley Labour Club with some bottles of beer for a drink; and when we come to this house, there's a fair few other people there; it's a proper party going on. I saw one man I knew well, and he asked me how I was going on, and I said "Champion" and asked after him and his family. Now, in the corner there's an old man reading a newspaper. It's Ann's father. And the minute he heard me speak, he dropped his paper and looked at me. And suddenly, he gets up, and he bursts out crying, and he's all shaking and trembling from head to foot. He comes running over to me, and he kneels down in front of me and he starts saying "I'm sorry, I'm sorry. It was all my fault, it was me who shot thee, and tha's come back to haunt me. I'm sorry, I'm sorry." He's at my feet, stammering and shaking, he says "Tha's Charlie Cansdale and tha's come back to haunt me. I never meant it." And it turned out it was this Sergeant Brennan; he was Ann's father, the man who'd given the order to the soldiers to shoot their own man, my father. He'd never said owt to anybody all these years. He thought I was my Dad, because although we weren't the same size, they always said I looked and sounded like him.

'I didn't know what to do or say. He were in a terrible state, very distressed and upset. I had to say to him I'm not a ghost, I'm Charlie Cansdale's son. It was a dreadful experience. The only person I've ever told that story to is my son because it chokes me up to think of it. That this man had gone round with this terrible feeling on his conscience; and he kept asking me to forgive him.

'And that poor old man, he was flitting with his daughter and Bill the next day to Southport. And they did, they went on the Monday, and the very next day, on the Tuesday, he died. It was as if he'd been living all those years just to get it off his chest. It had really been on his mind, preying on his thoughts all those years. And once he'd got it off his mind, it was as if he could die in peace.

'My Auntie Cissie, she tells this story about my father's death. I don't know what to make of it, but anyway . . . During the black-out in the First War, old Billy Blowflat used to come round to make sure they'd all got the black-out up properly; they called him Billy Blowflat because he had a great big belly. He always went round to make sure no gaslight or anything was showing. Anyway, he'd just been, and there came a knock to the door this neet, and my mother said "Who can it be?" And she went, and it was a gipsy selling flowers, a penny a bunch – paper flowers. My mother felt sorry for her, and she would have bought some, but she only had a penny in her purse – and it was an old black penny she kept for luck. So she calls up to Auntie Cissie and Auntie Beatie to see if they had a penny; but neither of them did. So she offered this black penny to the gipsy. But the gipsy drew back. "I can't take that," she said. But she gave my mother a bunch of the flowers, and she said to her "If you ever spend that penny, you'll spend your husband's life with it." So my mother kept it, she never spent it. Then one night, some months later, they were all sat there, and the gas started begging; and my mother was up to her neck in jobs that needed doing, she'd got to have light for them. So she thought to herself, "I've only got that black penny." But she thought she could put it in the meter. It wouldn't be like spending it at all because when the gasman came to empty the meter, she could get it back from him, give him another one in exchange. So she put this black penny in the meter. And the next day – that was the day she got the news that my father had been killed. According to my Auntie Cissie that meant he had been killed the night she'd put the black penny into the meter.

'Growing up hard, it made us tough, but not insensitive. There's nothing I can't stand, no pain or privation I can't put up with. All the years in the pit, the unemployment, illness, injury, I've never been frightened. I've always trusted to providence. I used to be a boxer till I got my arm smashed in the pit.' He rolls up his sleeve; the arm is thinner than the other one, withered and scarred. 'I got this arm nabbed between iron props. It was hanging right off. I was carrying it in my other hand. It took three years to mend. I've never complained about any hardship. They were the circumstances of your life, you had them to put up with.'

Mr Travis is seventy. He lives in Lower Ince, a council estate that has been built on the edge of ruined terraces that are falling down through age and subsidence. His house has a large garden: bluebells and wallflowers have just finished flowering, aquilegia and delphiniums are just coming into bloom. Inside, there is a big coal-fire blazing. A man in his thirties, Mr Travis's son, is just home from work; he sits at the table eating his tea – a pork chop and baked beans; Mr Travis is resting on the sofa in a corner of the room. He has had two heart attacks and has lost the sight of one eye. His glasses magnify the eyes, so that the impression is of a blue swimming colour behind them. Mrs Travis sits in an old rocking-chair: she is a beautiful elderly woman with a soft face, the ghost of a hairstyle from the 1930s, warm, welcoming. Mr Travis is not so well today; but he sits up and rallies as he talks; the old vibrancy and power seem to come back with remembering; but his wife looks at him anxiously, urging him not to overdo it.

Mr Travis was a miner all his working life, in spite of years of unemployment in the thirties. But he would have liked to be what is now called a graphic designer, what might then have been a sign-writer. He takes down a notebook in which he has practised every imaginable kind of calligraphy and lettering. He has copied pages of quotations from the *Wigan Observer*, fragments from famous writers and pieces of traditional wisdom, as well as various commercial logos all executed with minute care and skill.

He started work in Worsley Mesnes pit when he was thirteen; but the pit closed soon after he started. 'They just stopped the pit, closed it. There was my father, me and my brother working there. We'd all done a full week, and they just announced Friday, at one o'clock, that the pit was closing. They left everything behind, all the machinery, even the coal we'd been cutting that week. They just cut the ropes, left it where it was.' Mr Travis's son says 'They wouldn't have cared even if they'd left some of the men down there with it.'

'That was my first taste of the dole. We had to go to the chapel to sign on then. On Fridays the dole queue stretched right along the road, five or six deep, and they'd keep us standing there till nine o'clock at night, and even then you wouldn't get paid. You had to go and start again on Saturday morning.

'The dole clerks used to give you a card to take to places looking for jobs, and you had to get this card signed by the manager to prove that you had tried for the job. But when you got there, the jobs had always gone, even if they had been there in the first place. Every pit-yard you went to, there'd be fifty or 100 men. Some of the under-managers would be afraid to come up and face them because they could be in quite a rough mood; they were afraid they might get mobbed. But some of them used to come up and feel your muscles. Once in 1931, I went with my pal, a big-built lad, to see if we couldn't get a job at one pit. There were fifty or sixty of us. The under-manager came up. "Get back, get back," he said, and went round feeling people's calves and muscles and picking out those he wanted. He picked two others and myself, took us to his office, and we thought we were sure of a job. We went back next day, and there were fifty men again. Once again he picked out three of us; and it turned out there was no job anyway. It was just his bit of fun.

'I got on with my father working at Eden Green pit. I don't know if you know, but when they put a road through a gradient of coal, they do it so one way you have to go uphill with the coal, and the other way you go downhill with it. The lower side was harder work, and the control of the air was difficult; but you had one advantage – there was little or no gas there. It was the higher side where the gas accumulated; and that's what happened one night when I was working with my father. It was 1932; ten past two in the morning. There was a sudden thud, like a big hammer it sounded, and it seemed to shudder through you, like a deep vibration; you felt it with your whole body. My father threw his tools down. "Come on lad." We were working in just our shorts, so we grabbed our clothes. He said "Never mind the tools." We weren't allowed to travel on the main haulage, that was for the coal. I said "We shall get done," he said "Come on, come on." He knew there'd been an explosion on the higher side. We got out, and we hung about waiting to see what happened. It was about half-past five; the fireman came and asked if we would come and help identify the thirty-two men who'd been trapped. That was terrible. I can see it yet. We went into this place where they'd laid out all the bodies. It was like looking at tomatoes that had boiled in their own skin; it was horrible.

'We were on the dole again in 1933. Then the dole ran out and you had the Means Test. To get the UAB you practically had to beg for it. When the Means Test men were on their way, the word went round the district. They did cause resentment. You were afraid to let your neighbours know if you had anything a little bit extra, people were encouraged to report on each other. Mostly, they didn't, but there was always the few who would.'

'The woman who lived next door to us,' broke in Mrs Travis, 'she used to wheel out an old man in a chair once a day; he'd had a stroke or something, and he used to give her half a crown a week for that. Somebody reported her to the Means Test and she had her money stopped.'

'They always asked if you had any relatives as could help, aunties and uncles,' Mr Travis said. 'They more or less forced people apart. It broke families up. I was married on the dole. I was getting twenty-nine shillings a week for myself, the wife and the first child; and yet they wanted me to pay four shillings a week out of that towards supporting my father and mother. It got you so frightened, you daredn't let your right hand know what your left was doing.

'I had spasms on and off work. I went looking. Wherever there was new building going on, you could sometimes get taken on; but then there'd be some Irishmen brought over and they'd do it cheaper, so they'd sack us. I was on the Means Test till 1938. Then I got a railway job; they were building new signal boxes. But that stopped when war broke out. I did ARP work, and went about all over the country. I was in Coventry the night it burned. After that I gave over. I thought "I'll go back to the pit. I might as well snuff it near home than miles away if I've got to go."'

Mrs Travis took up their story: 'We had three boys. At one time when we were on the parish, we were getting twenty-five shillings a week. Sometimes you got a food voucher for 7*s* 6*d*. My mother and father helped me pay the rent and an occasional bag of coal, but you durstn't let them know. I used to make a rag-rug for the hearth. I'd made one of these one Christmas time. A neighbour came in just as I were finishing it off. She said "Ee, that's nice, will you let me buy it?" Well, it was Christmas, I thought it'd be the chance to get a bit extra for the children. I let her have it and she gave me £3. Well, when I went for my money that week, there was none for me. I was given a time to face the board in the afternoon. When I went in they told me somebody had wrote in saying I was making rugs and selling them. They wanted me to account for every penny of that £3. Well, I'd bought a new jersey for each child, and underwear for the winter. And being Christmas, I can remember exactly what I'd done with the money. I'd bought a plastic aeroplane, a plastic sailing boat and a plastic submarine, an orange and an apple each and a ½*d* bar of chocolate to put in their stockings. And do you know what they said to me? "Them were things they could very well manage without." That made me very bitter. That hurt me more than anything else.

'There have been times when I've not had a butty in the house. Once, my mother brought us some strawberries for us teas. And the man from the parish came just as we were eating them. There were four saucers, and each one had four strawberries on it, with just a little sugar and the top of the milk. This man, he looks at our tea, and he says "My word, we don't give you money for luxuries like strawberries." What can you say? "They're for our tea, I've not bought them"; but the rage and the humiliation, it chokes you up. And the strawberries, they tasted like ashes after that.

'The old folks durstn't go to the picture palace because they would be watched by the Means Test men. There was a balcony, and the Means Test man would go up this balcony and watch the people come in to see if there was anybody they recognized who was on relief. So people used to say "We'll have to wait till it comes dark before we can go in"; and then they had to leave before the picture finished so as not to get caught. It made you bitter; but everybody was fixed the same way.

'I was the youngest but one of eight children. I was a pit-brow lass when I went to work. There was a layer of dirt in the coal-seam, and they didn't bother with it down the pit; but they used to tipple it all down a chute at the pit-head, and there'd be women at either side picking out the coal from among the dirt as fast as they could; and the piles of dirt went into these waggons and then were thrown onto the waste-tip. You wore black aprons and clogs and black stockings and men's jackets. You stood there whatever the weather, snow and rain, just the same; the machinery never changed its speed. I got rheumatic fever through doing it. After the dirt was sorted, we had to rook all the coal, stack it all up. But even then, working in the dirt and the weather, there was some bonny lasses among us. Once, they mistook me for the Cotton Queen when I went to a dance. They were expecting her, and when I walked in they all clapped.'

She takes out an old photograh from her album, and wipes it with her fist, as though effacing the years; and although she is still a handsome woman, she really was lovely then, and a bit sad too. Her husband looks at her tenderly, and says 'I knew how to pick a good 'un.'

Mr Travis recalled the General Strike and after. 'In the '26 strike, there was a lot of hardship. A large number of people never really recovered from it before the slump started. They fetched blacklegs to work in the pit where we were then. All the miners'd be there booing them when they fetched them out of the pit. But nobody set a hand on them; there was no violence. Not till one day, a motor-van went down Queen Street with a load of special police they'd drafted in for some reason. They said they'd heard there was to be some attempt to stop these blacklegs. And, of course, a crowd gathered; and the police went among them. They ran after them with their truncheons out and started bashing everybody in reach. Woman and children, women carrying babies, they were all smashed on the head, old people – anybody who was in their road. The police even ran into shops where people was being served and laid about them. That day there were people injured, maimed for life. Some of them never went to any doctor because they didn't know if they'd be accused of starting trouble. They used to call the old chief constable Kaiser Bill. He looked a bit like him, moustache and all.

'If you ever had occasion to go and see the pit-manager, you had to go home and wash and change before he'd see you. He sat in his office; and there was a carpet with a pattern on it. There was a line on this pattern, and your toe had not to go one fraction of an inch over that line. I once had to go and see him, and I went with my pit-clogs on. I went plonking in; he nearly fell out of his chair. "How dare you come in here with those things on? Go home and put some shoes on." "I can't." "You can't?" "I've no shoes to put on, and I'm not coming here barefoot."

'They used to think more of a pit pony than they did of the men. But then they had to buy a new pony if they needed one. Them pit ponies, some of them were only three feet high, but they could make men sit down and cry like a child, if they got awkward, if they wouldn't budge or wouldn't go the road you wanted them to. They could open your tommy-tin faster than you could if you left it lying around – you know the tommy-tin, like two metal parts that fitted into each other. And you had a can with your drink in it with a flat-top lid, a two- or three-quart can. The pony could knock that can over and sup up your drink before you knew what had happened. And if your lamp went out and you had no light, you were lost; but those ponies would know exactly where to go to their place, and then you had to depend on them.'

Mr Travis's son, Victor, works in a factory. He is at great pains to distance himself from the conditions described by his parents. He repeats ironically 'The good old days,' when they talk of their past. 'It's all different now; it'll never come again, all that.' And yet he has more similarities with his father than he recognizes. We go upstairs to his room. The walls are covered with his drawings and paintings, drawings of locomotives in crayon, biro, pencil; and fantasy pictures of outer space. He has hundreds of books, mostly paperbacks, especially science fiction, witchcraft, the occult; he too is a gifted and intelligent man; but he has something of the obdurate independence of the earlier generation. All his creativity and interests are private, almost secret. It is difficult not to feel that with some training and more exchange with others his life could be much expanded; in many ways, he seems to be as much a victim of contemporary circumstances as his father was in his time: he has failed to realize his skills and abilities just as his father did. He goes down into the greenhouse, and brings in a cactus to show his mother: a tiny terra cotta pot, with a spiky leaf and a perfect tiny rose-coloured flower.

10
Bolton 1981

From the hills surrounding Bolton the dominating shapes on the skyline are unchanged – the cupola of the town hall, the towers of churches, the rectangular mass of mills, the black cylinders of chimneys. At a distance everything seems to express the lasting function of the town, and its semi-metropolitan status among the industrial towns and villages of the North-west. But close up you can see than many of the older buildings have been transformed – mills into garages and warehouses, churches into stores or car showrooms. Many of the streets are in the process of being cleared; a few old people stand out harshly against the red rubble: an old man on his way to the shop for a basinful of chips and peas; an old woman in carpet slippers wanders among the ruins; she is picking up brick after brick and then discarding them as though looking for something that has been absorbed by them.

On the roads that led from the town centre many of the shops are scruffy and second-hand: Pam's House Clearances, as though she were doing people a favour, with the crinkly china vases, the kind of furniture that defies even sentimental attachments, the old leather suitcases full of family photographs – a sad spurned heritage spilt among the dust and flies of a mud-spattered shop window. The butcher's shop, with its notice that civility and cleanliness are its motto, speaks of a time when shopkeepers were perhaps characterized by roughness and dirt. Some of the mid-Victorian streets still surround the mills, giant palaces of production, many of them now gutted, their machinery sold, their workpeople dispersed. In certain areas, where the streets have been demolished, there have been attempts at landscaping – which seems to mean the elimination of all traces of the industrial revolution: a grass bank with a grove of saplings, a car park, some prefabricated cash-and-carry warehouses or stores selling parts for Toyota cars.

In the town centre, the new style of glass and concrete imposes itself on an older more intricate architecture, and in its starkness seems to reflect the forces that are at work on people, paring them to the bone, stripping away the accumulated experience. The geometric blocks are dynamically related to that spill of once precious belongings in the junk shops; as the buildings become plainer and more denuded, so the spoliation of the working class continues, the plundering of people, the shedding of skills, the loss of human resource.

A council estate on the south of the town was built just after the last war. The houses are constructed with cement blocks and were designed to last twenty years. With its crude, spare design, in winter it has the aspect of a shanty town. The houses have been recently sprayed yellow or white, so that from a distance you can't see the porous concrete of their construction. The corners are of long concrete strips, but in many of the houses these are crumbling. The kerbs too are wearing away in a scatter of gravel and pebbles, and hollows have appeared in the roads, some of which have been filled clumsily with bitumen and gravel, while others overflow in the winter rains in great rippling sheets of water which spray passers-by as cars drive past. The pavements are uneven and subsiding, so that in places you have no choice but to walk through the puddles. Even where the road has been dug up to repair public utilities, traces of the disturbance remain in uneven infilling, causing ridges and depressions in the surface. Some of the roof slates of the houses have worked loose, as has the shingling at the side of the houses. The front doors are plain, with a rectangle of frosted glass. Many have a growth of privet; the summer grasses drained of colour by the frost are silvered with rain; a more lasting patch of green is submerged into an oozing marshland. The only local amenities are a few shops, a general store with a metal mesh at the windows, a chip shop with some yellow benches and a stone floor, where people queue for a midday meal, the spiky battered fish, chips and peas; and the grease soon shines through the wrappings of the *Bolton Evening News*.

The public bleakness is not reflected in the interiors of the houses. Most are warm and comfortable, even though few have heated bedrooms. Carpets in brindled green and yellow or crimson; bright curtains. Most have pictures on the walls, an autumn landscape, a Flamenco dancer or Chinese girl, or a Murillo-type child with huge tears on his cheeks. There are family photographs on most tv sets, children against a simulated sky, wedding pictures, a casual snap of Mam taken on a back porch before she died. Most of the houses have gas-fires, a wooden frame set into the wall. There is nearly always an ornament in the window — Capodimonte or a vase of dyed grasses. There is a three-piece, often too big for the rather small rooms, in black studded leather; sometimes a more old-fashioned sofa with coloured stretch-covers. Occasionally, older people retain something of a more austere style: an old box radio, antimacassars, embroidered cushion covers, a piece of crochet work as a sideboard runner, a brass plant-pot with a poinsettia given by a daughter as a birthday present. Some of the poorer families use a paraffin stove for heating, with the result that the windows are permanently frosted with condensation.

The context in which people are without work here should be so much easier than that evoked by those who remember the thirties. But it is the sense of loss and dispossession of those who have worked all their lives that strikes one; the affront to those who had always believed that their work function was indispensable, and who are now being told to prepare for a leisure society while they're spending their days wandering round town looking for somebody to talk to, or staying in bed till afternoon because there's nothing to get up for. If they always felt sceptical about the dignity of labour, they are insulted by the rhetoric about leisure – it looks too much like futility. And what makes it worse is to be told you have priced yourself out of markets when you've never had quite enough money to provide for the needs of those you love all your working life.

Mr Delaney is in his late sixties. He took voluntary redundancy a few years before retirement so that he could relieve his wife in the task of looking after their handicapped daughter. His wife died three months after he gave up work. His daughter has been the beneficiary of the discipline and stoicism which enabled him to work in the same factory for nearly forty years. Looking after her provides him with a sense of commitment and purpose, but he is lonely and regrets the loss of the old neighbourhood supports, the falling away of the wider family group.

Grace, his daughter, is thirty-six, hydrocephalic. She is small, with dark hair, and wearing a pretty dress and cardigan and thick crimson socks. She sits with two cardboard boxes of toys and Christmas cards. She takes out the cards one by one, looks at the pictures and tears them methodically. Flakes of tinsel spangle the worn chair and hearthrug. She smiles at her father, and he says to her 'You're a bad lot, you are', and she gurgles with pleasure at the depth of his feeling for her. She holds out her hand; and he knows how to interpret her every gesture. She wants the light on because of the gathering dusk. He keeps his eyes on her all the time. As she tears one of the cards, half of it lodges in the bars in front of the gas-fire. Grace can do nothing for herself. Her father feeds her, changes her, lifts her. The two rooms downstairs have been knocked into one; and the bed on the far side has a blue metal hoist to help Mr Delaney lift her in and out of bed. Because she cannot be left even for a moment, he shares the double-bed with her.

'When my wife died, it was terrible. I felt insecure, it didn't seem worth going on, just me and Grace in the house. It felt so empty without her. I asked for the district nurse to call. I think she came once. You'd have thought they would have wanted to keep an eye on her, but nobody seemed to care. The wife and I had been looking after her for thirty-six years. It's the only thing I've left to do. I couldn't shove her away in a home. Never. Not while I've the strength to see to her. I wouldn't want her roughly handled by strangers when she's only had hands of love touching her all her life. She might not know it, but she'd feel it, and so would I. They did offer to take her one day a week at a day centre, but when I took her there, they'd only got one attendant, and she needs full-time attention – they wouldn't take her. You'd think with all the people out of work, there's jobs to be done. It doesn't make sense.

'I'd like one day a week because I'd get out and do the garden. I can't do it, not this time of the year. I'm having to rush to the window every two minutes, to make sure she's all right. In the summer it's not so bad, she can sit out in the sunshine.

'I'm not badly off. It's not money. I was a progress chaser at Edbros and I took early retirement. I've got this lifting gear, I've always had to lift her, and now I'm not so strong as I was. My family's no help. I've two sisters, I thought they might take some of the washing. They live near by, but they don't come in. All the people in the street stop and have a word with me. They all say "You're looking well." That means "I hope you're not looking for help, because I can't give you any." They don't come in. It isn't that people aren't concerned; they just don't want to get involved.

'I miss work. Oh it's a break when you stop. That's what a married man never understands about a woman's life. I've learnt that, seeing to the house. Men don't know they're born. I did go depressed for the first year when my wife died. But you've no choice have you?

'People are not communal as they used to be. They'd not have been away from the door at one time; they wouldn't have waited to be asked, people would have done it. There's a woman two doors away, we've both lived here thirty years. She's never once asked after Grace. I don't know what people are frightened of. They've forgotten how to be with each other.'

The chicken soup which he has prepared for Grace's tea is bubbling on the gas stove. He says 'I must be getting help from somewhere. I'm not complaining. I've sacrificed my life for her; but what else would I have done? We did have a little boy, but he died at a few weeks old; and then, when Grace was born, we didn't want to have any more.' He looks at her with warmth. 'I think she gets up and walks about when nobody's here, don't you love?'

Mr Campbell is nearly seventy. He has been a labourer all his life, and has never doubted the value of the work he has done: it is still tangible – there in the buildings he has worked on, the houses, factories. He has been pitman, docker, building worker. He is still proud of his physique: over the fire, there is a colour photograph of him at sixty-four flexing his biceps. It is the body of a man of thirty. Mr Campbell's granddaughter, a beautiful dark-eyed child of ten, sits in the corner with her cassette recorder and earphones; so that even though he talks about her she doesn't hear, but is absorbed by the music. She was left with her grandparents at six weeks; her mother couldn't cope with the child and went away. Mr and Mrs Campbell adopted her.

'I've done everything in the way of manual labour that you can think of, navvy at the gasworks, steelworker; I went in the pits after the War; I worked on Manchester docks. The pit I worked was two miles deep, it's closed now. I've worked in factories too.

'What we're living through now, I've seen it all before. It's worse for the young 'uns now because they're not used to it. We had the cat and the birch and hanging to keep us in order. When I started work, you had to provide your own tools. I was a navvy with my own pick and spade. I had to walk three miles to join a queue of 300 men all waiting for a job; all men without work. They'd stand there all day while the overseer on his horse rode up and down; if your face fitted, he'd call you out and say "There's a man collapsed up there, you can go and take his place." And you were grateful for the chance to work; you used to stand there hoping somebody'd collapse. You got 1*s* 1½*d* an hour.'

Mrs Campbell comes in from the kitchen. The first thing she says is: 'When I was a young woman with kids, your neighbours'd do anything for you. If you had no work, they'd help you out. They'd bath your kids, they'd fetch gruel for you if you were sick. They used to send for me if anybody had a baby, ninety out of 100 kids were born at home. If anybody went for the midwife, she'd ask who was with her, and if they said "Glad Campbell", she'd say "Oh, that's all right then." Neighbours are not neighbours today.' Mrs Campbell repeats what everybody has been saying on these estates for years now. It isn't recognized as the political statement it is because people have to believe that we have voluntarily set aside the capacity to care. It is too terrifying to think that, on the contrary, this is something that has been done to us, this winnowing of our feelings is an inseparable part of the improvements that have been granted.

'What I miss most is the old-time Vault in a pub; if you only had 2½*d*, you could go and buy a gill and sit there all night, and there'd be somebody to talk to. Working people talked, exchanged ideas. You were a psychiatrist to each other, you didn't have these depressions, the mental and emotional problems.'

Mrs Campbell says: 'In the War, we worked from six in the morning till five-thirty in the mills. We were told that it all depended on us, victory, survival. And now they can just get rid of us and close down the mills. Textiles are finished. Bolton means textiles. It takes your whole meaning away. It's enough to make people bitter. They tell you we're pricing ourselves out of the market, and people aren't even getting a living wage. I clean the frames in a mill. I have a power gun to do it with. I started work when I was fourteen and now I'm fifty-nine. That's forty-five years. I started in a spinning mill the day after I left school. I started as a setter-on in the card room – that is taking the full bobbins off and putting clean ones on. It was very fine work they did there. My first wage was 3*s* 6*d* a week. Now I take home £36. I'm working for less than a pound an hour. If that's pricing ourselves out of markets, it means only one thing. It's slave labour they want back.'

'I've seen all this before, cock,' Mr Campbell said. 'I've seen tradesmen thrown out on the streets, glad to take a labouring job. This is what unemployment is all about. Mrs Thatcher's version of a wages policy. Make the working people grovel. In the thirties it was the same. Nothing for the lads to do until they arranged another war for them. That could happen again. A conventional war; there won't be a nuclear one. They could fix another conventional war. After the General Strike I went in the army. It was the only way to escape from unemployment.'

On the same estate, Adrian Colqhoun lives with his wife and son. The whole family are out of work. The house is comfortable inside; everything about the interior symbolizes the turning away from the bleak estate, the introspection, the closed front door, the rejection of public areas and communal values.

Adrian Colqhoun was an electric-arc welder until he was made redundant in October 1980. 'A year before we were made redundant, we were told the jobs were safe. We got an agreement that if there was anybody to go, it'd be through natural wastage; then it became voluntary redundancy; then the last-in first-out principle. But when it came to it, it really meant getting rid of all those they didn't like. They got rid of the shop stewards first; they do that, then they can do as they like with the rest of the workforce; they know they'll have no more bother. I'd worked there twelve years; my mate had been there twenty-five. Get rid of those who'll stick up for the workers, those active in the union.

'In the end, they kept some men on over retirement age, those who are docile, cause no trouble. The company uses the recession as an excuse for a witch hunt.People should back their shop stewards. But they're frightened. That's what the present time is all about – fear. I got disillusioned. I wouldn't be a shop steward again. I wouldn't do it for people, they don't appreciate it. I wouldn't do it again. I've learnt a lesson, it hasn't done me any good. Too many people are in the union for the same reason they're in the Labour

Party, for the sake of their career. You lose sight of its purpose, you lose the idealism.

'People brand you as a communist, an extremist, if you say anything critical. It's so crude. I'm a socialist; but they try to brand you; they'll do anything to kill any real argument about the way the system works. That means they'll call you a wrecker because you say humanity is more precious than the system.

'I served my time, I did a five-year apprenticeship. I enjoyed the job while I was doing it. I can do the job a damn sight better than a lot of them who are still working there. That hurts. They'd rather keep on indifferent workmen who'll keep quiet, rather than somebody who knows the job but won't knuckle under to any shit they care to hand out. I took pride in my work. They came to me to work on a pressure vessel, an air compressor; I had to weld together two half cylinders to stand pressure of 200 lbs per square inch; the metal was ¾ inch thick. It had to be perfect; to get the Lloyd's insurance certificate, it had to be to a very high standard.

'The damage that's being done to skills, the workpeople who've done their apprenticeships, who've acquired the experience – what a waste! They blame the workpeople for everything. They blame the workers because there's a lack of investment in industry, for the running down of companies, for investing abroad where they can get cheap labour – they actually blame the workers for all the inefficiencies of capitalism, and people believe it. People don't usually blame themselves, they blame each other. Work has become so divided, it's the car-workers unless you're a car-worker, the miners' fault unless you work in the pits, the steelworkers' fault if you don't happen to be a steelworker, it's the blue collar workers if you're a white collar worker; and the workers in general if you're not one.

'I can't understand why people are not more militant. They're not angry, even the way things are. You hear them parroting Thatcher – as if running the economy was like running a household. We've lost faith in ourselves, that's the trouble. Working people have lost their sense of being able to offer a more humane alternative. It's no good blaming the Labour Party or the unions – it's us lost faith in what we can give each other. That's what the system has taken away from us. We believe that capitalism is the only thing that can give us the jackpot.

'People have stopped caring for each other. There is a mate I used to work with, he's lying over there in the hospital. He was with the firm forty-two years. Out of all the people we worked with, I think there's three of us been to see him. He'll never get up again. He got his redundancy notice while he was lying there.

'Since I left the firm they've got rid of five apprentices. Anyway, apprentices aren't being trained properly; most of them are just taught a few elementary jobs, then told to get on with it. Five years' cheap labour they get out of them, then chuck them out. Maybe I'm too hard, too blunt. That's what the wife says anyway. I don't use big fancy words I don't know the bloody meaning of, but I can see crystal clear what they're trying to do to us.' Mrs Colqhoun interrupts, 'Yes love, but it's the attitude you take, I mean, they are the bosses, they run the place.'

'Yes, and we're the workers, and we make their money for them.'

Dennis, their son is twenty-three. He sits in the chair doing the crossword in the *Daily Star*. He says, 'I was lucky, I did my apprenticeship with my Dad. He taught me properly.'

'That's right. A lad should be close to a journeyman while he serves his time. You pick your trade up as you go along. Most firms just get a lad doing the job, and leave him to get on with it; there isn't the close supervision and instruction and teaching that there should be. It's like all the other work relationships – ruined.'

'The trouble with me now, I've been a year without a job,' says Dennis. 'I've got age without experience, that's the worst thing. I went to Holland on a contract. The English worked the night-shift because the Dutch wouldn't; you knew what it felt like to be an immigrant. The Dutch learned all the short-cuts from us, then chucked us out. I get embarrassed when I go to sign on.'

In Bolton I met several people who said they felt their redundancy was connected with their trade union activity. They felt betrayed and disillusioned. Their commitment had been absolute and passionate to the union and the men they served. Able and intelligent people, their trade union work had given their dedication to work a dimension which was not there in the rank and file; and while they were enthusiastic to resist closure and redudancy, they found, on the whole, that the support was not there. Some of them found this a wounding experience. Their sense of work was strengthened by what to most people in the workplace seemed extraneous activity. It perhaps blinded them to the diminishing sense of function to which the men they were leading were more vulnerable.

Some of these men, now in their fifties, feel they will never work again. And they spend their empty time re-living past experience, recalling old triumphs and successes, how they scored off management, got someone unfairly dismissed re-instated, got some irksome regulation rescinded. But as time passes the relevance of past achievements fades; they find that people no longer seek them out in the pub or Labour Club, or they turn the conversation to different subjects.

Of these sad meetings, I can see a kind of composite front room in a terraced house in the old parts of various towns and cities; the room where such men, mostly dedicated shop stewards, did their administrative work. The wife brings in some tea, and effaces herself, observing a residual respect for husband's work, even though that has now gone; and he, irritable without occupation, keeps her at a distance so that she should not see his despair and loss. There is a file of dusty papers, correspondence, the documentation of past disputes and victories. In the bookcase, there are copies of 'Rights at Work' and the 'Hazards of Work'; but now he is more likely to be leafing disconsolately through the pile of *Readers' Digest*. There are the Country and Western records, Barry Manilow, the rubber plant, the mixture of time off and the extension of work. All the efforts of his life have been concentrated on the workplace, the classic locus of capital in its continuing struggle against labour. But the struggle seems to have become hermetic, enclosed; the classic pattern froze; to him, unemployed, the elaborate defensive structures built against what were felt to be known patterns of exploitation look disturbingly distant. And he wonders if he has not been too complacent; has failed to see that classic patterns have begun to dissolve; that the indispensable function of the working class has been weakened, and with it, the source of labour's strength impaired. Perhaps capitalism requires a dilution of that function now, a relaxing of those old coercions that forced him and his father to be up before daylight every morning for forty years. It is true that the mills of Bolton that still blot the town with their implacable red geometry are increasingly fossils, no longer exercising their discipline on those who live in their shadow. Has capitalism become more benign; or does it damage and destroy in other ways?

Graham Deacon, twenty-five, is a tall, fair-skinned young man, passionate and committed. He has recently married, and lives on a small private estate on the edge of Bolton. The house is immaculate; floral three-piece, wall units, bookcases full of volumes about kings and queens of England; ceramic tiles in the kitchen, hi-fi units, open staircase. In the newspaper rack, a somewhat incongruous juxtaposition of *Woman's Own* and the *Morning Star*. Graham says, 'We've only been married a year. My wife shares some of my ideas, but she doesn't go all the way with me. She is a royalist. I'm not.'

His father was a pitman; but had a heart attack and was forced to leave the pits. He had to stay out of work until he could find an undemanding job; and now he works as a cleaner, earning £60 a week. Graham's mother was a local girl, who won a scholarship to the grammar school, but whose family were too poor for her to be able to go there; so she left and worked as a clippie on the buses. She is now a night-care attendant in a hospital.

'They were both Labour people; but that didn't mean much in political terms. The first time I bought the *Morning Star*, my Mam went mad. "That thing's not coming into this house." I said, "Well if I can't read what I want, I'm not staying." She said, "If you start reading that and going about with those sort of people, you could easily fall into the wrong hands." "What do you mean by that?" "Never you mind." Then when my grandma found out, she went mad as well. She said, "We were fighting them so-and-so's in the War." I said, "No we weren't, we were fighting the Nazis." It was as if they'd forgotten.'

Graham is full of restless energy. He talks emphatically and with conviction. He is a mixture of modern young man and the old enquiring working-class spirit. He was brought up only a mile away from where he now lives, and is proud of his local roots. He is ambitious, not for money, but for the improvement of working people. He failed the eleven-plus, and many of his mates went to the grammar school. 'They were only the same as me; it didn't seem fair. The only thing is I was worldly wise as a youngster. That's what you learn at secondary school. My wife and I were in the same class. I used to be a real nonentity. She can't even remember me from school.

'I fucked up my school days. I got seven CSEs, but my mate got expelled so I left when he did. I got a job shelf-filling; you've got to be a right Wilbur to hold on to a job like that. I had some mates at an engineering firm, and I got an apprenticeship there.

'I learnt my trade as a plater. It's a dying trade really. There aren't the opportunities now. It was a structural engineering firm; they made the superstructure for factories. It was a family firm, the kind of firm I thought only existed on tv – you know, father builds up the business from nothing, tycoon son takes over. Mr Grimshaw, old Harry, used to walk round the shop floor once a month, and he used to stop and talk to certain people if they hadn't buggered off to the bog when they saw him coming. The first time I spoke to him I was surprised that I was a bit overawed by him. He was a bit of a Santa Claus figure. He had a deep voice, and he always said the same thing, awkward sort of bloke. "Hello there. Are you getting on all right? Are you going to the match on Saturday?" When he said, "What are you doing?" if you started to tell him, you could see he couldn't wait to get away from you. Patronizing, no danger. He had no idea how to talk to working people.

'Anyway, I got my apprenticeship there. The firm had its own training school. It was a better system then than it is now. Now the firm picks you out to go to Tech for a year full-time. Then you spent the first year in the charge of the training officer, and went to Tech one day a week. You were separate from the shop floor for that first year in the training school. You learnt turning, welding, plating, developing, drawing. After that you went onto the shop floor. It was a big place, half the size of a football pitch. You rarely visited the shop floor in your first year. Then after twelve months, you specialized, fitters, welders, platers, and you'd be assigned to your place in the works. But then the EITB – the training board – took over, and I got moved round the works. You had a module book and recorded all the jobs of a certain nature that you did to make sure that you got a balanced experience. That was the best training you could get: the blokes were interested in the young lads. Mind you, if the supervisor didn't like you, you got left with all the dead-end jobs. I was lucky. I got a good apprenticeship with a shop steward.

'The factory fabricated steel: the raw material comes out of the steel mills, and we made it into whatever was needed – joists, angle-iron, T-bends, you make the structures for the buildings. A lot of the work is dying now, because a lot of it is done mechanically now, shot-blasting, cleaning the steel. Once it was done manually, but it's all automatic and mechanized now. Plater is more of a shipyard term really. A lot of the drilling is done automatically; you used to have to mark the holes and then do all the drilling by hand. Now you just check. You can see more and more things get taken over by machinery all the time; when you work with it, you become aware of your own job being eroded. It's a continual encroachment on what we've always regarded as our skill. A lot of strikes are defensive reactions against what's happening. You can feel your own skill going, it's almost a physical thing. And then, a lot of the work is taken over by pre-stressed concrete, especially things like motorway bridges. Then there are too many firms competing for the same work. They'll always need platers, but the days of the big yards have gone. But those skills, they are a marvel, what men can do – it has to be seen to be believed. The unions must fight to keep works open. The traditional skills are there, and they're being thrown on the scrap heap. So much is lost every time a firm is put out of business.

'But I don't subscribe to the dignity of work. I didn't work for the love of it. I wish I didn't have to. I don't want people telling me I need work for dignity. I'm a person in my own right without work. You don't cease contributing to a society if you don't work. But I'm lucky, I can do something politically, that's work as well, and that's something that I do enjoy.

'The unemployed should get together. But they're not militant, that's the trouble. I think that the unions stand indicted for what they've failed to do. The boilermakers, my union, don't cater for the unemployed. I tried to introduce a discussion on what we could do. They didn't want to know. I said we need to get the shop stewards of all the different firms together, we need a common front to face the onslaught of the present time. The older ones – and they're nearly all older – said "Tha'll never get people doing that, lad, tha'rt naive lad. Tha'rt reet, but tha'll never do it."

'The unions haven't kept up with the sophistication of capitalism, they've let it outstrip them. You can't get a political discussion going. They'll not take notice of you.'

Graham has an inner burning energy; the kind of passion which you don't often find in young working men. As he talks, he evokes an older Bolton, the intensity of the Shakers, the radicalism of the old weavers. 'The inner toughness has gone from the working class; there's only the frivolities left. There's an outer show of toughness, but that's all bluster. I don't say that living easier has made people softer, that's too simple. There's nothing wrong with liking things, enjoying a decent life; but it's when you get so's you can't do without them, you grow dependent. Even in a community like this, you don't know people. They seem afraid. They don't seem aware of what they can do if they unite.

'The trade unions seem to dwindle in stature at the first sign of significant unemployment. And then the management dictates terms. All we've been trying to achieve, it's all been pushed back by years and years. There's been a lack of response. OK, they had a march, Liverpool, Glasgow, the March for Jobs. But what's come of it? In the future, people will look at the trade unions and say "What the fuck did they do?" Young people, when they come to think about the unions, will say "Oh well, they couldn't stop unemployment reaching 2½ or 3 million, they didn't stop these cuts in wages. What the fuck did they do? Why should I join?" All the confidence we've built up, it's melting away overnight.

'In a way, yes, the working class has lost something. The Left has been a bit inadequate to fight the poison. But there's still a lot there in people. I'm not religious, but I think there is some morality there, at the root. I remember when we had this NF pisspot at work in our place; he was working on the guillotine, and he used to go on, and some of the blokes used to listen. I really had a fucking go at him one day, and there was no doubt on whose side most of the blokes were. But there's always a danger that the Labour movement will get like the Labour movement in the United States – no balls to it. I think it's true that where most working men used to carry a two-foot rule in their pockets, they now carry the *Sun*. On Mondays they get the *Star* for the starbird in colour, the rest of the week it's the *Sun*; the young ones, anyway.

'I was only twenty-two when I took on active trade unionsim. I got a lot of aggro because I was young. Management hated it. The managing director said I was too young. He said he didn't consider me to be a suitable representative, because I hadn't been tempered by experience. I said "Will you write that down, I'll use it as a reference." I had a struggle when I first became shop steward. One time when the works manager and foreman were going to tell the blokes about some decision that had been made, I said "*You* don't tell them, the union puts it to them." The foreman said, "Thee shut thee fucking mouth. Tha doesn't tell me what to do. I've spent more fucking time at union meetings than tha's lived." I said, "It doesn't make you any wiser though, does it?" He grabbed hold of me: "Come outside." Being a shop steward, I had to prove myself more than a forty-year-old would have to; and to the workers as well. The safety rep. said to me, "You're so fucking bigheaded, even if tha was doing something dangerous, I wouldn't tell thee." And then, if you've won something, a good concession from management, you can't go round saying "I did this, I got that." There's no credit for anything you do; but if you do anything wrong, you soon hear about that. When management treat you like a joke, they're psyching you out, and the blokes do the same. It's only when you get respect from management that you get respect from the men as well. I think that says a lot.

'Losing the job, the closing down of the works was really traumatic. It wasn't made easier by the fact that the company had two factories, and only one was closing, so you'd got a split workforce. I'd been shop steward for two years. I first got notice of it out of the blue. I mean, they'd mentioned that order books weren't full, but then order books have never been good since Noah built the ark.

'When it happened, I thought "Jesus wept, it's happened to me. What do I do about it?" I got every book and pamphlet I could find on redundancy. Your first thought is "Have I caused this? The things I've got them to accept, is it my fault? What about those poor blokes?" I couldn't believe it. I'd broken my leg at football at the time, so they sent a taxi for me to get me to the meetings. But not actually being there at the time, it magnified the tensions of work in my own mind. I'd get calls in the evening from the blokes, and I was stuck here in the house: it got amplified, bouncing back off the walls at you. I know the tension at work must have been greater, but at least they shared it. That's the great consolation about work – you share it; you don't share unemployment.

'We wanted to fight the closure. But I thought, what would happen if we fought and got fuck-all? I couldn't admit it, but I knew there was fuck-all fight in the men. With the split works, they'd got us divided. Even the two shop stewards at the Top Works knew they weren't getting the sack; so the management threatened them at Top Works that if there was any reduction in the Bottom Lane works, there'd have to be more at the Top.

'We tried everything to prevent it. We offered to go on short time, work sharing, ways of spreading the work – anything to avoid redundancies. Then early retirement, then voluntary redundancy, then, as a last resort, last in first out. That was the order of priorities, but at first you say you're fighting closure – full stop – on principle. But they cut the ground from under our feet because of the split site. While the shop stewards were in the middle of negotiations, management said to us "The lads at Top Shop don't want to support you." It got me so angry. It gets you to such a pitch; I was terrible at home, I lost my temper with my wife. I was so angry. Fucking bastards, I thought "We're strong enough, we'll do it." Then, when it was obvious we'd get nowhere, I still couldn't give in. I said "Are we such fucking sheep?" And the answer was "yes". And we'd been one of the best-organized workforces in Bolton. All those books, 'Rights at Work', the ACAS guide, they're very good, but they don't put an argument together for you. You might as well have the fucking *Beano* in front of you unless you've got the backing, the solidarity.

'The way they do it, it works by rumours. Blokes start grabbing you physically and saying "What's this I've heard about somebody's got a job, he's going?" or they say "How can we fight them? Anyway, they've promised no redundancies." Then they look round and see somebody is not there, so they jump to the conclusion "So-and-so's fucked off." He might only be in the toilet, but everything flares up, it's so volatile. People start behaving like children; mature blokes are running around "I've heard there's so many thousands of pounds going. We want to know this, why's that not being done?" All hell breaks loose.

'People seek their own individual salvation, and we're crushed. It's as if we were being crushed by nutcrackers – management on one hand and the decay of support on the other. There was no sign of collectivism except from the stewards. As soon as it was announced that one works would close, the other stay open, it was just like the opposite poles of a magnet – they flew apart. They might agree "Occupy the factory", but behind their hands, they're saying "Thank fuck it isn't the Top Shop."

'I thought to myself "You fucking bastards". I'd never sworn so much in my life, I felt against the blokes. I thought, "Management, that's their job to be bastards, but not the blokes." Later, I was disgusted with myself for having had that reaction. I can say that now, but I still feel bitter that we didn't stay together and fight. It made me feel inadequate. For all my rhetoric, I couldn't hold them together, I thought what a fucking pisspot I must be. Management did their job well, but mine was just a cock-up.

'I was there nine years. I got £500 plus nine weeks' back-pay from the date of the notice. And we negotiated a loyalty payment. While you're trying to fight, at the same time, the idea of the money is in your head: taking action could jeopardize that. They didn't make everybody redundant; they kept some blue-eyes on. I went back to see what was going on after I'd finished, and they told me I had no right to be on the premises. Well, to me, responsibility didn't end just when I stopped.

'I could have left a long time before the end. I didn't because I'd just been made a shop steward. My wife thought I was mad. She works as a secretary, she earns good money. When I left, it wasn't the firm I missed, it was my responsibility as a steward. I loved the contact with people, sorting out claims for people injured at work, that sort of thing. I like following the issues through.

'I love talking. When we had the engineering strike last year, the stewards addressed the staff to explain to them the reasons for the strike, we wanted to get their support. And the guy who was talking to them, you could tell he wasn't getting across, you could feel the meeting going against us. He was clouding it, not talking directly to them. So I asked if I could have a word. And I spoke for twenty minutes. I felt so strong; I felt great because I knew I'd done OK. I didn't even know afterwards what I'd said, but it all came spontaneously. Then, when I was back on the picket line, I heard some people talking, and they said "That Deacon lad is a good speaker." "Aye, and he really knows his stuff." I felt good. That's what I miss most. Maybe when I say I don't care about work, maybe that's not the whole of it: I need the kind of work I care about.

'I don't know where this feeling comes from; it's just there. Bolton has a long radical tradition, it's sort of there, you talk to the older people, and that kindles something in you. I feel I want to be in there, fighting for people, those who've got nowt, those who'll get crushed by the system. I have to be doing it. I always had a romantic ideal to be in a union when I was a kid. I know that isn't very common; but then, when you hear the unions knocked and rubbished by the media, the papers, that's not surprising. You know there's a lot wrong with the unions – but what's wrong is the opposite of what the media say is wrong – they've lost the real fire, the real concern with people. They've been bought off with money. It isn't that they're a threat to society, are they heck. They should be. The old 'uns don't want to lose their power. They make the young 'uns feel they couldn't possibly fill their boots. They like to give the impression they're irreplaceable. They do the work, but then some of them, old Len, he's saying in one breath "Too many blacks, they breed like rabbits"; then the next that he's the champion of the working class. It doesn't add up.

'I've never been unemployed. When I went to the job centre, there was fuck-all jobs there. I thought what can I fucking do? I wrote to British Aerospace. They said they'd put me on a waiting list for six months. It's only just beginning to hit me. I'm an active person; I like to play football. I've got a lot of energy. Carol feels it as a stigma. She's inclined to chastise me because I don't. She's the only wage-earner. I don't care. I don't believe in all that macho shit. I used to go out with some of my mates on Friday night, a lot of them were married; and they'd say "Eh, let's get some jars down me", they were glad to get away from their wives. They actually needed to get away from their missus. I couldn't understand it. And then, when I was out with the lads at a dance, chatting up a girl, they'd say "What did you tell her you did?" I said "I told her I was a plater." "Oh, I said I was a draughtsman." It shows what a lack of confidence they have in themselves as working men. I think you should bring the best of yourself to work, it doesn't matter what you do.

'People want to be in steady work, but not for the aesthetic thrill. I'm like my Dad. I mean, you could say he was the noble pitman come down to a rubbish job. But he's never downhearted, it hasn't depressed him. He's a happy person; and so am I. It wouldn't get me down. I feel my life is only just starting.'

Jim Corcoran is thirty-two. He was made redundant from the same firm as Graham Deacon. A skilled welder, he did five years' apprenticeship, and then worked in a factory which was working on an order for machines that shelled, sorted and graded the peas for Bird's Eye foods. He was made redundant there in 1973. He then worked at arc welding for a company that was making container tanks for breweries, with a 90,000 gallon capacity. The factory was a converted mill; the floors had been removed to accommodate the bulk of the tank, which was two storeys high.

'You had to work inside it. It was very specialized work. The conditions were terrible. You had to wear a respirator all the time. There was a perpetual fog in the factory, a haze of fumes and smoke. I stuck it there for two years. It was the time when the health and safety legislation was passed, but even with that they're not going to apply it so stringently that the firms go bust are they? It didn't make the place either healthy or safe.'

He left to go to his last job, where he stayed five years. Jim is diabetic; and when he became redundant, he was having a day off most weeks because of a bad reaction to insulin. The work was too heavy for him anyway, making cranes and compressors. 'They had a big contract in Saudi Arabia, installing pylons right across the desert. Some of the lads went out there to work. I could never do that. The firm wanted me out. Once, when I was fainting from diabetes, I asked for a cup of sugared water, but they wouldn't let me have it. They said "Oh no, you're not allowed to have sugar if you're diabetic." The first ones they get rid of are those who are sick or strong union blokes, so if you fall into both categories, that's it. Under cover of the recession, they'll dump all those who are a nuisance one way or the other.'

Jim has now been out of work for a year. He tries to get home most evenings before the rest of the family who are working, so that the house is warm and welcoming. He lives on the early post-war estate with his mother, younger brother and sister. He does some shopping for tea. The wind drives the rain over the tops of the hills, and gusts across the sweep of concrete streets. The grass verges are muddy, and almost cover people's shoes as they cross them; the drains echo with the water swirling in the road.

The house has been empty all day and is cold when Jim gets in. He lights the gas-fire, and puts the kettle on. Mrs Corcoran comes in first. Jim makes tea; strong, almost orange with the tang of sterilized milk. His mother comes from Liverpool. One of a family of sixteen, she is a formidable woman with short blond hair and tinted glasses. She is a traditional working-class Mum, protective, warm, proud and authoritative. She has worked in Social Services and a hospice for the elderly; now she is an industrial nurse. As soon as she gets in, she starts cooking tea.

Dave follows her in from work a few minutes later. He works for the same firm as his mother; it was she who got him the job. Dave is in his early twenties. He is thin, with glasses and dark curly hair. He sits on the sofa and yawns. He is bored rather than tired. He was in the Royal Navy for four years; an intelligent and able young man, but restless, unable to find expression for his abilities. He had an apprenticeship in painting and decorating when he left school, but gave it up because it bored him. 'The paint got on my stomach. I had a mate in the Navy, so I joined up.' He came out in 1979, and was out of work for a few months. Then followed a short spell with Group Four Security, twelve-hour shifts patrolling industrial premises all night. After another short spell without work, he went into the warehouse of the mill where he is now. Towels are made there. His job is behind the manufacturing area, where the towels are sent for packing when they have been checked. It isn't hard work, but it involves a lot of walking about during the day.

Dave has tried to get into the police and the Merchant Navy, but so far without success. He went for an interview for a job deep-sea diving off Texas. He passed the interview, but now has to take a medical with a private doctor which will cost £55. Dave feels bitter at the under-use of his capacities. And he is learning the lesson which so many able working people have learnt before him – that the needs of the economy bear no relation to the needs or abilities of people. He feels hurt and rejected. He is slightly incredulous that his worth has not been recognized. He is working for a net wage of £43 a week, forty-five hours; less than a pound an hour. And yet he has no choice. 'I hate what I do. Every day I hate getting up to go to work. I know there's nothing to look forward to. I know exactly what's going to happen. It makes me bad-tempered. The family get on my nerves, and I get on theirs. If you haven't got a trade by the age of twenty, you're knackered.' His mother says 'You'll have to sit at your O-levels.' Dave sits with his head in his hands. 'I can't. It's no good. I haven't got the concentration. It's too late.'

Mr Corcoran died twelve years ago, when Dave was twelve, and Carol, the youngest child was four. Mrs Corcoran is devoted to her children. She says, 'When they were growing up, I went out five times in twenty-two years.' She sends Jim out for some shopping he forgot to do. She criticizes his ability to shop properly: the role of child unable to carry out a commission dies hard, even though the children are grown up.

Mrs Corcoran grew up in appalling poverty. 'Some weeks, a ten shilling food ticket was the only money we had in the house. It's made me proud. I wouldn't ask anybody for anything. When I was a kid, we lived in a little row of houses, with a shop on the corner; and the shopkeeper fixed up a speaker from his radio in every house, and we all paid sixpence a week to listen to the same radio. When the man from the Public Assistance Committee came round – I shall always remember, we were listening to Henry Hall; and the PAC man looked round and he saw this speaker on the wall, and he said "Get rid of it." You were allowed nothing. We had no comfort in our house – red tile floors, wooden chairs, a scrubbed table, nothing else. If you had a cushion, it was "Sell that"; if you had a rug on the floor, it was "Sell that" before you got a penny out of the PAC; even the bowl and jug on a marble stand in the bedroom, it had to go. You were allowed a bed in your bedroom and nothing else.

'My father was sick; he was in hospital fifteen years. He was hit over the head by a policeman's truncheon. It did something to him, some damage. He finished up in the bin. My mother was a big woman, powerful. She was forty-five when I was born, and there was another one after me. Once, when I was just a little kid, I was the only one in the house with her, and one day she collapsed; fell on the floor. She was hefty, I couldn't do anything. I didn't know how to help her. I remembered not far away seeing some big houses, and on one of them I'd seen a brass plaque saying DOCTOR. So I took off; I rushed through the streets till I came to this house, rushed up the drive and rang the bell. A woman came to the door, and she looked down at me – this raggety little kid. I was always clean, but my clothes weren't top drawer; and she looked at me and said "Out". She looked so tall to me, but I said "I want to see that doctor man." I wasn't going to be turned away; and the doctor came out to see what all the commotion was. I begged and pleaded with him; and he got his bag, and he took me by the hand, and he walked home with me. I learnt then that you had to do things in life if you wanted to survive. You had to push yourself, act thick-skinned, however sensitive you were underneath. But they did push you around. Usually, you went to the PAC doctor.

'I went to see the PAC doctor once with my mother when I was about fourteen. I told him I'd got a sore throat. He told me to strip off. "But she's only got a sore throat." "Strip off." "I will not." "Get your clothes off." "I won't." I said to him "I think you're a dirty old man." They docked five shillings off my mother's money for that. The humiliations they suffered. It stays with you. When my mother got her PAC voucher for clothing she had to go to a certain shop to buy underwear or whatever; and the other half of this shop was a pawn shop, you just had to go round the other side. So she'd take the brand new clothes she'd just bought with this token and pawn them. And the man who'd just served her on the other side of the shop would take them and give her something for them, and not bat an eyelid, just as if he'd never seen her before. And with that money she'd go and get us something to eat.'

Jim and Dave have heard the stories before. 'Come on Mum, let's have tea.' Carole comes in. She has a job typing, and is enjoying it. Many of the girls she was at school with are unemployed. Carole is seventeen; she is earning £30 a week.

Supper is Cornish pasties, mixed vegetables and beans. The family eat together at six o'clock, so that even if they are going out, there is still time to sit around, have a cup of tea and exchange news. Although they are on the edge of town, it takes only a few minutes into the centre. You have more time in smaller communities than in cities. You don't spend hours travelling, and there is more opportunity to be together casually, to call in on relatives without prior arrangement. Tonight Carole is going out; her boy-friend is calling for her in his car. Her brothers tease her mildly: 'She looked at the car first before she looked at who's driving it.' Mrs Corcoran doesn't sit down until everybody is served.

Dave says, 'Doing a useless job like mine, you can't even take a girl out. I've no money and no prospects. This experience has racked and ruined me. I feel, I don't know, disappointed in Britain. I thought I wouldn't have any problem getting work. I thought I'd get given a job. I know it was peacetime when I was in the Navy, but it's still the services. I developed a lot of skills there, but they're no use to you as a civvy. I learnt radar, and I mean learnt, you have to learn in double quick time in the Navy or you get a boot round your arsehole. I've got training in security, fire-fighting, damage control. But you can't use it, it's not recognized as a civilian qualification. I feel I'd've done better if I'd been in the nick for four years; you're trained but you can't be properly employed. I've done radio operating. I was paid £60 a fortnight in the Navy, which was spending money. Out of the £43 I get now I have to pay my keep and everything. Getting honest work doesn't pay. I've spent the last eighteen months writing letters. I detest the life I have to lead. Get up at six o'clock. It's the first time I've ever had to work cooped up in the same building all the time. I can't leave because they depend on the money at home.'

Mrs Corcoran sits down at the table with a cup of tea. She doesn't seem to have eaten very much; perhaps a habit of self-denial. She talks about her husband. 'I've been better off than I ever was while he was alive, bless him. When he knew he was dying, he looked at me and said, "I haven't been able to give you anything, love." I said to him, "You've given me everything." Because he knew the poverty I'd come out of. We had a loving life together and a loving family. Since he died, I've never wanted another man. For me, that's it, he was the one for me, and there's no more to be said about it.

'I looked after the children, five of them. They were my life, and they still are. I don't know though. I look on Jim and Dave as my failures. "Why failures?" "Well, I think all the protection I gave them, it's made them too hesitant. Not self-confident enough. It was perhaps too much. Our Dave had to go into the Navy to break away from it. Your life gets so entwined with theirs. Perhaps not failures. You can have too little love, but can you ever have too much? Perhaps I should have shoved them out, made them fight it out for themselves.'

Mrs Corcoran looks at them. She says, 'The spirit of those who've loved you lives on even when they're dead. I can hear my mother in me sometimes. That's the only immortality you can be sure of, whatever happens to you when you die. In that sense, nobody dies, except those who've never been loved or never loved anybody else.' Even as Mrs Corcoran talks, you can feel the pain and uncertainty of what is neutrally referred to as 'social change' reaching into the hearts of the people together in this house. It is an almost physical presence, the tug of individuals in different directions, away from each other, and her resistance to it. At one point, when we are discussing whether family strengths have weakened, she says fiercely 'Not in this family'. She is proud that she holds them still together, but at the same time, wondering whether she hasn't perhaps been 'too protective' is like becoming aware that the strengths of the old poverty could become weaknesses in the altered context and over that she has no control. The decay of shared purpose destroys their anchorage in a society in which people feel they are part of one another, and the individual project becomes a substitute; and in order for this wound to be healed, they have to look for comforts they would never have needed if that sense of shared venture had not been broken.

Carole and Dave say they are not interested in politics. Mrs Corcoran and Jim are strongly committed Labour supporters. You can see how the two younger ones have become detached from the tradition. Dave says, 'I've never voted. I might now because of Margaret Thatcher.' But the anxieties of Dave's life seem to him to belong to an area over which politicans have little control. To him, what he describes as 'the way things are going, the modern world, the development of technology, progress' have their own independent force, and nothing can stop them. Because capitalist development seems to have fused itself with these things, it appears to have taken on an unstoppable dynamic of its own, almost as though it were no longer susceptible to human influences. Dave says 'Your political allegiance is only a reflection of what your parents think. And things have changed so much you don't need to accept them any more.' Dave is inclined to bait Jim's more passionate commitment. And it is difficult not to be aware of that process at work wrenching people away from commitment to each other, this time through the assault on the shared values of collective project. How can they feel any relationship with the Labour Party, when the process of spoliation of their values, their culture, their solidarity has gone forward with such relentless force; and in the vacuum, what is left but the ubiquitous and strident values of the capitalist machine? Jim and his mother are baffled and hurt by the indifference of the younger ones; Mrs Corcoran lived through that poverty, and Jim has absorbed so much of her experience that they both still feel it; but Dave and Carole, in spite of the love that has been transmitted to them, have not been formed by the same social values, the generosity and humanity of Mrs Corcoran.

After supper, Dave's friend, Stephen arrives. They are both interested in photography. They compare cameras in a corner of the living-room. There is no real privacy: they inspect each other's camera, and read their photographic magazines while everything else is going on at the same time; but their conversation is quite self-contained and doesn't cause any friction. They are looking at Dave's Japanese camera: it has its own self-regulating light meter, its exposure is automatic; and they compare it with Stephen's German model, which, although in its time a masterpiece of advanced technology, has been easily displaced by the superior Japanese creation. Everything about this new camera – design, size, weight, efficiency, decreased skill needed to operate it – offers enormous fascination. Reduced human involvement in the use of it is matched by increased perfection in the product. You can see people being humbled by the things that can be bought: whatever the virtues of these artefacts, you can't help feeling that this is not the lesson that human beings ought to be learning from them.

After supper, Mrs Corcoran talks about the past. 'Of couse, when I was young, children didn't count in the family. I was fourteen before I had my first cup of tea. I can remember it; it was one of the few happy moments of my childhood. It was the day war was declared in 1939. When we came in, my Da was sat by the fire, and he'd made a cup of tea, and he said "Come on in and sit down." Until then the children only drank water, and until you left school, you never sat down for your meals. Oh no, you ate standing at the table. You had to earn your right to sit down.

'They were an Orange family, all my brothers and sisters; I was the only one not to get baptized. The reason for that was, they were very fanatical, and they always had this saying "Be baptized in Paddy's blood." I was an impressionable child, and I took it literally. I thought they really did baptize you in Catholic blood; so on our way to church I ran away. My grandmother – she was a fanatical Orangewoman – she chased after me, and she bit me. She bit me on the cheek, just under my ear, I've still got the scar. My grandmother was so extreme that the only flowers she would have in her garden were orange lilies, and golden privet for the hedge, she wouldn't have anything green. She even used to go and pull up the grass. My father had religious mania. In the end he went mad.

'I haven't kept up with it. I think we were a funny lot. Of course you grew up in great ignorance. When I was pregnant with my oldest boy, my sister was pregnant at the same time. And do you know, she would never say how she'd got pregnant? She denied that she'd ever been with a man. She wouldn't say how she'd got that way. She was strange. She said they'd cut her open and put the baby in there.

'I don't see them now; we've not seen some of them for years. My other sister, she sent Jim a birthday card once when he was fourteen. It was the first time she'd ever sent him a card; and there was a postal order for ten shillings enclosed. We thought "Oh that's good, that's generous of her." A few days later, a letter comes asking if we could send back the postal order; she'd intended to enclose a postal order for half a crown; the ten shillings should have gone to the bookie's.

'I will say though that people used to take responsibility for each other. When I was young, my brother Peter, if he saw me walking out with a boy, he'd call me a dirty slut and start a fight with the chap. Once, I remember, I was coming home late from a dance, and it was a foggy night. I saw my brother and his mate, they were out looking for me. I turned round and fled. I went into the police station because I knew Peter would give me a good hiding if he got hold of me. I ran into the police and said "There's these two men chasing me"; and so the police went out and got them. And when they got them inside, Peter said "I'm her brother"; so out I ran and left him there. But I knew I should get a pasting when he got home, so I went off, out of the window, over the sheds, and I ran into a convent and told them I had nowhere to go. They let me stay there for three weeks. It was wonderful, one of the best times I ever had.

'I've lived on this estate since we were married. My husband died eight years ago. It was terrible how he died. He had a disease of the kidneys and they never diagnosed it. They didn't know what it was. And he died on the toilets in the hospital. He should never have been allowed to go there on his own; he slipped and fell. God knows how long he must have stayed there before they found him. Everybody said we ought to have sued them. But that wouldn't bring him back again.'

Mrs Corcoran feels her husband's presence. She says he has helped her bring up the children on her own. Since he died, she won't sleep in the room they shared, but stays downstairs and sleeps on the sofa. She is the kind of person who has suffered, but never lets the tragedies and disappointments reach the core of her; she remains strong, a support to everyone who knows her, the one you turn to in trouble. The value of Mrs Corcoran to her community cannot be calculated in money terms; and she has the scarcity of an endangered species. She says: 'A Pakistani family moved in a few months ago; and there's a lad down here, he thinks he's the cock of the estate; and he said "Oh, we'll soon get rid of them." I said to him: "They live opposite me, you cause any disturbance and I'll disturb you." I would. If I hit any kid on this estate while mine were little – not that I did very often – and they went home and said "Connie Corcoran hit me", they knew the kid deserved it. I never had anybody knocking on this door to complain.'

But most of the Connie Corcorans have gone. Perhaps their

vigour and energy have been absorbed into the professions that have opened up to women; but it is not easy to say that they are more effectively applied there. Connie has been doing a university course. She shows me an essay she has written on the trade unions and the origins of the Labour Party. But she belongs to that older tradition with that wisdom and knowledge that deals spontaneously with human problems. To see the way she works is moving and powerful; and a measure of the loss can only be seen when you see her abilities dispersed through social work or community work or teaching. The process of things being taken away from the working class can be felt strong as a gravitational pull, the draining away of abilities that are then turned into marketable skills. That Connie would express herself more fully only in a career is true only in so far as the context makes it inescapable. We delude ourselves if we imagine that this makes the accumulated knowledge and wisdom of working-class women more effective socially: these things are not enhanced by being decanted into the market-place and sold. In the end, there will be a loss of a resource to the working-class community.

Mrs Corcoran knows this. 'You still know all your neighbours, you know what happens to them, but you can't always do anything to help. This street has seen its share of tragedies. There was a girl lived over the road, there; she was a beautiful girl, friendly, a bit shy, she was really good-looking. And she hadn't had any boyfriends really until she met this man. He moved in with her. It was the first time she'd ever really loved anybody, you could tell. She glowed. And he seemed to love her. He moved in with her and her parents, and they were all getting ready for the wedding. She got pregnant, so they decided to bring it forward a bit. Then one night, he never came home from work. It turned out that he already had a wife. But it broke her heart. From being a happy, beautiful girl, she just turned in on herself. It was terrible; you could see it happening, but you couldn't do anything to stop it. The baby was born, a beautiful little boy. But it didn't change her. One night she just hanged herself. She tied a rope up from the top window, and jumped out. It was the room where the little boy was sleeping as well.'

In a pub in the town centre, a group of workers are talking about unemployment. An elderly woman says, 'In the Depression me and my husband went to London to look for work. He got a labouring job, twenty-one shillings a week; and we had to pay fifteen shillings for a room. We had a baby, so I had to get a job as well. I went in service. I used to be coming home just as he was going to work, so we used to pass the baby to each other as we passed by. That was practically all we saw of each other.'

'Was it harder then?'

'You didn't expect so much, so that made it easier.'

'They don't know what to do with themselves now.'

'There was work to be done at home when we were young. I'd the little ones to look after. I might have resented it, but it was a bloody sight better than hanging round town looking for some kind of rough-house like they do now. They've nowt to do.'

'At our place, they made 500 redundant. It was like Russian roulette, you didn't know who was next. They told us individually. Sent for us to the office. The supervisor came up to us individually, "Will you report to personnel?" Then we were escorted individually from the works. They said it was because of the fear of reprisals. A lot of the men had worked there years. They were scared they might smash the machines. Promised to send their pay on. It was like kicking them out and accusing them of being criminals at the same time, to help them on their way. It shows what they really think of you. We bloody soon got that stopped. Since then they've been sending out letters, and they go up, still one at a time though, to collect what's owing to them.'

'They talk about extremism. What about their extremism? Treating people like rubbish, isn't that extremism?'

Cold winter afternoon. Snow and mist on the hills around Bolton. The snow hangs like bandages over the wounded fabric of the town. It falls in melting splashes over the roof-tops onto the pavements below. The chimneys and mills look darker against the whiteness. On an estate in a town a few miles away I was taken by an out-of-work labourer to where his mate shows blue video films two or three afternoons a week. It was in an ordinary council house, like its neighbours; grass overgrown, snow covered. A dog was tied to a stake in the garden. The house was badly in need of paint; but like most of the houses I went into, it was warm and comfortable inside. The curtains are drawn, but because of the dark afternoon that doesn't look incongruous. In the living-room there are about eight men. At first, it looks almost like some secret political meeting, a clandestine group at which revolutionary speeches are going to be made, oaths taken. We pay £2 and sit down on the leatherette chairs and sofa and four dining-room chairs. The lights are turned out, and the film begins on the big colour tv. It's about a young girl who leaves home after having been beaten by her father and brother, and she gets a lift in a truck to London. She is subjected to all kinds of brutalities – rape and beating and humiliation. She becomes a prostitute in London. One day she picks up her own father, and he doesn't recognize her until they are about to make love. He breaks down and says how sorry he is, and begs her to go back home with him. She agrees, and they go to the station to wait for the train; but she meets a man and has it off with him in the waiting-room, and disappears with him leaving her father standing as the train pulls in. It is a messy and horrible piece of work. Some of the men in the room hold their groin and groan when they see her undressed and when her legs part. There is a close-up of the man's cock entering her, and one of them says 'Christ I wish that was me'; but on the whole they are not very impressed. There is a lot of laughter. The colour of the film is appalling; all the flesh looks bruised, unnatural violets and reds seem to predominate. But there is something disturbing about the whole event. It is like a caricature of why working men should meet together. The fact that they are all out of work was an ugly irony. The fantasy that fills the vacant spaces of time, the parasitic relationship to the capitalist processes, the oppressive power of a technology that is used to subject people and not to liberate them, the wasted energies and the fantasies that luxuriate in the inaction and emptiness; even the enterprise of the man with the video – bought with redundancy money; and the fact that we are near Bolton, the old stronghold of working-class radicalism – everything underlines the enormity of the task confronting the Labour movement, which, for the most part, it hasn't begun to come to terms with.

In this place, there is a powerful sense of what has been pared away from people, except those appetites which only capitalism can answer. So many of the cultural attributes of the old working class have been peeled away; we have been reduced; we are truncated and vulnerable; and only what we can buy through the capitalist market-place will make us whole again. The film we have seen, in suggesting that everbody is venal and worthless, that everybody wants only money and sex and sensations, and that everything else is pretence, faithfully reflects the values of the society that produced it. Of course, there is resistance to this cruel message. Afterwards, the men in the room are slightly awkward. They say they have been conned and, half-joking, say they want their money back. But everywhere you can feel the ebb of what Connie Corcoran and those like her stand for. This is where we need to concentrate and reinforce our resistance: not only to the relentless driving of working people to extract a maximum of labour from them, but the ugly obverse of it as well, the deformity of leisure that will shape us into bottomless receptacles that will absorb all the products that have to be so swiftly used up and replaced. The creation of wealth is matched by an impoverishment of human beings: just as it always has been. The resistance has to be constant and on every front. If we forfeit that, we become dependent on capitalism, and we don't even have our old indispensability as a counter in that future struggle. In *The Uses of Literacy*[34] Richard Hoggart in the late fifties was talking of the responsibility of the minority of political activists and convinced trade unionists within the working class, when he said:

> I have recalled their work for social reform, and have stressed that it was inspired not primarily by a search for material goods but by a sense of the need for higher satisfactions by working-people, satisfactions which could be more easily obtained once material improvements had been made. The greatest need now is for this minority to reassess the position, to realize that the ideas for which their predecessors worked are in danger of being lost, that material improvements can be used so as to incline the body of working-people to accept a mean form of materialism as a social philosophy. If the active minority continue to allow themselves too exclusively to think of immediate political and economic objectives, the pass will be sold, culturally, behind their backs. This is a harder problem in some ways than even that which confronted their predecessors. It is harder to realize imaginatively the dangers of spiritual deterioration. These dangers are harder to combat, like adversaries in the air, with no corporeal shape to inspire courage and decision . . . It is easier for a few to improve the material conditions of many than for a few to waken a great many from the hypnosis of immature emotional satisfactions.

Mrs Tysoe lives in a 1920s house in a steep street in Bolton; in fact the road falls away so sharply that it has been blocked off into a cul-de-sac. There is a small front garden, beds of honesty and hydrangeas. The front room is plainly furnished, and without ornament: the result of a long period of unemployment during which nothing could be renewed. A grey three-piece in cut moquette with a red border, an electric fire with artificial coals stands in the buff-coloured fireplace, a china cabinet and bookcase. On the bookcase there is a little notice in Gothic script. It reads 'Out of the Gloom a Voice said unto Me "Smile and Be Happy; Things could be Worse." So I smiled and was Happy; and Lo, Things were Worse.'

Mrs Tysoe is in her forties. She was trained as a nursery teacher, but left the profession – temporarily as she thought – to get married. By the time she was ready to start work again, with the decrease in nursery school provision and the fall in the number of children, she found it impossible to get work. She went on a TOPS course to be retrained in office skills, and found a job as an accounts clerk. When she was made redundant, she was out of work for eighteen months; but she has recently found work in a textile factory – another sector suffering in the current wave of unemployment; but this firm specializes in uniforms and clothing on government contracts which are less likely to be imported.

'Being without work was a horrible experience. It came to me as a complete surprise. I was brought up in a shop. My parents had a small grocery business. It never occurred to me that I would ever receive unemployment benefit, or any other kind of benefit for that matter. While you're still working you think "Oh if I lose my job, I'll soon get another." That colours your attitude to the unemployed; you think they can't be trying hard enough; and then you get all the stuff in the papers about scroungers, it's very comforting.

'I was made redundant in 1978. I'd been an accounts clerk with a firm of electrical engineers. They made things like weatherproof lamps. They'd started in mining equipment years ago. It had been a little family business; and then they started making lamps for oil-rigs and the railways. The Coal Board had been their biggest customer.

'I was a teacher originally. It was a shock not to be able to get a job in what I thought of as my chosen profession. But I went on a commercial and clerical course, bookkeeping, typing, I thought,

"Oh well, I'm safe now." I was there just over a year. Then orders were going down, and the company was sold to BICC. And like so many firms when they're taken over, they're rationalized. My job disappeared. It moved to head office.

'I put my name on three registers. I thought something would soon crop up. But there was nothing. I was told I was at a problem age. They think you're senile at thirty-five these days. They only want to take on young ones. I'm forty-four. There's no chance that I'll get back into office work now. I've had one or two interviews, but I get a note saying I've been "unsuccessful" – that's the word they use. They never tell you why. I suppose there must be a hundred applicants for every job. You get to the stage where you feel it's an achievement just to get an interview.

'For a while I didn't feel too bad. But after a number of rejections I started to think "Well whatever's wrong with me?" Your self-confidence goes lower and lower. You start to think that even applying is a waste of time. You're sure you won't get it. Then you get diffident and start to avoid people. I felt I was worthless and useless. It got pointless even trying for work.

'My finances soon led me to look for any kind of job. I wasn't choosy. Wherever I went, they said they wanted experience. I went for a job as a folder in a clothing factory. They said "Have you ever folded before?" You fold things every day. But of course they were on piece-work, even the folding has to be done perfectly. With so many unemployed, they'd probably be able to find a hundred people who'd never done anything but folding all their lives.

'You start to envy people who are working. I even went round factory sites that were just being built, making enquiries about who was going to lease them so I could be first in the queue; but nobody knew if anybody was ever going to rent them. I went to Ashton, St Helens; I wrote, I phoned, I visited. I thought "Oh heck, the word'll go round, they'll know me before I get there." I imagined they'd be on the phone to each other: "that unemployable woman is on her way."

'The way I got the job I'm doing was sheer luck; chance. I was in the launderette doing my washing one day, and the woman who runs it was saying "Why don't you try the sewing factory in Darlington Street? My sister works there." "Oh," I said, "do they need anybody?" I went down. "Are you a machinist?" the manager asked. "No." Oh, well, I thought, that's it. To my amazement, he said, "Well that doesn't matter, we can train you." I nearly fell through the floor. He said "There's a divider's job coming up"; a woman was retiring. But I'd lost even the confidence that I could do that. The cutters cut the garments in layers, groups of anything from ten to 200 at a time, and the pieces are not all cut from one roll of cloth; there might be three or four rolls being used at any one time; and each roll, although the same colour, is a slightly different shade. So you have to separate out all the different pieces and make sure that there's not an arm from one roll and a front from another. So we get all the layers on the table, and there's paper between the rolls, so you separate them out into backs, fronts, sleeves and so on; and what we do is bundle up so many backs, fronts and everything to make up one garment, in bundles of ten, put the trimmings in, collect it all up and give it to the machinist. It couldn't be more simple. But I thought "I'm bound to do something wrong." I was terrified. The first day I went to work it was like going to an exam. Then I thought to myself "Don't be so stupid." Of course after a day or two I was all right. The manager was a bit lackadaisical; other people had phoned or written for jobs, but I happened to be there on the spot, that's why I got it, not because of merit and not because of experience.

'I've been there twelve months now. In one way I enjoy it; but in another I'm frustrated and bitter. I mean, I worked hard for my qualifications under difficult circumstances; and I feel all that was wasted effort. I had to give up teaching, not just because I got married, but to look after my parents too. Then when I tried to get back into teaching, I tried for two years. I felt let down. You feel you've got the qualifications, you're safe. Then you find it's not true. You feel you've been misled. Your parents make sacrifices so you can do what you want to do; then you pay them back by looking after them; then there's nothing. And the reason why I did office work was because I thought that meant certain security. I felt even more let down when that went.'

The telephone rings in the back room. Mrs Tysoe goes out; she is away for several minutes. When she comes back, she looks shaken. She sits down and says, "I'm glad there's somebody here. I've just heard something horrible." A friend had phoned to tell her that a neighbour, a man a few doors up the road had committed suicide. He had hanged himself. He has been out of work for fifteen months; Mrs Tysoe is disturbed and angry 'Of course I've no evidence it was anything to do with his being out of work, but I could understand it if it was. If you're able-bodied, you've got to have a reason for living; and for most people, their job is their main reason for living. If you can't do that, you feel you're on the scrap-heap; you feel a burden to society.'

A few days later the report of the inquest on Mrs Tysoe's neighbour was in the local paper. It said that he had been depressed by his inability to find work after having been made redundant eighteen months earlier. He was forty-eight. The inquest was told that he refused to go out of the house when his father died. He was a bachelor and lived with his widowed mother, and had been receiving psychiatric treatment. He was found hanging from a rope in an out-house. The coroner said: 'He had been depressed partly due to being unable to find work and the death of his father.'

Later, Mrs Tysoe continued: 'In one place where I worked, there was a woman who was obsessed with scroungers. "Oh," she'd say, "there's always two pages of jobs in the evening paper every week", without stopping to wonder whether those people could do those jobs, or even what two pages of jobs means when there's thousands out of work. Then when you went for your dole money, on the wall outside somebody had painted "Get a Job you lazy Gits". You felt bad enough without that. There's a man where I'm working now, he's another one who goes on about the work-shy and scroungers. He said his uncle, who is an old-age pensioner, couldn't manage, and he was told to go and claim supplementary benefit. He went down and came straight out again. "Oh, why was that?" "Well," he said, "who do you think was behind me, a man from a bit further down our street, and I know for a fact he's only fifty-two. I said to this man "I've been drawing unemployment benefit for over twelve months, I got £21 for six months, then £18.50. Could you live on it? When I was working earlier I'd saved a little. I didn't apply for Social Security when I stopped work, not till I'd used up all my savings. But if I'd gone any longer without a job, it would have been a case of drawing Social Security or killing myself." He never said a word. A few days later though, I heard him telling someone else the same story. "Disgraceful," he was saying, "a man of fifty-two drawing Social Security."

'When I got this job, I had less than £100 left. I was dreading the moment when I'd have to go to Social Security. I did go once. When I saw them all sitting there, I came out. I couldn't bear it.

'Even though I've got a job now, I'm not using myself to my full capacities, nor anywhere near it. This happens to a lot of women. It's being stretched that gives you satisfaction. Not using the skills you have, you feel it's such a waste. All that needs to be done in the world, all the things you thought you could do, and it's not wanted. What a waste. I mean, I'm no machinist, when I do a cut it looks as if I've used a knife and fork. On the other hand, the people I work with are very friendly. They're the best people I've ever worked with. It's the people who have bucked me up. We laugh and joke and have the wireless on. But the fact remains, I'm not using myself, here I'm the lowest of the low. Don't get me wrong – the people couldn't be nicer; but there must be other people out of work who could do the job better than I can. It makes me sad; all those exams, all the time I spent studying; all the hopes your parents cherished for you. I have to think now how lucky I am to have a job at all.

'Oh it's changed me. Before I was unemployed, there was no way I'd ever do anything wrong. I'd never have broken the law. I suppose I believed everything was for the best in society. I don't believe that now. I take after my father; he was always honest, and to those people he met in business who weren't he always said "I can sleep at night, can you?" But now, if I saw someone drawing Social Security or supplementary, and doing a bit of work on the side, I wouldn't blame them, and I certainly wouldn't report them. It is impossible to live on unemployment benefit. I don't live it up on what I earn now, I have to scrimp a bit. I earn £54 a week gross; for forty and a half hours I take home £42 a week. If I'm ill, have to take a couple of days off, I'll only get £27. I have to mollycoddle myself, I can't afford to lose time. It makes me cross when you hear people say "Save for a rainy day." They tell you to cut down your living costs, but I live as frugally as I can. Why should people suffer? If people can get a little job on the side when they're out of work, good luck to them. At one time I would have thought talking like that was shocking.

'I was offered bar work, three nights a week, £18.50 a week. It would have been Thursday, Friday and Saturday night; and that wage would have been deducted from benefit in such a way that I'd be getting just £4 a week more for working those three nights. That would have meant twelve hours a week work for £4.

'It made me bitter, and having to suffer the attitude of people who have never known what it's like only made it worse. You can understand youngsters not bothering, saying they don't see the point. My mother and father used to talk about the thirties. They said they thought it would never end. You wonder now if some of the young people ever will get jobs. It was only the War that made things pick up anyway. You do wonder. The girls and women at work, I talk to them, but you can talk till you're blue in the face – people don't take it in. They don't understand other people's suffering until it happens to them. You've got to go through it personally. Even now, I can tell who's experienced unemployment and who hasn't – just talking to people; all the bitterness and frustration come pouring out.

'But I was the same before I went through it; a "let them eat cake" sort of attitude. And I considered myself to be rather "feeling" towards people. Yet I still felt if they tried a bit harder, they could get what they want. But one day when I came out of the job centre, I was so pent-up, I felt a sudden overwhelming desire to smash every window in the street. It was quite overpowering. I just stood there and said "Calm yourself down, this isn't going to get you anywhere." But I felt I suddenly got a great insight into vandalism and violence, because there it was in myself. One day I was in the job centre, I saw a girl go raving mad at the girl behind the desk. She said to me afterwards "People think we're sitting on jobs, but we're not."

'Then I had the problem that although you might not be fussy about what job you take, some employers won't take you on if you're above a certain level. "You're too highly qualified." I used to promise "I'll stay." "But if a job comes along that suits you better, you'll leave." "Well, I'm not going to say I won't." "We won't risk taking you on."

'My job is in textiles; they're taking a bad knock at the moment. Before Christmas we thought we were going to get our cards. We know more or less what orders are coming in, and it went really low in the autumn. There are three factories in the group; each factory has to make a profit, or they'll shut us down. Fortunately, we're not working on a belt, but machining. A girl makes the full garment so you can diversify. We make trousers and jackets for Nuclear Fuels; they're only worn once and then thrown away because of contamination, so that's a constant source of work; we make nurses' uniforms for the Health Service, brownies' and guides' uniforms that are specific to England, so they haven't been undercut by imports. They've just got some new cutters, so we look all right for the moment. But who's safe these days? I don't know what would happen if I had to go through it again. I don't think I could.'

Mrs Tysoe illuminated the experience of many people, especially women and school-leavers: unemployment has the effect of making people grateful for any work. It inclines them to accept jobs far below their abilities, and blurs the fact that negligible skills are required, that the new jobs offered may bear little relation to any perceived human need; it give another twist to the spiral that distances work from anything that is demonstrably useful or valuable to humanity, and makes the alternatives to profit seem even more remote and unthinkable.

As if the loss of dignity and self-esteem were not enough, many people who lose their jobs are humiliated further by the insensitivity and indifference of the agencies that are supposed to help them. Kathy McGuire is in her late twenties, a bit overweight, with dark hair and fair skin. She lives in a terraced house in a poor street in a small Lancashire town that has been badly neglected in recent years. She wears a pink summer dress and plastic sandals. Nervous at first about talking of herself, she becomes more confident and articulate with the anger at the way she has been treated. Why is it, she wonders, that so many of the organizations intended to help the poor, take on all the features of the evils they were supposed to remedy?

Until January 1981 Kathy was working in a factory making motor-cycle number-plates. 'Then they started a new way of doing the transfers direct onto the Perspex. Even though I'd been there three years and never had a complaint, they started sending a lot of my work back, saying they weren't satisfactory, even if they were only one-tenth of an inch out. Next thing, a young kid comes up to me, he says, "I'm going to work with you." I said, "Does that mean I'm out of a job?" "I'm working with you." I said, "Wait a minute." I went upstairs to the manager. I said, "What's that young kid doing down there?" "I'm making you redundant as from today." "What for?" "It's your asthma, all the time off, the fumes affect your asthma." They'd never bothered about the fumes affecting my asthma for the three years I'd been there. Anyway, they did it, they made me redundant and kept this kid on, which they're not supposed to do. I should have taken it to the tribunal, but I settled out of court for £150.

'I can't get a job now. I'll turn my hand to anything. I've done bar work, I've done burning radiators down for scrap, cleaning, filing in offices. I'm getting £43.80 a week, including family allowance and child benefit, single-parent allowance. My ex-husband is supposed to pay maintenance. I don't get it. He's just been sent down the line for six weeks for not paying. I've got my boy-friend living with me, but he's never helped me to pay the bills. He just gives me £20 a week for his board and that's that – that's supposed to cover everything. I'd put him down as a lodger. They said to me "are you cohabiting?" I said "No". I want to keep my independence. They put pressure on you to get married. They keep on at you.

'My husband went down last week for maintenance. He's living with a woman who has four kids. She's a widow; she had two kids to her husband, and then two to another boy-friend before she started living with my ex-husband. She gets her widow's pension and she has a part-time job; and she gets whatever she wants, no danger. Because she's a widow they don't ask her if she's cohabiting. She told my kids, she said, "I'm sleeping with your Dad, you know." My kids are eleven and nine, Wayne and Michelle. I pay rent of £25 a fortnight, £3.50 a week milk, £3 a week for bread. You can get a meat-pack for £3, and in that there's a bit of everything – stewing meat, liver, sausages, neck of lamb, that'll last me a week if I can afford it on Saturday. I get a sack of potatoes for £3; they'll last a month maybe. So the kids always have one meal a day, then it has to be beans on toast, spaghetti on toast at night. But the kids can't do anything without spending money. It's a pound for them to go swimming; so what happens? In the holidays the clothing club money has to be missed to let them go. What I have to pay out every week for tv, electricity, gas, washer, that comes to £35 a week. And I'm getting £43.80. My boy-friend has lost his job now, so he's getting £20.65. I'm already worrying about Christmas – how can I pay anything into a Christmas club?

'I'm still getting unemployment benefit, but that'll run out by the end of the year. I can't stand being on Social Security. I've been through all that. Your boy-friend stays more than three nights – you're cohabiting. I've had the snoopers. The neighbours have been to the police saying I'm locking the kids in all day. A woman phoned the children's people – the NSPCC – when I'd just gone up to the shop one Saturday morning. People spy on you. There's always somebody saying you're ill-treating your kids. People are scared you're getting something they're not. They've got nothing else to do but keep their eye on you, they jump to the wrong conclusions. On Social Security your life's not your own.

'When my husband left me, I was here one day, sorting out some of his old things. I'd found a heap of old shirts and things. The Social Security visitor decided to come at that minute, and I had to answer a bloody string of questions: What are you doing, who do those shirts belong to? I said, "They belong to my husband, I'm throwing them out." I dread the end of the year when I shall have to go back on the Social. It's bad enough with us both being out of work. We have rows. I feel I want to walk out of the house some days and never come back. I threaten him sometimes, I say I'll put him out. I pack his bags, that's the only way to get through to him. I've done it several times lately.

'My daughter wets the bed. I have to go to the hospital with her. It affects the whole family. You try and keep it to yourself, but it gets through to them. The trouble is when you're in work, you take on debts. I didn't know I was going to lose my job; and neither did he. They don't like paying us our unemployment benefit separate because we get a bit more as two single people than we would if we were a married couple. The Social Security try to put pressure on you to get married because it would be more convenient and cheaper for them to pay us as a married couple. They actually put pressure on you to go into another marriage that might well be just as much a disaster as the first one. I want my independence, and I don't see why I shouldn't keep it.

'It was because of them that my husband and I got together again after we'd already split up and separated. But things got even worse; and the final break was even more bitter and unpleasant than it would have been. My husband used to drink, he used to get drunk on the labour money. He'd get really paralytic, so he'd be trying to walk up the wall thinking he was going upstairs to bed. Then when he got to bed, he'd wet it and ruin the mattress. In the end I had to tell him to get out. I couldn't stand it. It just couldn't be patched up. I was on nerve tablets, and it was upsetting the kids. Anyway, he did go. I went down to Social Security to tell them he'd gone, and this time it was for keeps. And you won't believe what happened.

'He'd got nowhere to go when he went from here at the finish. He's only a skinny bloke. And what he was doing, he waited till the kids and me had gone to bed. And then he was lifting up the grating in the street, what they use to put the coal down in the cellar; and he was jumping down into the cellar, then up into the living-room; and he was sleeping on the sofa. Then he'd clear out in the morning at six o'clock while we were all still asleep. I never saw him. I never had the slightest idea what he was doing. We had a dog, and the dog recognized him, he'd only have to say "It's all right Patch, it's only me", and the dog wouldn't bark or anything.

'One morning two blokes came knocking at the door. I was upstairs, and I saw them from the window coming down the street. I was scared stiff, even though I'd no idea what they were coming about. It was just their manner like. I let them in. "We want to see your family allowance book and your Social Security book." I handed them over. "We're keeping these." "What for?" They said I'd made a statement that was false. I said "Oh, why, what's that?" They said my husband had been seen coming out of here at six o'clock, seven o'clock every morning. He'd been followed down this road, down that road. They'd followed him, every step he'd taken. Well, I knew he was doing a bit of window cleaning. But they could tell me exactly where he'd been. I said, "But he can't be. I've got the keys to the house." Which I had – the spare ones as well. I didn't know anything about it; but they could tell me exactly how long it had been going on. When I told them, they wouldn't believe me; I don't know if I expected them to. But they got hold of him, and told him he was going to be taken to court for failing to maintain his wife and family, and I was going to be prosecuted for making a false statement. Later, they said to me if I would have my husband back, we wouldn't be prosecuted. So I had him back. We needed the money. Then after six months they said they'd dropped the case against us. But it was terrible. He drank, and we got on each other's nerves and he started knocking me around. In the end I had to fetch the police to get him out of the house; and the magistrate told him he'd go down the line if he laid so much as a finger on me.

'I've been with Bobby, my boy-friend for two years. I mean, everybody needs somebody to cuddle up to at night, don't they? He's a painter and decorator. Since he lost his job, he gets £20.65 a week. They threatened to cut off the electricity: I've got an immersion heater, and we had to use an electric fire for three weeks in the winter; and the quarter's bill came to £80. I had to borrow money to pay it off because I'd got a tax rebate to come from where I was working, so I could pay that off all right.

'It gets complicated. My husband was taken to court for non-payment. He owed me £330. With his unemployment benefit, how's he ever going to pay that? They cut it down to £300. The woman he's with, she's got widow's pension, maintenance for the two kids from her ex-boy-friend, family allowance for four. My husband had paid me £30 in four years. And I was getting taxed on maintenance money I was not receiving. I had to take him to court to get all that sorted out. I didn't want to. I was in tears when he was being sent down. I don't owe him any grudges. I mean, he has his problems; he had an ulcer, and needed a special diet. And then he was supposed to be paying me £5 a week out of benefit of £19. It wasn't reasonable. But I had to take him back to court every six weeks; they reduced the £5 to £3. They threatened him with gaol because he still couldn't pay. "Well pay what you can", they said. He paid £6 in nine months.

'I had a phone bill that mounted up to £120. I got taken to the county court; it was cut off. I still haven't paid it. I went to the housing to apply for a rent rebate. They told me not to pay my rent until the rebate had been sorted out. Then another department at the Town Hall sent me a letter telling me I'm going to be evicted for non-payment of rent, which they had advised me not to do in the first place.

'I don't know what'll happen. I say to Bobby "Come Christmas, tha's got to keep me." I don't know, I'd do anything rather than go back on Social Security. I don't go out; the odd game of dominoes or crib down the pub. Some days I stop in bed to stop myself from eating. I'm on steroids for my asthma, and that gives me a false appetite; and then if you get depressed, the first thing you want to do is eat. And then I've got these tablets for depression. At one time, I got so that I was waking up, giving the kids their breakfast, and then taking more tablets just to get back to sleep again. I'm supposed to take one a day; one day I took six. You know, it's a temptation to take them just because that's the only way to escape from it, sleep.

'The way I look at it, I'm fighting to keep my independence. I don't want to get married just for their convenience, and then find out I've made a terrible mistake, go through that all over again. But why should I also have to give up having somebody to cuddle up to at night? I mean, we both want our independence. We lead our separate lives, we go out with somebody else if we want to. But we are a comfort to each other. Not so much just lately, now we're both at home all the while, we've been getting on each other's nerves; the least little thing blows up into an argument.

'I worry about it. We're down as man and wife in the housing department for the sake of getting somewhere decent to live; but I get the single-parent allowance, that's £3 a week on top of the £4.75 for each child. The summer holidays, it's a time you should look forward to, but you can't afford to do anything with them. The kids go on to the play scheme, that's a godsend. I'd like to take them to see *Clash of the Titans*, but you can't even afford to go to the pictures. The other day I was playing bat and ball with them in the street. Some old woman comes out and "Get back in your house" she says to me. I mean, one time over, everybody used to be out in the street on summer evenings. Now it's "Get back in your house." The holidays are the worst times. All these rapes, children being murdered, you daren't let your kids go anywhere.'

11
The Eighties

If we want to understand why unemployment remains such a distressing experience despite the more favourable material conditions of the eighties, we have to realize that it is precisely those more favourable conditions which make it so disagreeable; not only because the plight of those without money is mocked by the stridency of all the buying and selling, but also because a deep hidden price has been paid for the improvements working people have seen.

With the mitigation through time of the exploitative, relentless labour of the working class, there has also occurred a considerable weakening of function and purpose; and it is important to distinguish these overlapping but separate processes. The decay of function has actually been concealed by the very success of the Labour movement itself in its long crusade against work as tyranny. But in addition to the concessions it has granted, capitalism has smuggled in this subtle counterfeit as well – this erosion of the older strengths of the working class. It should not be exaggerated: it is a tendency, if a strong one, not an absolute and complete process. It has already a long history – every mechanical and technological innovation has in some measure been designed to replace labour. George Orwell[35] recognized the distinction though:

> The truth is that when a human being is not eating, drinking, sleeping, making love, talking, playing games, or merely lounging about – and these things will not fill up a lifetime – he needs work, and usually looks for it, though he may not call it work. Life has got to be lived largely in terms of effort. For man is

> not, as the vulgar hedonists suppose, a walking stomach; he has also got a hand, an eye and a brain. Cease to use your hands and you have lopped off a huge chunk of consciousness.*

It is just in this spirit that so much of the rhetoric about leisure has been aimed at working people in recent years, a great deal of it from the Left.

What has been happening to the function – and hence the sense of identity – of the working class has been even more deeply submerged by the noise and display emanating from the market-place in recent years. The exaltation of the material concessions yielded by capitalism has meant that those improvements have been used, not primarily as a relief from that older poverty, but as a means of creating a different kind of subordination of the working class. This has been achieved by a series of penalties and forfeits which the working class has paid, the extent and significance of which are only just now being grasped. Among these losses, apart from the damaged sense of function, have been some of the humanizing responses to that older poverty, the solidarity and sharing, the living practice in the daily existence of millions of working people of values – dignity, frugality, stoicism – which offered an alternative to the brutalizing destructive values of capitalism. This has been the greatest loss of all because it means that the option of that alternative as something that could have grown organically out of the way people lived out their lives has been crushed. And by contrast with the material concessions, which are temporary, perishable and insecure, the intangible things that have been taken away begin to look more serious and enduring.

In place of those losses, market relationships have encroached as a main determinant on working people's consciousness. Now the idea of market relationships as an end result, the reflection of people's needs being answered might be more defensible if you could start from scratch with each new generation. But that is clearly impossible, with the result that many younger people have grown up with the strident hymning of commodities, the selling and buying of things ringing in their ears from the moment they were

*Compare E. F. Schumacher, (*Good Work*, Anchor Press, 1979)[36]: 'After all, it is work which occupies most of the energies of the human race, and what people actually *do* is normally more important, for understanding them, than what they say, or what they spend their money on, or what they own, or how they vote.'

born. So what is supposed to be a way of answering human needs becomes a determining influence, and a very powerful one in the lives of the young. It comes to seem to many of them that nothing exists, and certainly nothing is of value that cannot be exchanged for money. Nothing has worth but that which can be priced; and the risk is that they develop as diminished shrunken dependants, and not as full human beings. Of course, like all the other controls and oppressions that working people have suffered, there is resistance, but like the other, older poverty, this too takes its toll.

What we have seen happen is that material improvement for its own sake and not for the sake of human need has become a substitute for that lived alternative. Instead of allying the vast possibilities of increased production to the old frugality and modest wants of the old working class, that earlier response has been crushed because it was a threat to the capitalist dynamic. And in its place a profound dependency has evolved on the goods, the commodities and services which capital can provide. And because these depend in their turn on profit, they become more and more disjointed from perceived human need; and, as a result, the working patterns of people follow them, become more and more broken from any sense of purposeful or explicable activity. One effect of this upon those who work is that many of them despise the product they make or resent the service they give, while at the same time they use not a fraction of their real powers and abilities in the process.

The 'creation of wealth' has become an almost mystical obsession, and it has come to constitute the sole subject matter of all political debate. One observable result of this in all working-class communities has been a disruption, discontinuity in the old ties, the old associations, the bonds of kinship, neighbourhood and workplace, without any serious political resistance. The enormous forfeits which have been exacted as a condition of material advance have been separated from it, neutralized, disconnected from the processes of which they are an integral part. In this way the exaltation of things has deeply damaged the care for people. If this has indeed happened – and everywhere you go, in Sunderland and Birmingham as in Bolton and the East End, people are still saying this is so – then loss will have cancelled gain over the years.

It need hardly be said that this new condition of the working class is not going to lead to socialism. Socialism could have been an organic expression of the way people lived and worked together; why it failed to emerge is a subject of almost infinite conjecture and debate. But one thing is sure: we shan't build socialism out of those values now, out of that endurance and frugality, out of that pride and solidarity. The moment has passed.

But the idea is not lost. That practice, those values, the power of people to mitigate each other's suffering and console each other, to abate the worst visitations that either nature or their human oppressors can devise, constitute an abiding response to human existence itself. The way those people lived has a resonance and power that goes beyond the experience of the working class in one part of the world for a mere couple of centuries or so. So even though those circumstances have been changed out of which socialism might have been constructed, and although the socialist project seems to have become such a theoretical and intellectual exercise, yet the values which the old working class embodied in its resistance to the circumstances of its life retain an inspirational, spiritual significance. It may be a bitter thing that such an opportunity as we had should have been lost; it is sad that the battle fought by so many selfless people should have to be fought all over again, and in a very different and difficult context.

The reason why the loss of that older working-class practice is such a grievous one is that it is the only model we have had in recent centuries in the West that would have fitted in with the need to conserve, to live modestly in a world threatened by ruin and depletion, waste and pollution, poverty and hunger. The whole world is the poorer for the eclipsing of those values, of that solidarity, of that caring.

Because the old working class expressed something lasting and profound about the nature of human life this response must be re-discovered. This cannot be done by imposing an intellectualized version of it as conceived by some sections of the Left; nor is it likely to be achieved through the institutions which grew out of that earlier response, but which have now become rigid and ossified. It has to be revitalized with an ardent and living impulse. The endless argument on the Left about how to reach the mass of the people strikes shrill and repetitive; and it drowns out the sound of the people who have been trying to reach their leaders and sympathizers alike for as long as I can remember. People have been talking about the loss of brotherhood, the damage that has been inflicted on human relationships as the price of the capitalist material improvement they have seen. But it hasn't been heard; or if heard, not taken proper account of, certainly not integrated into the political argument where it belongs. Instead of trying to compete with capitalism in its vain promises of growth and wealth, the Left should listen to what is said about the other side of the equation – the losses and forfeits which working people have lived with for so many years. The issues must be reformulated to take account of the way people have actually experienced the cruel distraints in their lives, not only as a result of material insufficiency, but as a result of this capitalist way of improving the condition of the people: that violence and distrust, the cruelty and the loneliness, the breakdown of relationships, the mental illness and pain, the ugly gulf between the generations, the sense of futility, the ruin of fraternity, the breaking of belonging together. If capitalism could create this hurt during the years of greatest buoyancy, is it any wonder that when it is in decline, it leaves such human wreckage as we now see? And still we haven't begun to confront these political questions because we don't recognize them as such.

The damage to the function of the working class is profound and vast. It isn't confined to the work role, but to everything that stems from it, above all to its capacity to forge a more human alternative to the impositions of capitalism. It is this absence which makes the lives of so many of those people in this book more bereft, more numb and powerless even than the loss of work itself would involve. Unemployment in the eighties is an outcrop of these deeper losses; and these cannot be made good by any amount of creation of jobs or wealth on the terms of capital. The only consolation is that the real work still remains to be done.

It has been painful to write about these things. Those of my generation have been instrumental in the process of taking away much of what the working class has lost. We were actually a part of those losses; and no amount of sympathy, commitment, devotion to 'the caring professions' can restore more than a fraction of them. The guilt remains. This is perhaps why it is so difficult for many of those on the Left to accept the argument about the intangible losses; and they are content to restrict political argument to the question of measurable material gains. By doing this, they can ignore the moral, spiritual and human losses which, however immaterial, are nevertheless the very substance of our lives.

Notes

1 Adrian Sinfield, *What Unemployment Means* (Martin Robertson, Oxford, 1981), p.18
2 Cook and Stevenson, *The Slump* (Quartet, 1979)
3 George Orwell, *The Road to Wigan Pier* (Penguin, 1975), p.76
4 J. B. Priestley, *English Journey* (Penguin, 1977), p.87
5 E. F. Schumacher, *Good Work* (Anchor Press, 1979)
6 W. W. Daniel, *New Society*, 19 March 1981.
7 Raymond Williams, *The Long Revolution* (Penguin, 1965), p.64
8 E. P. Thompson, *The Making of the English Working Class* (Penguin, 1968) pp.487–8
9 Priestley, op. cit., pp.341–2
10 Emile Zola, *Germinal*
11 Priestley, op. cit.
12 Robert Roberts, *The Classic Slum* (Manchester University Press, 1971), pp.10–11
13 Richard Hoggart, *The Uses of Literacy* (Chatto & Windus, 1957)
14 I. Illich, *The Right to Useful Unemployment* (Marion Boyars, 1978)
15 Ibid.
16 Thompson, op. cit., p.485
17 Harrison, quoted Adrian Sinfield, op. cit., p.89
18 Marie Jahoda, *Bulletin of the British Psychological Society* (1979), **32**, 309–14.
19 Sinfield, op. cit., p.53
20 Orwell, op. cit., p.104
21 Southwick Neighbourhood Action Project, Sunderland: Report on Fuel Cut-Offs, December 1980.
22 Illich, op. cit.

23 Guy Debord, *La Société du Spectacle* (Buchet/Chastel, Paris, 1967)
24 Thompson, op. cit.
25 Williams, op. cit., p.131
26 Hoggart, op. cit., p.17
27 Ibid., p.175
28 Thompson, op. cit., p.111
29 Ibid., p.127
30 R. H. Tawney, *The Acquisitive Society*
31 Jahoda, op. cit., pp.309–14
32 Clive Jenkins and Barrie Sherman, *The Collapse of Work*
33 Tony Benn, *Arguments for Socialism* (Penguin, 1980), p.44
34 Hoggart, op. cit., p.322–3
35 Orwell, op. cit., p.173
36 Schumacher, op. cit., p.3